Mary Elizabeth Atherstone

The dramatic Works of Edwin Atherstone

Mary Elizabeth Atherstone
The dramatic Works of Edwin Atherstone
ISBN/EAN: 9783743346406
Manufactured in Europe, USA, Canada, Australia, Japa
Cover: Foto ©ninafisch / pixelio.de

Manufactured and distributed by brebook publishing software (www.brebook.com)

Mary Elizabeth Atherstone

The dramatic Works of Edwin Atherstone

THE DRAMATIC WORKS OF EDWIN ATHERSTONE,

AUTHOR OF

'THE FALL OF NINEVEH,' 'ISRAEL IN EGYPT,'
'A MIDSUMMER DAY'S DREAM,'
'THE HANDWRITING ON THE WALL,' Etc., Etc., Etc.

EDITED BY HIS DAUGHTER,

MARY ELIZABETH ATHERSTONE.

LONDON:
ELLIOT STOCK, 62, PATERNOSTER ROW, E.C.
1888.

CONTENTS.

	PAGE
PELOPIDAS; OR, THE DELIVERANCE OF THEBES	1
PHILIP	119
LOVE, POETRY, PHILOSOPHY, AND GOUT	195

BETWEEN sixty and seventy years have elapsed since the following dramas were written. They were many times, between 1824 and 1834, offered to the then *great* London theatres; and I have a clear recollection of seeing letters from Kemble, and—I think *several*—from Edmund Kean, expressive of their approval; and of their willingness to take a part in either of the two first plays.

The character of the last Philip of Macedon was by them—as also by other great tragedians—considered to afford scope for the exercise of an actor's best abilities.

It was suggested—I fancy from Covent Garden—that the comedy would be more likely to succeed were the scene laid in England.

Therefore, under my father's direction, I (who from childhood had been his copyist—his 'Secretary' according to our most valued friends of those old days—) had to fairly transcribe the whole,—changing names and scenery: but ere the task was completed, the Manager—at whose suggestion it was undertaken—seems to have left the Stage.

I much prefer—for many reasons — the comedy in its original form.

My father never, by look or word, manifested disappointment at the rejection of these works: but probably some disappointment may have been FELT—and testified by a little note I now find on the last page of the *original* manuscript—and which I will here insert :—

'My third, and *last*, attempt at the Drama—none having been accepted.—E. A.'

It seems strange my father should not have thought that—even if unsuited for the Stage—the three plays might still make a fit volume for the Library : but I remember no hint as to his having any idea of their publication.

To *me*, their perusal in Book-shape will be far more pleasant than in the various copies of manuscript—the yellow pages, and faded ink of which suggest the propriety of my seeing them safely in type ere I, also, pass away.

M. E. A.

PELOPIDAS;

OR,

THE DELIVERANCE OF THEBES.

A PLAY IN FIVE ACTS.

Persons Represented.

LEONTIDAS
PHILIP } *Noblemen of the Aristocratic faction; and afterwards Tyrants.*
ARCHIAS

PHILIDAS—*Secretary to the Tyrants.*
CHARON—*A Noble Theban, of neither Party.*
HIS INFANT SON.
ISMENIAS.
EPAMINONDAS.

PELOPIDAS
ANDROCLIDES
GORGIDAS
THEOPOMPUS } *Noble Thebans of the Democratic Party; and afterwards Liberators of Thebes.*
DEMOCLIDES
PHERENICUS
MELON
CEPHISIDORUS

PHŒBIDAS—*The Spartan General.*
ABAS, ACHILLES, AGAMEMNON—*Tailors.*
TELEMON—*A Cobbler.*
CLONIUS—*A Poor Theban Youth.*
MENON—*Servant to Archias.*
PROTUS—*A Rustic.* A BAILIFF.

WOMEN.

CLYMENE—*Wife of Charon.*
THULIA—*Wife of Androclides.*
DORIS—*Wife of Protus.*
A PRIESTESS.
LORDS, SOLDIERS, SERVANTS, A MURDERER.

Scene—At and near Thebes.

ACT I.

Scene I.—*The fields in the vicinity of Thebes.*

(*Enter, on one side,* ABAS *and* CLONIUS; *and on the other,* PROTUS *and* DORIS.)

ABAS. Now, where's your wager, Clonius?
A good morrow to you, Protus, and to your lovely wife, who is this morning doubly lovely, for that she hath bestowed on me two skins of ruby wine.

PROTUS. Aye, truly! as how?

DORIS. Not I, in sooth. He doth but jest.

ABAS. In sooth, he doth *not* jest, fair mistress. Yet, in a sort, he doth jest; and yet he doth not.

PROTUS. Come,—here's a riddle—doth—doth not—and doth; who reads it first?

CLONIUS. Oh,—that will I.

ABAS. Nay, boy;—that wilt thou not; unless, indeed, thy wit have a longer reach than thine eyesight.

(EPAMINONDAS *enters behind.*)

CLONIUS (*aside*). Conceited old ass! I wish the wine may choke him.

DORIS. Why, he is young enough to be your grandson; sure he should have the better sight of the two.

ABAS. A raw conclusion, young mistress; yet natural enough too, for a young woman to think the worse of an old man, and the better of a young one. But there's no exception without a rule—as I heard the noble Pelopidas say t'other day in a question about the tusk-teeth of a wild boar, though I don't quite bear in mind what the matter was. But, as I was saying—no rule without a deception; and so it is that, of all the youngsters in Thebes, there is not one with such a thorough-piercing eye as mine—for a distance-object, you mark me,—for, as to things at hand, I make no particular boast.

EPAMINONDAS (*aside*). No such remarkable peculiarity, my honest friend! I know hundreds who can distinctly see the failings of their fellows afar off—though they should be no larger than an acorn;—yet are blind to their own faults, though they would overtop the oak.

ABAS (*looking out*). I marvel that I see nought yet of the Spartan soldiers.

PROTUS. But what of the wine, master?—tell us that.

CLONIUS. Why, see you, as you were coming on——

ABAS (*putting his hand on the mouth of Clonius*). Why! wilt thou now? Thou know'st well enough I tell a tale better than any man in Thebes;—and that has been said a hundred times.

CLONIUS (*aside*). I've heard *you* say it, nobody else.

ABAS. Let the winner tell of a battle;—not him that lost it.

CLONIUS (*aside*). The old wide-mouthed villain! I'll put a viper into his wine.

ABAS. And now, mine honest Protus, will I show to thee how it is that I did *not* jest,—yet, in a sort, *did* jest;—and yet again did no such matter:—how it is that your sweet-faced young wife—whose progenitors Jupiter bless!—did, albeit she deny it, bestow on me the foresaid two skins of ruby wine. Also will I make apparent to you how that, for a clear-spying eye, this youth doth in no way match my age, and also——but by the great Apollo! there is the noble Epaminondas,—the bravest of our philosophers, and the wisest of our soldiers, as the valiant Pelopidas hath ofttimes said. Wait awhile,—for I must have speech with him touching great concerns. I will return anon, and discourse further with you.

> (*He walks to* EPAMINONDAS, *who sits on the root of a tree, a book in his hand.*)

CLONIUS. A meddlesome—prating—overbearing—conceited old fool! I owe him money that I can't just now pay him, and so he plays the lord over me. He would tell me how many paces I should take during the day;—and count out my breathings—and regulate the number of my heart-strokes!

PROTUS. But what's this about the wine-skins?

CLONIUS. The noisy—prating old swaggerer! He's for ever raising a thunder-storm inside a soap-bubble. 'Tis just this. As you came tow'rds us, and when we could barely see you through the mist,—'Bless us!' said I; 'here comes Protus with his sister! what brings them to Thebes so early?' ''Tis not his sister,' replies old Backstitch; ''tis his wife.' Now I,—not knowing you were married,—said again 'twas your sister; and he, thereat, bets me two skins of wine—which I have lost—and there's the whole matter. But what make you at Thebes so early this fresh morning?

PROTUS. Oh! just to see the procession to the feast, and to shake hands with some old friends. My wife has relations here whom she has not seen since her wedding. You come, I suppose, to take a look at the Spartan troops yonder?

CLONIUS. We do. How far are they off?

PROTUS. Why, you might see them now but for the fog. They may be perhaps a thousand paces off. They have been marching since peep of morning, and are just going to put up their tents.

CLONIUS. What may their number be? Hast heard, or canst give any guess?

PROTUS. I have not heard, and truly have no guess. Were they corn-sheaves instead of soldiers, perhaps I might have better chance to count them. Let the tailor stick to his needle, and the weaver to his loom—and we then may have good cloth, well sewn: and so good morning to you, sir; and Ceres send us a bountiful harvest.

CLONIUS. Good-morning to you, friend; good-morning, pretty mistress, and a happy day, though I have been a loser by those light-treading ankles of yours.

DORIS. Good-morning, sir; and may your wine be good, though *I* shall be no better for it. [*Exeunt* PROTUS *and* DORIS.

Clonius. What does the wench mean? No matter! I am sure *I* shall be no better for it; but I have a good mind that somebody else shall be the worse.—Ah! you infernal old rascal! you everlasting—babbling—wide-chapped tyrant! I'll have done with you;—I'll defy you. This day is the last of your reign. Sooner than be your drudge, and your butt any longer, I'll go to prison and curse you.—He is coming away. I'll not wait for him.—How the old knave will froth at the mouth! Ha—ha—ha! [*Exit.*

Epaminondas. Then be it as you say. So, or in any other fashion that affects not singularity. I love not these discourses. —For the slave you spake of;—rebuke her if you will, but chastise her not. The whip is an odious instrument, even when used to the brute animal alone;—when applied by man to torture his fellow, it becomes as a fire that consumes both the victim, and him that throws it on the pile.

Abas. Your wisdom speaks most wisely; and I will rebuke the slave. For the fashion of the——

Epam. My good friend, no more of that, I pray you. If in aught I can render you service, say it:—if not, I have matter for reflection here, and would gladly be left at leisure.

Abas. Of a surety, my lord! and I humbly take my leave, and wish you a good-morning.

Epam. Friend, farewell. (*He returns to his seat.*)

Abas. And now, my honest Protus, will I read to thee the riddle I—— Hey! how's this? gone off? singular ill manners —even in a clown;—but Clonius gone too! the ungrateful fellow—whom nothing but my foolish kindness keeps from the society of a jail! As I am a true Theban! there he walks with as much majesty as if his body were his own property. Holla!— holla—holla—I say! By the glorious Apollo! he heeds me no more than if I were a wood-louse! A pestilent—ungrateful scoundrel!—Within this hour shalt thou see the dungeon-grate for thy prospect; and thy music shall be the clink of fetters. A horrible—heartless—thankless—impudent fellow!

[*Exit, towards the city.*

Epam. Ye gods! of what strange stuff have ye made man!
Yet some o't's excellent.
    Pelop. (*without*).   Lead back my horse;
And gently—for this run hath tried him hard.
    (*He enters slowly, still talking to the grooms without.*)
And see that Nimrod's wound be tended well:—
I never saw a better mettled dog.
Here—take my boar-spear too; and let the smith
Secure the rivets.—Ha! my placid friend!
Kind soldier,—brave philosopher,—good-morrow!
    Epam. The same to thee, Pelopidas. Look here.
Dost see yon man-shaped thing, cleaving the mist?
'Tis an old tailor,—an anatomy
That cuts out cloth,—and holds discourse of sleeves,
Shreds, remnants, hems, and tucks—backstitch, and gussets;
Yet to himself he's a divinity.—
Jove rules not with a lordlier hand the fates
Of helpless man, than doth that shadowy thing—
Now melted in the unsubstantial fog—
The lives and actions of whom Fortune puts
Into his grasp. ' I have a slave '—quoth he,—
' A female slave—a disobedient wretch:—
But, if to scourge her deep, or put to death,—
I am in doubt:—will you resolve me, sir?
For you are wise.'
    Pelop.   A most dispassioned lord!
And what was the offence?
    Epam.   His slippers brought
Ofttimes uncleaned;—his mantle badly brushed;—
His needles lost;—his goose ta'en from the fire;—
His witty sayings mock'd behind his back,—
And twenty such abominable things,
The least a crime for death.
    Pelop.   And what said you?
    Epam. 'Doubtless,' said I—' these are most serious things!
Slay her;—and do it by some curious death,
Shall mark to after-times her heinous sins,

And your rare vengeance. Then erect a tomb,
And on it have engraven the whole tale.
Say, how a much-respected man of Thebes—
A tailor, old and wealthy—had a slave ;—
There give your name and hers—a female slave,
Of such, and such offences guilty :—there
Note down—' your slippers dirty—needles lost—
Jokes laugh'd at,'—note them all ;—let times to come
See all the villainies ;——and then conclude,
' This horrid wretch was justly flogged to death,—
Roasted—or boil'd,'—just as your whim shall be,
' A warning to the disobedient.'

  Pelop. How took the tailor that?
  Epam.   With most grave face,
At first,—like one who listens with quick ear
To some wise judgment, whereto he assents.
Now would he nod, and twinkle his small eye ;
Now lift his furrow'd brow ;—now turn aside,
With head aslant hard-gazing on the ground,
Filled with prodigious greatness ;—but, erelong,
The light came o'er him, and he saw, asham'd,
His judgment-throne changed to a tailor's board,
His sceptre to a yard. Enough of him !—
I wish there were not thousands such as he !—
Where hast thou been ? and what hath brought thee here ?

  Pelop. What ! hast not heard the Spartans are at hand?
  Epam. No, truly !—how ?—what Spartans ?
  Pelop.   Can it be?
Or dost thou want more tailors for thy wit ?
  Epam. In very sooth I nothing know of this.
  Pelop. Why I—an hour back—and three leagues away,
Hard in pursuit of a most noble boar,—
A monster bristled like a porcupine,
Tusk'd like an elephant,—and with a——
  Epam.   Stay !—
No more of that ! I join not in the chase,
Nor hear of it with pleasure. To the rest.

Pelop. Well, 'twas a noble brute! But, as I said,
Thus distant, thus employed,—I hear the news
Which thou, an idler, and upon the spot,
Art ignorant of.
  Epam. So chances it sometimes.
For Rumour's couriers do not always hold
The broad, straight highway;—but, like drunken knaves,
Oft turn aside to where a welcome waits.
Yet less an idler do I count myself,
Discoursing with divine Pythagoras,—(*pointing to his book*),
Or to these solemn trees, or cloud-swept hills,
Putting mute questionings—albeit my limbs
And muscles move not—than Pelopidas,
Hot from the chase,—and reeking with the spoil.
Think'st thou the mind hath not its exercise?
Aye! and far nobler game to chase! The spoil
Far richer, and not bloody!
  Pelop.   There are birds
That shun the day, and go abroad at night;
Others, whose wings are spread with the first dawn,
And folded at the sunset;—some that fly,
With dull, slow pennon, ever nigh to earth,—
And others that seem couriers 'twixt the stars,
So pierce they the blue sky;—some sweetly sing
All the night through,—and some but in the day;—
In winter some,—and some sing not at all:—
These in the hedge, or low grass, build their nests;
And those in rocks that overhang the clouds.
Even of such various natures are we men:
Spendthrifts, and misers; fools, philosophers;
Idlers, and busy; soldiers, men of peace;
Cautious, and headlong; fierce as raging flame,
And quiet as the night-breeze, that scarce moves
The down on the young redbreast where he sleeps.
  Epam. Go on—I like thy rare philosophy
Far better than thy boar-hunts.
  Pelop.   Nay—'tis done.
The nightingale can never change his note

With the hoarse raven—nor the gloomy owl
Bathe in the sun-stream with the fire-eyed eagle ;—
Nor more can *we* our proper natures change.
Thou'rt a philosopher ;—a soldier I—
A hunter—and a wrestler——

  EPAM.   Nay—but hold !—
Thou *art* a soldier, and a good one too,—
And passing brave,—for thou dost beat thyself,—
Talking philosophy by th' hour, to prove
Thou'rt no philosopher.

  PELOP.   Then be it so !
Men bear with patience *blows* they give themselves ;
Yet, if their neighbour do but wag a straw
To threat them, swords must kiss,—and wounds must ope
Their bloody lips to answer it.—
          But see !
The thirsty sun, who all the night hath chased
The darkness that still flies as fast away,
Drinks up the fog. Would I had such a throat !
I've had a chase almost as hot as his—
I'd quench my drouth with the great Indian sea,
And show its depths to daylight.

  EPAM.   Those are arms
That twinkle so in this dim sunshine. Look !

  PELOP. In truth they are. I see spear-heads,—and glance
Of polish'd breastplates.

  EPAM.   I spy helmets too ;—
And now they put up tents ; and I can see
Scarlet apparel.—'Tis the force you spake of.
What make they here ? Hath it been well considered ?
What say the Archons, and the Senate to it ?

  PELOP. All men know of it,—and consider it
According to their humours. Of the Senate,
Some blame, and some approve. The Archons, too,
In this, as in all other matters, jar ;
Ismenias, and our party like it not :—

Proud Leontidas, and his purse-gorg'd crew,
The haughty Aristocracy, commend.

EPAM. Who leads them on? and whither are they bound?

PELOP. What! hast thou drunk of Lethe, that thy brain
Doth hold no figures of the past? Bethink thee!
When—'tis not yet a month,—for yon worn moon,
So thin and sickly, was then two nights old—
Eudamidas, with his two thousand, pass'd
Against th' Olynthians——

EPAM. Ha! I know it all.
These, then, are the fresh troops whom Phœbidas
To reinforce them leads.

PELOP. Rather, I think,
This is the army's self,—of which the first
Was but a handful;—the thin end o' th' wedge;
Keeping the place till this, the broader back,
Were ready for the stroke.

EPAM. I like it not!
This Phœbidas is a vain, shallow man:
Will swallow flattery as the glutton shark
Gulps the small fry by shoals. Nought comes amiss;
No compliment too vast;—none too minute.
Call him a god,—he rubs his hands, and smiles:—
Commend his perfumes, or his glossy hair,—
His toothpick, or his sandals;—still he smiles:—
Or say Achilles had not such a thigh,—
Or Helen such a lapdog;—'tis the same—
He smiles, and takes it all.—'Tis dangerous
To trust such men with power. Who comes this way?

PELOP. Ha! 'tis a worthy man,—a friend of mine,
And shall be your friend. I've oft promis'd him
To bring him to you. But, for a rare piece
Of Nature's workmanship, look to the dame
That leans upon him; 'tis his new-wed wife;
The daughter of rich Thrasymed of Corinth.

EPAM. As well as from this distance I may see,

She seems, indeed, a jewel for a crown.
With what a grace she bends her to that flower!

PELOP. And rises now like—oh! like nothing else
But her own loveliness. Yet 'tis no flower
That she has gather'd—but some stone or gem :—
See how she holds it in her delicate hand
Betwixt the sunlight and her sunny eye.

EPAM. Will they come hither, think you?

PELOP.   So it seem'd
As they advanc'd; if not, we'll seek them there.

EPAM. I never saw a shape so like to what
The poets in their verses make us dream of.

PELOP. Oh! she is *more* surpassing beautiful!
Hast thou not seen a willow, by the brink
Of some bright stream when the warm south-west comes
To toy, and whisper with it;—how each leaf,
And long, down-drooping branch waves gracefully :—
Bends inward now,—as from the breeze it shrank
For that it kiss'd too lovingly :—now wafts
Sidelong its feathery hands, as it would say
Farewell—farewell :—then downward drops its leaves
Into the dimpling stream,—and, lifting them,
Seems as 'twould rain a shower of crystal tears,
For that the fickle zephyr had gone by.

EPAM. I' faith, a rare and most pathetic tree!

PELOP. Now, with a proud humility, bows down
Its regal top, like to a jewel'd queen
That courtesies lowly to her throned lord,—
And now, lets go its tresses to the breeze,
Like joyous flags that wave on festivals. . . .

EPAM. I see one such on the Cadmea now.
But, in Apollo's name, what means it all?

PELOP. Oh! you perplex me!—for my meaning, *that*,
I' faith I scarce can tell ;—but, yester-even,
I rode from Copæ, coasting by the lake ;—
The waters look'd so beautiful, beneath
The gawdy-colour'd sky, I could not leave them.

EPAM. It was indeed a gorgeous firmament!

PELOP. You saw it? Well, just where the river runs
Out of the lake, there is a willow-tree
Such as I pictured. The last sun-tints burn'd
Upon it;—and the evening wind so moved
Its delicate branches, that I stood to gaze,
Saying within myself: 'Sure never thing
Moved with such perfect gracefulness!'—And then,
I know not why—this lady's image came
Into my thoughts:—so now, beholding her,
I think of *it* again.

EPAM.   And is this all?
The little hillock had a mountain's bulk,
Seen through your mistiness. Yet so it is:—
The beautiful doth conjure up its like
Ofttimes in things that do seem opposite
As heaven to earth. A little flower shall—
Sprinkled with shining points—bring to your mind
The starry firmament; a grassy field,
Waving before the breeze on a May morn,
Shall make you think on ocean's plumbless deeps.
Yet look not, gentle friend, too oft on things
That shall recall that lady to your thought.
Sweet-looking fruit may have a bitter taste,
Touch'd by unholy lips.

PELOP.   Oh Jupiter!
May not one gaze at some bright-twinkling star,
Nor wish to steal it?—She's my dear friend's wife,
And *so* fenc'd round with rock of adamant;
But, were such fruit my own,—by heavens! methinks
I'd swallow it at once.

EPAM.   Soft—soft—they come.

(*Enter* ANDROCLIDES *and* THULIA.)

PELOP. Good-morrow, Androclides;—and, sweet Thulia,
A thousand, and ten thousand happy morrows.
I've promis'd oft to bring you to the shine
Of our bright Theban sun.—Epaminondas,

This is my good friend Androclides ;—this
The goddess who to young Anchises here
Hath given her hand ;—although, on further thought,
'Twas not the fashion with that dame to wed,
And these *have* been to th' altar—so, at once,
I'll name her as the lady Thulia—
The wife of this same blushing friend of mine.

EPAM. They're both most welcome. Often have I heard,
In the mad talk of this our *hunting* friend,
Of your true worth, and shall esteem me rich,
Possessing such a friendship.—Your fair lady
Oft makes companions of the morning hours,
If that her cheek tell truth.

ANDRO. She's nought but truth !

THULIA. What ! Androclides ! You turn'd flatterer too ?
I've heard you say such things were but base coin
With a fair impress ;—nay, you call'd them trash,
Such as the merchants give to savage men
Of Ind ;—expecting, for their worthless toys,
Gold-dust, or costly jewels :—knaves, and fools,
You call'd the parties—ha !—what say you, sir ?

ANDRO. That you're a little knave, to use those arms
Upon your friends, were given you 'gainst your foes.

PELOP. Hark, Androclides—I've a rare conceit
Just hatch'd, and it must forth. We'll call thy wife,
For that she is of Corinth,—and to thee,—
A plain, strong pillar—the chief ornament—
We'll call her thy Corinthian Capital.—
What say you, lady?—Shall it not be so ?

THULIA. The Capital is nought without the shaft
That gives it eminence ; nor would I wish
For better name than Androclides' wife.
But, good my lord, jest on, if so you will.

ANDRO. Look ! here's the man who pass'd us even now
With such vehement gesture :—sure he's mad !

EPAM. Ha ! 'tis our wrathful tailor.—Honest friend,
Whither away so fast ?

(ABAS *enters with a Bailiff bearing off* CLONIUS.)

ABAS. I'll hear nothing. You are an ungrateful and insolent villain! Ask the iron bars shortly, and you'll find them as soon to be bended as I am. If you don't like to go to prison,—why, pay the money—that's all.

CLONIUS (*holding back*). Wait but a moment while I speak to these gentlemen;—they may perhaps assist me.

ABAS. Drag him along, bailiff: a horrible miscreant—gentlemen assist you indeed! Drag him along;—and if you'll put the heavier fetters upon him, why, your fee shall be the heavier. Thankless! saucy! proud-stomach'd!—Ha! my good lords! I did not see you. Bailiff, let the youth rest a moment;—we have time enough,—and such offices should be gently administer'd— As I've heard you often say, my lord—for you are always kind.

EPAM. So are not you. Fair maxims in the head,
With a foul heart,—are but the golden spots
Upon a deadly serpent.—What's your debt? (*to Clonius*).

CLONIUS. A hundred drachms, my lord;—I undertook to pay it upon the death of my father—for it was a debt of his.

EPAM. Who was your father?

CLONIUS. He was of Thebes—and his name was Mydon. He was slain at the battle of Coronæa.

EPAM. At Coronæa?

ABAS. Yes, my lord, I——

EPAM. Peace!
Now,—Androclides—this hath happen'd well
To put the seal to our new covenant
Of friendship. You are wealthy—I am poor;
Nor, but for such a purpose, would be rich,
Save in the treasures of philosophy.
Discharge this youth, and take him to your home.
I'm sure he's honest, and will serve you well.
I read his heart.

ANDRO. More joyfully I give,
Than he can take his freedom,—for I am

The greater gainer—gaining the proud right
To call myself Epaminondas' friend.
What is your debt?

CLONIUS. A hundred drachms, my lord.

ANDRO. Here are two hundred. Satisfy this man,
And keep the rest as earnest of your hire,
If you incline to serve me.

CLONIUS. Oh! my lord!
I'd serve you, were't to swallow fire, or hack
My limbs to pieces. While I live all thoughts
Shall be towards your pleasure. And—kind sir!——

EPAM. Nay!—throw me not again the coin I gave:—
I did but utter a few quiet words
That cost me nothing. Let them rest.

CLONIUS. Oh! heavens!

PELOP. So!—I'm discharged from office,—and you, sir,
Are the new treasurer——

THULIA. No! you shall be
Joint partners in this holy ministry;
And I your humble servitor. How say you?

PELOP. Lady—your slightest censures are strong laws
That bind rebellious thoughts. But now, my friend,
Where are you bound?

ANDRO. Our sauntering had no aim
But the fresh morning air; yet now, we hope,
'Twill turn to noble purpose:—our new friend
Will grace our house with you:—

THULIA. If that be 'nay'—
To bring forth which you have purs'd up your brow,—
I do forbid it.—'Tis an ugly knave
That stabs young friendships often to their death—
I *will not* hear it.

EPAM. 'Twas indeed a *nay*,
That I had fashioned,—for my purpose was
To make the fields this day my study room :

But to that *nay* I'll say another *nay*,
And go along with you.

ANDRO.   We thank you, sir ;
And hope our entertainments shall approve
The love we bear you.—*You* will go with us?

PELOP. Ev'n as you will.   I came to see yon camp :
But I spy others going the same way—
Whom I were loth to meet——   Let them pass by.

(*Enter* LEONTIDAS,—ARCHIAS,—*and* PHILIP.)

LEON. You look hard at us, gentlemen, this morning.
Have you been anger'd somewhat at the sight
Of our good friends i' th' camp?

PELOP.   Who looks *not* hard
If a foul scaly dragon pass him by?—

LEON. Hot-headed youth! beware the dragon's teeth!
His eyes are on thee, and thy factious crew.—
Farewell—farewell.

PELOP.   Foul dragon, take *thou* heed!
Thine eyes are charmless,—and thy venom'd teeth
May be pluck'd out.   Hence to thy friends, black snake!
The air is poison'd round thee.

LEON.   Mad-brained boy!
Thou'lt hear of this anon.   Come friends—away!

[*Exit* LEON.

ARCHIAS (*to* PHILIP). Didst ever see a thing so beautiful?
Whence is she?—what's her name?

PHILIP.   I'll tell thee all
As we go on.—Good Democrats—adieu!

[*Exeunt* PHILIP *and* ARCHIAS.

PELOP. Foul Oligarchs—to hell!—
   (*To* EPAMINONDAS) Give me a word.

ABAS (*aside*). I'm glad of this ; and will cut close, and try to save good cloth by 't.—What a tiger this boar-hunter is, being roused! And yet I think the dragon shall bite his nails for

him. But, till then, I must stroke his paws, and pat him on
the back :—and, maybe, I shall come in for a share of his skin
after he is killed. Now, good youth (*to* Clonius), thou'lt not
forget to say to thy master what I have expounded unto thee :
—and be sure I'll not forget my promise to thee :—and—more
than that—but come this way, and I'll let thee further into the
matter.

    Thulia. Oh! my dear lord !—these rough encounters shake
My nerves almost to death.—What dark, stern man
Is that your friend so bitterly reviled ?—

    Andro. 'Tis Leontidas :—and the other twain
Are Archias—and Philip.

    Thulia.   Which was he
With the red beard ?—he bore his sword up thus,
Under his arm.—

    Andro.   Oh ! that was Archias ;
A loose, debauched man.

    Thulia.   I'd rather see
Toad—adder—newt—or aught more loathsome still,
Than that man's countenance. Oh ! it is bad !

    Epam. (*to* Pelop.) That will be well. I'll call on you at night
And hear how you have sped. And, if the Senate
Should favour you,—then stir Ismenias up
To bolder questioning.—Shall we attend you ? (*to* And. *and*
    Thu.)

    Thulia. We shall be proud to be *your* satellites.

    Epam. Come, then, fair lady ; I'm your guest to-day.

    (*Exeunt* Androclides—Thulia—*and* Epaminondas.
    As Pelopidas *is going out* Abas *detains him.*)

    Abas. Most honor'd lord !—May I entreat one word ?

    Pelop. Quick then, for I'm in haste.—

    Abas. Oh ! my dread lord! I fear that I may this day have
fallen under your most terrible displeasure.—

    Pelop. Thou hast :—for thou art a tyrant to thy slaves, and

wouldst be a slave to tyrants. I know thee now, and cast thee off. [*Exit.*

ABAS. But, most valiant, and honor'd lord! be not so terrible in punishing so awfully for such a little sin! Think—good my lord!—for fifty years yourself—your honor'd father—and his father—have my poor hands been favor'd to clothe in rich habiliments—wherein, of a surety, most gracious and honor'd —— What! is he gone?—A foolish, raw-brain'd boy! I'll give him up,—him and all his party!—I see, clear enough, what color'd cloth will be worn next, and they shan't find me out o' th' fashion. Aye—aye—my hot mettled lad! my old thimble may outlast thy young head yet. I'll pay my court to Leontidas now, and to Philip, and to the yellow-bearded Archias: —and I'll lose no part o' th' sunshine for want of going betimes to work.—Cast me off—indeed!—poor green boy!— Cast me off!

(*As he is going off, the* BAILIFF *stops him.*)

BAILIFF. Tarry one moment, master o' mine. You promised me double fee, you know, for coming out o' my way when I was about other business. Your rich promises are apt to stink if they be not sometimes stirr'd.

ABAS. Why, thou most unconscionablest low fellow! Hast thou taken him to prison? thou knave! If thou say'st another word, I'll let the Archons know of thy neglect of duty; thou vile, avaricious—and over-reaching villain! Pay thee double fee?—Oh! thou doubly double-faced knave! Out o' my sight!

BAILIFF. Then, my old goose-iron, I'll get my fee out of that yellow, parchment hide o' thine: thou vile, stinking old weasel! [*Exit* ABAS, *pursued by the* BAILIFF.

SCENE II.—*The Lacedemonian Camp.*

(*Enter* PHŒBIDAS, *with a* SOLDIER *walking a little behind him.*)

PHŒBIDAS. Then let them move a little farther west: Is the brook sweet and clean?

SOLDIER. 'Tis as bright as diamond, my noble general: and, for sweetness, I never tasted its fellow, except from a small gush that I found one sultry day as I was climbing one

of the hills that rise out of the vale of Tempe ; and that of a
surety was . . .

 Phœb. Well—well—then let them move. But see the
ground
Is firm and dry—or else their bones may rue it.
And look they rear my tent beneath the shade
Of yon huge chesnut,—for these misty morns
Bring ever a fierce sun.
     (*Enter another* Soldier.)

 2nd Soldier. Three gentlemen of Thebes, most noble
general, desire to be admitted to you.

 Phœb. Who are they? Ha! my noble friends! good-
morrow.
This is most kind.

    (*Enter* Leontidas, Archias, *and* Philip.)

 Leon. Archias *and* Philip (*speaking together*). Good morrow, Phœbidas.   [Soldiers *go out.*

 Leon. Why, Phœbidas !—have you some charm or drug
To make the years run backward ? By my troth
You are a younger man than five years back
Presented you. Is't not five years ?—'tis more—
When was it we met last ?

 Phœb.   No—'tis but four.
'Twas the third year o' th' last Olympiad,
At Mantinea, was't not ?

 Leon.   So it was.
And well can I remember how you fought
That glorious day. By Mars ! I flatter not ;
But you outdid what I had e'er conceived
Of the great captains that beleaguer'd Troy !

 Phœb. Nay—nay—you flatter now ! I did my best,
And that was all.

 Leon.   So thousands did their best,—
But yours was best of thousands.—Philip—you
Can never have forgot how, when our wing,

Broken—gave way before the Arcadian horse,
And all seem'd lost,—then, like victorious Mars,
Came Phœbidas upon his thundering steed.

PHILIP. Snatch'd from the flying standard-bearer's grasp
The glittering pennon :—with a dreadful shout
Rush'd on th' astonish'd victors ; drove them back——

LEON. Scatter'd before him like the dust——

PHILIP.   Trod down—
And vanquish'd utterly.

PHŒB.   Well—well—kind friends,—
And if 'twere so, there were brave men besides
Who have most well deserved.

LEON.   Yet but one
Who did the best deserve.

PHŒB.   Oh ! still you flatter !
Yet, in a sort, I do confess your praise
Not undeserved quite :—but still you flatter !

LEON. Far from it !—Your deserts above our praise
Still soar, as, over the high-climbing waves,
The broad-hull'd ship ;—go they as high as heaven,
It still o'ertops them. . . But, brave Phœbidas,—
Would you all former glories quite eclipse ;—
And draw on you the gaze of all mankind,
As on a new sun in the firmament—
Listen to me.

PHŒB.   Most patiently I'll hear.—

ARCHIAS (aside). I wonder what's the color of her hair ;—
I think 'tis golden :—something near my own :—
Her eye was blue,—I'm sure on't.

LEON.   Now, my lord.—
You go against Olynthus, a small town,—
Whose conquest yet shall cost you many lives,—
Much time,—much treasure :—be controlled by me
And you shall vanquish a far greater city ;—
The time almost o' th' instant ;—the cost nought ;—
The victory sure and bloodless.

PHŒB.   You speak wonders!

LEON. Which you may *act*:—and for such services
Your country shall applaud,—nay worship you.

PHILIP. Be sure on't! or all men will hold them base.

PHŒB. Go on.

LEON.   Then thus. You know how in our Thebes
Two parties stand at deadly variance:
One, friends to Sparta, and just government,—
In which we rank ourselves:—the other wild,
Fierce brawlers-out for loose democracy,
Which they call freedom;—in whose faction stand
Ismenias—Pelopidas——

PHŒB.   Go on—
I know it all. What follows?

LEON.   This, my lord.
Either we must crush them, or else be crush'd.
The frenzy now is at its height; and blood
Must be drawn forth to cool it.—Would you aid
Your country's enemies?—pass on your way:—
They are the stronger, and must soon prevail;—
And Thebes shall then be Sparta's bitterest foe:—
But, would you now befriend your country's friends?
Which, done, makes Thebes to Sparta like a child
To a beloved father,—say but so—
I'll shew you how to do it.

PHŒB.   Pray you, on!
You know I'm yours in all things.

LEON.   Then, at once—
This day the women hold the feast of Ceres
In the Cadmea. At the hour of noon,
When all will be reposing from the heat,
And the town still as night, have ready then
Your heavy armèd men as for a march.
I'll meet you here again, and lead you straight
Into the Citadel.—No man is there,
In reverence to the mysteries of the feast:—

The women we can quiet,—lock the gates ;
And Thebes is yours !

  PHILIP.   Now, valiant Phœbidas,—
Looks it not well ?

  PHŒB.   It seems indeed most fair !

  LEON. It cannot fail. And mark the consequence :
You masters,—*we* are masters,—and shall do
As Thebes to Sparta should. You know it well,
A proclamation hath been sent abroad,
Forbidding any citizen of Thebes
To join you in your march against Olynthus.
But, do as I advise ;—and we will send,
To aid you, numerous troops of horse and foot ;—
Staunch men that you may trust.

  PHILIP.   What say you to't ?

  PHŒB. Ha ! truly 'twill be well !

  LEON.   It *shall* be well !
Thus, with a powerful army, will you march
To reinforce your brother ;—and, ere he
Can take Olynthus, you shall capture Thebes,
A far more mighty city.

  PHILIP.   Think but then
How all tongues shall be busy with thy praise !
' The hero Phœbidas '—from mouth to mouth
Shall go, in every city, where'er Greece
Is known, or valour talk'd of :—all——

  PHŒB.   Great Mars !
I thank thee ! Gallant friends, it shall be done !
It shall be done ! This instant will I go
About the work ;—and at the noontide hour,
Look to behold me.

  LEON. Wise, and valiant man !
Then hie thee to the task : and the great Gods
Prosper our just designs ! Till noon adieu !

  PHILIP *and* ARCHIAS. Adieu, most noble Phœbidas.

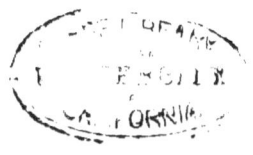

PHŒB. Kind friends—
Farewell,—we soon shall meet again.

LEON. One word.
Coming to you, we pass'd the factious chiefs:
Lest they should aught suspect of our intents,
Give orders through your camp for a new march;
Be the tents struck :—and show all outward sign
Of hasty going hence.

PHŒB. 'Tis wisely urged,
And shall be done. Once more adieu. [*Exit.*

PHILIP (*speaking loud*). A brave and noble man!
(*Then, after a pause*) The shallowest ass
That ever walk'd upright, and gossip'd Greek!

LEON. But still he bears our gold.—Go after him,
And stay with him. Some wise forethought, or scheme
May blaze up in his brain, that, of *our* plan,
Would soon make dust and ashes. Thou, being by,
Mayst pour upon it streams of quenching words
That shall extinguish it.

PHILIP. If he take fire,
I'll wash him well, be sure on't. Fare you well. [*Exit.*

LEON. Now, Archias,—let's away! We've much to do,
The Senate will soon meet, and we must speak
To every separate friend of this high matter.
Stay,—you shall call on—No! I'll do't myself,
He'll like it better. Come, away. [*Exit.*

ARCHIAS. By heavens! he dies! she must—she shall be
mine! [*Exit.*

END OF THE FIRST ACT.

ACT II.

SCENE I.—*The Citadel. Women holding the feast of Ceres.*
Hymn—sung in Chorus.
(*Enter* LEONTIDAS, *and* PHŒBIDAS,—*in armour.*)

PRIESTESS. The mysteries are profan'd! break off! break off!
(*The women shriek and run to and fro.*)
Oh! Ceres, Proserpine, and Pluto, haste!
Avenge! avenge the violated rites!—
Cry, women, cry! let the heav'ns hear the deed!
Ye horrid men, detested by the Gods!
Get hence! get hence!

LEON.   Good priestess! hear one word.

PRIESTESS. I will hear nought, profaning wretch! get hence!

LEON. I *will* get hence,—so thou wilt hush this noise,
And hear me speak.

PRIESTESS.   Women, forbear! forbear!
Now—what hast thou to say? irreverent man!
Quick—and depart!

LEON.   Most gentle priestess; list
With patient ear.—With no unholy thought,
No over-curious eye,—no foul design
To interrupt your hallow'd mysteries
Are we come here.—

PRIESTESS.   What then?—intruding man!
Thy life may answer this!

LEON.   Sweet priestess! hear!
My life *may* answer it;—but that is nought
Where lives of thousands are upon the die.
In brief:—A giant sword hangs in the air,
And is about to fall.—When the sea chafes,
The stateliest barks must be content to toss,

---

* Probably never written, as a vacant space for its insertion is left in the original MS.—*M. E. A.*

As giddily as cock-boats :—and so now,
In this turmoil and tempest of events,
Your dignities, and reverend privilege
Must yield like meaner things.—

  Priestess.   Ye Heavenly Powers!
Have ye no scourges left?—Who art thou, man?

  Leon. (*taking off his helmet*). Chaste priestess! know'st me
  now?

  Priestess. Immortal Gods!
The Archon?—the stern Leontiades?
Can *he* be the profaner of the rites?—
The cold,—severe—the proud?—

  Leon.   Stay, priestess! stay!
Thou know'st me; and shouldst know that no loose thought,
No madman's freak, hath moved me in this act.
Time's hour-glass now is dropping golden sands;
And I must hence. What is about to be
Ye cannot know. Enough, that it *must* be.
With that content you. For your better peace,
Thus much I say:—this tempest hath no bolt
'Gainst you, so you provoke it not. No hand
Shall touch you,—not an eye shall look on you,
So ye but keep retir'd. The place you hold
Must be left free.

      (*To* Phœbidas) Now lead your soldiers here.
Lock fast the gates,—and let none enter in
Save such who bear my passport.   [*Exit* Phœbidas.
         Factious crew!
Your good deeds now shall have their guerdon due.

  Priestess. My lord—these actions are most strange!

  Leon.   They are.
All things are strange; their causes being hid:—
But, known—are common matters. Is't not strange
That the bright sun—the moon—and all the stars
Should, like a monstrous wheel, roll round this earth?
And is't not passing strange that the great sea——

      (Phœbidas *brings in his troops, behind.*)

Many voices of women. Oh! heavens! arm'd men! arm'd men! we are betray'd!

LEON. Silence! ye cackling geese,—and get ye hence! Priestess, away with them;—and let them know They're safe while they are silent.
                      (*To* PHŒBIDAS) I go now
Straight to the Senate. Look to hear anon
The thunder burst that way. Farewell.   [*Exit.*

PHŒB. And let the peal roar till all Greece shall rock.
Now, soldiers,—lock the gates, and make all safe.
Sure never fortress was so lightly won!
    (*The women go out. The troops continue to pour in till the next scene drops.*)

SCENE II.—*An anteroom leading to the chamber in which the Senate is assembled.*

(*Two* GUARDS *enter, and pace before the door.*)

1ST GUARD. Hark! didst ever hear such a noisy debating? —That's the voice of young Pelopidas. He's teasing Philip about the Spartan troops. Hush!

2ND GUARD. Who is't speaks now?

1ST GUARD. Ismenias—and now Philip—and now Pelopidas again, as if he were cheering on a boar-hunt. If thou and I, now, were to be as noisy over our potations, as these be over their disputations,—why, the fetters—you know;—or a kiss from the whip for us.

2ND GUARD. And reason good! Are not these all lords? and are we not poor men? Zounds! man—'tis quite a different matter! Your poor man is nothing but dregs at the bottom of a barrel;—and your rich man is the wine above it.

1ST GUARD. Which is the reason, as I take it, that your dry-throated Death commonly draws off the rich man first: leaving the poor dregs at the bottom to dribble away drop by drop, so slowly that one hardly knows when the barrel is quite empty.

2ND GUARD. I know *thy* barrel is empty: for thou wentest to bed sober last night.

1st Guard. I wish thou hadst risen so! I tell thee I was as drunk last night as any gentleman need desire to be.

(*Enter* Thulia.)

Thulia. The young lord Androclides is within,— I' th' Senate: pray you call him out.

1st Guard. No! lady. I think he is not here this morning. I think I may say he is not here.

Thulia. Good friend—I know he *is* here. Call him forth, For that I have to say imports him much.

1st Guard. Lady, it cannot be:—for how can water be drawn out of a well that hath no water in it?—or the lord Androclides called out of a place in which the lord Androclides is not?

Thulia. Here, friend, is gold,—so thou wilt call him forth.

1st Guard. Faith! and that's a chain that will reach the very bottom of the well. I'll see if he be there—perhaps—while I was away—or before I came—'tis possible—What shall I say to him?

Thulia. Say that his wife would speak to him in haste.

1st Guard. His wife!—I cry you mercy, gracious lady!

(*Goes into the door of the Senate chamber.*)

Thulia. Oh! heavens! what passionate voices do I hear! Is there aught ill within?

2nd Guard. Oh no! my lady—no! Nothing but a little flustration about the Spartan soldiers in the fields yonder. We never take heed of this sort of hurly-burly. 'Tis only a kind of thunder-clap high up i' th' air, my lady,—that, maybe, cracks a cloud or two, but never comes to the earth.

(*Enter* Androclides *and the* 1st Guard.)

Andro. Well, sweet—what is it?

Thulia. Oh! my dearest lord! I'm much alarm'd.

Andro. You are not come alone?

Thulia. Oh no! my maids attend without. But first bid these rough men retire.

ANDRO.   Friends, by your leave,
We would be left an instant.   [*Exeunt* GUARDS.
                    Now, sweet girl,
Despatch, for there's a hot debate within,
And I am wanted.
    THULIA.   But, my gentle love,
Why will you mix in these intemperate broils?
Yet do not tell me.—Deeply I suspect
Some wicked scheme in progress. I had climbed
Our garden wall, to th' south, by a large knot
Of purple grapes allur'd—nay,—do not smile,—
'Twas not to please *my* palate. . .
    ANDRO.   Sweetest girl!
I did but smile to think what hideous giant
This dwarf would usher in.—Pray now go on—
By this dire bunch allur'd—what next?
    THULIA.   Nay--nay—
I pray you do not mock me, gentle love!
But listen now :—yet shall I be most glad
To have deserv'd your mocks. I had climbed up
To look if snail, or any harmful insect,
Were in the leaves, or fruit : 'twas all untouched,
Purple and bloom most beauteous. As I looked,
Admiring how each full distended grape
Glow'd like an amethyst in the bright sun,
And thinking how delightful 'twere——
    ANDRO.   To pop
One after t'other in that pretty mouth——

THULIA. Shame on you, love! I meant them for your friend.
You know he tastes no meats :—and when you went
So hastily unto the Senate-house,
He would not stay,—but to the fields walk'd forth,
Nor could my best entreaties more obtain
Than promise of return ere evening fall.
I hope he went not anger'd.
    ANDRO.   Oh! no--love!
He would have urg'd us rather, had we lagg'd.

But now for thy catastrophe !—this ladder
Is very hard to climb.—

THULIA.   Yet, to descend
To me was harder still ;—my limbs so shook,
And every muscle so appear'd to fail :—
As when, in dreams, you would attempt to run,
And cannot ;—you have dreamt so,—have you not ?

ANDRO. Aye, dearest Thulia,—many times.

THULIA.   But now
To the chief matter.   Resting on the ladder,
I heard a sound that, for the rustling leaves,
I took at first,—or it might be the brook
Across the meadow,—or some harmless snake
Brushing among the long grass :—or some bird
Bringing her fluttering young on their first flight :—
You know there are a hundred little sounds
Among the fields and woods, that seem to be
Voices of men far off,—or whisperings
Of nymphs or goddesses i' th' air unseen.

ANDRO. There are, my love.

THULIA.   And so I heeded not ;
But, on the ladder leaning, trained the leaves
To shade from the fierce sun the glistering grapes
Lest with o'er-ripeness they should burst ere night :—
And, sooth to say—but you will mock me now.—

ANDRO. No love ;—if it displease thee, I'll not mock.

THULIA. And if you do I care not.—I was lost
In a long reverie of that blest night
When,—sitting on the shore of the Piræus
To watch the sunset in the ruby waves,—
You,—travelling then to Corinth—stay'd your horse
To look upon it too.

ANDRO.   I did so, sweet !
But, seeing thee, forgot the setting sun.

THULIA. So was I lost, methought I heard anon
The hollow trampling of your horse's hoofs,—

And, turning, saw the grey steed pawing on :—
And then I looked again upon the waves—
And then anon I heard your first soft words,
Breath'd in my startled ear :—and then the sun
Was gone down ere I knew it ;—and my maids
Told me the night would fall, ere we reach'd home ;
Which seem'd most strange,—for I thought not of night,
Nor anything but what you told me of—
And, all the way to Corinth as we walked,
You seem'd to talk to me,—and pointed back
To the deep ruddy sea,—or up to heaven,—
Telling of wondrous things,—as then you did.—
And last I saw you in my father's hall—
And the dear good old man, with a glad smile,
Hastening to welcome you—— Oh ! heavens ! what noise !
Sure 'tis some mortal quarrel !

  ANDRO.   No, love, no.—
There's a hot war of words,—but nothing more.
Hush ! hush !—I thought 'twas Archias speaking then—
But 'tis not he. They'll push him hard anon,—
And 'tis a chase I'd gladly join :—so, sweet,—
Put spur into the side of thy slow words,
And let them gallop to a close.

  THULIA.   Well, then :—
From this sweet reverie I was arous'd
By a harsh, horrid laugh, just underneath,
From whose most loathsome dissonance I shrank
As from the touch of newt, or bloated toad,
It had such foulness in it :—one quick step
In my descent I'd taken,—when thy name,
Distinctly syllabled, came to my ear.—
I paused :—there was a low, dull, humming sound,
Like a monotonous reader,—but no word
Clear-utter'd as before ;—so once again
I was descending, when another voice,
Not louder, but articulate, and slow,
Arrested me. 'I thank thee for thy care '—
Such were the words,—' they shall be look'd to close ;

Thou shalt have ample vengeance;—and yon sun
Shall not set ere it falls.'

ANDRO. Well!—Is this all?

THULIA. All?—dearest Androclides?—Is't not horrid
To hear thy name, and such terrific threats
Coupled together?

ANDRO. But, dear Thulia!
'Tis not enough that they have stood together
In such disparted talk, as thou hast heard,
To prove affinity.—They might have named,
At such wide interspace, th' Eternal Gods,
And some new snare for vermin,—then wouldst thou
Infer great Jove turn'd rat-catcher!—Why—love—
'Twas some foul beggar threating broken heads
On those who had refus'd him broken meats—
Some tinker,—or some cobbler——

THULIA. Oh! no—no—
Excess of terror made me bold. I climb'd
To the wall's height, and, over-peering, saw
The dark-brow'd Archon,—and the loathëd face
Of Archias—and with them the thin old man,
From whom this morning you redeem'd the youth,
Our servant now.—

ANDRO. Indeed! they saw not you?

THULIA. No—for that instant they were taking leave,
And parted different ways.

ANDRO. 'Tis odd enough!
A tailor, and two lords of Thebes, conjoin'd!—
Some dreadful purpose, doubtless!—Shall we send
To Persia—to consult the Magi on't!
Three such malignant stars, conjunct, must point
At revolutions—deaths of mighty kings—
And fall of Empires!—

THULIA. Oh! my dear, dear lord!

ANDRO. Go—get thee to thy happy home, sweet wife :—

Enjoy the present;—for th' unknown *to come*
Trust the good Gods! Adieu—and go at once.
(*He embraces her, and returns to the chamber.*)
THULIA. I will, love;—yet my heart sinks utterly:—
What can it mean?
(*Enter* ARCHIAS.)

ARCHIAS. What! do the Graces deign to visit us?—
Or is't not rather love's sweet Queen herself?—
Bright Goddess! thy celestial presence fills
This chamber with ambrosia!

THULIA (*aside*). Thine with poison! [*Exit.*

ARCHIAS. What a delicious wrath was on her brow!
Her anger is more sweet than others' love!
Gods!—there's more brightness in her darkest frown,
Than in another's smile!—There is more music
When she most chides, than when another sings!
Oh! thou most excellent witch! I'll forge a wand
Shall over-charm thy charmings:—and to-day
It shall be done. [*Exit into the Senate-chamber.*

(*The foregoing scene draws, and discovers* SCENE III.—*The Senate-chamber.*)

PHILIP—ANDROCLIDES—PELOPIDAS—MELON—DEMOCLIDES
—THEOPOMPUS—PHERENICUS—ISMENIAS—CEPHISIDORUS
—GORGIDAS—ARCHIAS—*and other Senators.*

ISMENIAS, *as Archon, sits on an elevated seat. Another, near him, for* LEONTIDAS, *is empty.* ARCHIAS *stands whispering to a Senator who is just going out.*

PHILIP. I do deny it!—and your empty threats
Hold with the threateners in contempt. We never....

ISMENIAS. Stay, Philip—stay—You've spoken for yourself;
And made a plausive tale.—Let Archias
Speak also for himself:—but with no prompting!
[*Exit Senator.*

ARCHIAS. I understand you not;—nor is't my use
To put my words beneath the pilotage

Of any man—I need no prompter, sir ;—
Needing no clue to lie by.

  ISMENIAS.   Fairly spoke !

  MELON (*aside to* DEMOCLIDES). He means that he can lie without a prompter.

  ISMENIAS. Now, sir.—It hath been charg'd 'gainst certain Thebans,
Yourself o' th' number,—that for traitorous ends
They did, this morning, seek the Spartan's camp ;
Encouraging, by every friendly mark,
The bad design he undertakes :—'gainst which,
As a most tyrannous and foul attempt,
The Theban state has set its face,—and made
Wide proclamation that no citizen
Shall give thereto his aid.—Sir, to this charge
Philip hath made denial,—and, withal,
Out of his courtesy, hath reasons given
Why you did so—and so. Beseech you, sir,
In the simplicity of your rare truth,
That ' needs no clue to lie by '—tell us now
Why went you to yon camp ?—what did you there ?
When came away ?—with other lesser things
That, by coherence with this first report,
Shall make your innocence clear.

      (*A Pause.*)

  (*Several voices.*)   Speak, Archias.

  ARCHIAS. Hath Philip spoken,—say you ?

  ISMENIAS.   Yes, he hath ;
And we would hear you also :—that his words,
Finding their counterpart in yours, may stand
Unchalleng'd by the doubtfulest.

      (*A Pause.*)

  (*Several voices.*)   Speak, Archias.

  ARCHIAS. But was there not a third ?—Best question him
Before I answer. He hath readier speech,
And will convince you sooner.—See—he comes.

(LEONTIDAS enters, in armour, and remains near the door as if arrested by the words of ARCHIAS.)

They call us traitors, Leontidas,—friends
To Sparta, and the Persian,—and demand
Our business in the camp this morn.

    ISMENIAS.   We do!
Who sees the vultures gathering, but suspects
They have mark'd out their prey?—But, good my lord—
If you come arm'd against our questionings
With such strong mail as clasps your limbs about,
The contest must be short,—for we've nor words,
Nor swords, to pierce such proof.—Wilt please you say
Why this poor, peaceful company, and place,
You honour by this most unwonted pomp
And blazonry of war?

    LEON.   'Twill please me much
To answer thee, and all of you. My tale
Is short, and plain;—but, therewithal, hath pith
May make it well remember'd.—Gentlemen—
The Spartan troops are in the Citadel—
                          (The Senators start up.)
Be not alarm'd!—They are not enemies
Save to the friends of war and anarchy.—
This act had my advice.—And, furthermore,
As general of the State,—and, by the power
Lodg'd in me by the laws to apprehend
All traitors,—for a public enemy
I do attach thee here, Ismenias!—
                      (He steps up and seizes ISMENIAS.)

    PELOP. *(rushing on him).* Villain! thou'rt the traitor! Loose thy grasp,
Or I will tear thy soul out,—spite thy mail.

    LEON. Off! boy! or thou shalt rue it.—Soldiers—here!
Secure him,—and convey him,—you know whither.
    (The Spartan soldiers rush in. Great confusion, and cries of 'Treason!—treason!—fly!—we are betrayed!')

ISMENIAS. Thou damnëd villain!—Friends—away! away!
Thy hour shall come for this!—Haste—haste away!

(ISMENIAS *is dragged out. The friends of* PELOPIDAS *rush out at different doors. In the confusion* ARCHIAS *attempts to stab* ANDROCLIDES; *but misses him.*)

PELOP. (*standing by the door in a threatening attitude*).
Abhorrëd dragon! Thou hast stung us now:—
But mark me!—I will find a time to rend
Thy sting and life at once:—thou hellish pest!
Mark me! I say!— [*Exit.*

LEON. I will, so thou take not the speedier flight,
Thou factious democrat!—Now, friends—away—
Let's follow them:—the sight of us shall be
A spur in their gall'd sides to make them plunge
And hurry to the precipice.—Let them fly! Their blood,—
Being so many,—would breed hatred to us,
And stain the reputation of this act,
Which else shall shew most holy.—But—away!
[*Exeunt all but* ARCHIAS.

ARCHIAS. I think I touch'd him:—but the dagger's bright.
He will escape.—What then?—she stays behind:—
That's not so well:—the thought of him alive,
Would fret me in Elysium:—he *shall* die—
By heaven and hell I swear it—he *shall* die! [*Exit.*

SCENE IV.—*The city gate leading towards Athens.*
(*Many persons pass hastily out, flying from the faction of* LEONTIDAS.)

(*Enter* EPAMINONDAS—*from the fields.*)

EPAM. What means this headlong flight,—and these wild looks?

(*Several voices.*) Fly!—fly! Epaminondas.—Thebes is lost!

EPAM. Stay—stay—I charge you.—They are gone. Just Heaven!
What may this mean?—Pelopidas——

(*Enter* PELOPIDAS.)

PELOP. Good friend!
Turn back, and leave the city. As we go,
I'll tell thee all.

EPAM. What!—play the runaway—
And then ask what 'tis frights me?

PELOP. We're unarm'd,—
Or I would stay and beard them. The black Archon
Hath seized Ismenias,—brought the Spartan troops
Into the Citadel.—yea, to the Forum,
Whence armëd men have chas'd the Senators.
Still they pursue us :—we've nor arms nor soldiers,
And must submit.—Hark to yon blood-hound cries!
(*Shouts at a distance.*)

(*Enter* DEMOCLIDES, THEOPOMPUS, *and* PHERENICUS, *in haste.*)

DEMO. Fly! fly! Pelopidas.—They call for you.

THEO. Haste! for Heav'n's mercy haste!—they seek your life.

PELOP. But shall not have it. Make what speed you can
Tow'rds Athens—I am safe :—My horses wait
By this time in the palm-grove near the gate.
(*Shouts at a distance.*)
Hence! hence! Heaven guard you, friends!

DEMO., THEO., *and* PHER. Adieu—adieu!
[*Exeunt at the gate.*

EPAM. Pelopidas—I shall not fly with thee.

PELOP. Then wilt thou perish?—As my friend, thou'lt die
Wert thou as harmless as the new-yean'd lamb.—
Thou shalt not stay.—By heaven, I'll force thee hence
If thou resist!—

EPAM. Pelopidas—these times
Are like fierce fires, that separate the dross
From the pure metal.—'Tis no wondrous thing
To lead an honest, quiet life ;—read books,
And dole forth scraps of wisdom to one's friends ;—

Wive—and bring up good children ;—pay one's debts ;—
Give unmiss'd alms to the unfortunate ;—
And so live on a comfortable life
Of virtuous indolence,—at a small cost
Buying the kind opinions of the world :—
This may be only glittering hollowness.
The bubble that the children blow for sport—
Seen in the sunshine, and the unmov'd air—
Looks bright and hard as crystal :—but, a breath
Dissolves it.—I've known many men, my friend,
Who have led decent lives,—and, at their death
Been held up as examples,—who but lack'd
Courage or industry to have up-climb'd
Guilt's steepest precipice.

  Pelop.   But, my dear friend,—
You need no fire to prove your metal pure——
            (*Shouts again.*)

  Epam. Stay—stay—the moments are but few. Now—mark me!
Though the sky bend its arch, and threat to fall,
I'll not leave Thebes,—till I shall be made sure
I serve my country so.—

  Pelop.   Then I will bid
The groom lead back my horses.—I can die
As well as wiser men.   (*He goes to the gate.*)

  Epam.   Pelopidas—
Thou hast thy duties,—and I mine : the paths
May join again, tho' in their setting forth
Averse as North from South.—What is our goal?
Our country's good.—You seek it hence,—in arms,
I—here—by patience and mild argument.
I ask not you to tread my path :—forbear
To urge me upon yours. Each, separate,
May trip on lightly to his journey's end ;—
But,—forc'd together ;—one will lag by th' way,
And drag his fellow backward.—Now get hence !
            (*Shouts again.*)

I hear thy name, with no kind accent, call'd.—
Depart—I charge thee !—

PELOP.   Will your life be safe ?

EPAM. Unless you stay with me, to lose your own.
Their fangs, being flesh'd, might hunger for more food ;—
I have no other fear.—From time to time
Let me hear of you.—You're for Athens too?

PELOP. 'Tis our best refuge.—It were vain to beg,—
And you're the wiser.—Be it as you say.
Farewell, Epaminondas—dearest friend—
Farewell—farewell !—   (*They embrace.*)

EPAM.   Both shall, I trust, fare well,
Though th' heavens look frowning now. Adieu—adieu !
Dear youth—farewell—farewell !   [*Exit* PELOP.
   (EPAMINONDAS *stands at the gate to look after him.*)

EPAM. Heaven never wrought a nobler piece of work
Than thou art :—save thy huntings ;—that's not well :
And somewhat over-fiery art thou too,
Being provok'd,—or in the battle's rush :—
But thou art full of every nobleness ;—
Thy very gait bespeaks a lofty soul ;—
Thy kindling brow is like a sudden burst
Of sunshine on a cold and cloudy day.—
The just Gods prosper thee ! (*Shouts again.*)

(*Enter* MELON—CEPHISIDORUS—*and* GORGIDAS, *from the city.*)

MELON. Epaminondas, have you seen your friend ?

EPAM. Melon, I have. Look there ;—he rides as cool
As if he took an airing for his health,
Or to make sharp his appetite.

CEPHIS.   Who is't
That stops him now?

MELON.   'Tis Charon.

GORGID.   Heaven be prais'd !
The harpies yonder would have drunk his blood.

Epam. Perhaps not, good Gorgidas ;—we've sins enough
In what we *do ;*—let our *intents* lie still.
Were each man's guilt weigh'd by his enemy,
The monstrous mass would burst earth's ceiling in,
And crush th' infernal Gods. . . Cephisidorus,
You look not well.   I hope you ride.

Cephis.   My strength
Hath been much shaken by an obstinate ague ;
And this strange business doth me little good.
Farewell !—our horses wait.

Gorgidas *and* Melon.   Farewell—farewell.

Epam. Kind gentlemen, adieu !   Heaven be your guide !
                [*Exit* Epaminondas, *towards the city.*

Cephis. In sooth I'm very faint.

Gorgid.   Come, lean on me.

Cephis. I thank you.

(*Enter* Charon, *from the fields.*)

Charon. My noble friends, I grieve to hear of this !
Have you seen Androclides ?—Ha ! he comes.
                [*Exeunt* Gorgidas *and* Cephisidorus.

Melon. Charon, adieu !—you're on a slippery path,
Yet strive to walk alone, or he who stays you
May trip your heels up.

Charon.   Melon, thou art kind.   [*Exit* Melon.
Adieu—adieu !   I thank thee.—Androclides,

(Androclides *enters from the city*)

Where hast thou lagg'd ?   I saw Pelopidas
An instant back, nigh to the grove of palms.
He waits for thee, and wonders at thy stay.
Art thou not well ?

Andro.   Oh ! Charon.—I am sick !—
Sick to the heart.   I hasted to my home
To snatch from ruin the sole thing i' th' world
For which I care to live ;—and she was gone !—

But that I hope a friendly hand hath borne her
To some safe hiding,—I would perish here ;—
For life, without her, were but agony
Passing endurance !—

    CHARON.   Hope the best,—dear youth !
If she be left behind thee, all my power—
And, as a neutral 'twixt your adverse parties,
Thou know'st I *have* power—with what sway beside
Wealth, and a noble ancestry may give,—
All power and influence mine will I employ
To shield her, and, at fitter season, guide
Where thou shalt point the way.

    ANDRO.   Charon—dear friend !
Thou giv'st all comfort I can take.—Oh ! God !
                                      (*Shouts again.*)
Must I then go?—Mad hell-dogs ! ye would tear
Your grey-hair'd fathers, or your prattling babes
When you are raging.—Aye !—you call in vain !
He will not bleed beneath your tiger-claws——
                                      (*Shouts again.*)

    CHARON. Hence—hence :—your name is call'd. To linger here
May cost your life, and his. Beside yon clump
Of dwarfish oaks I left my horse : your flight
May be pursued ;—take him, and leave your own :—
You may defy all chase :—twice hath that steed
Been victor at th' Olympic games.—Hence—hence—
Your foes are close upon you.—Stay not now
For a leave-taking,—but farewell at once.

    ANDRO. Farewell—kind friend !—Oh Thulia ! where art thou ?   [*Exit through the gate.*

    CHARON. Unhappy youth !—There may be sharper stings
For man t' endure than thine ;—but oh ! not one
That with a deadlier sickness swells the heart
Almost to bursting !—I have known that pang.

(*Enter* LEONTIDAS, ARCHIAS, *and* PHILIP.)

LEON. Charon, good day.   Hast seen Pelopidas?

ARCHIAS. Hast thou seen Androclides, gentle Charon?

PHILIP. Who wast went hence ev'n now?

CHARON.   Good gentlemen,
Good day to all of you.   I wish 't may prove
Good day indeed.   But oft a wicked noon
Follows such morning, and a woful night
Closes what dawn'd so fair.

LEON.   True, noble Charon:
Therefore, to have a still and pleasant eve,
We shun the guilty noon.

CHARON.   I joy to hear it.
You shed no blood then?

ARCHIAS.   Philip—Philip—look!
There rides the wretch who sought my life—

CHARON.   Your life!—
Who's he that did so?

ARCHIAS.   Bloody Androclides!
Ev'n in the Forum!—see where his fell dagger
Hath pierc'd my robe,—aiming to pierce my heart!—
I'll after him;—his life shall answer it.—
(*Going to the gate.*)

LEON. Stay, Archias—stay—I do not think 'twas he.

CHARON. I'd stake my life he's free of this!

LEON.   Think, Archias,—
In such turmoil how soon the steadiest eye
Might be disturb'd, and see unreal things:—
And of the danger think, if private broils
With this great public question be mix'd up.
Desist, I charge you!

ARCHIAS.   To the public good
My private must bow down:—let him go free!—
But wilt thou then pursue Pelopidas,

Forbidding me my chase?—Is yours not, too,
A private broil?—

LEON.   No—Archias.—Went he not
Through every street exciting to revolt,—
Calling us tyrants;—bidding men take arms
And slay us on the instant? No one stirr'd
To act his bidding:—but his guilty aim
Not less deserv'd the penalty.—Yet, mark!
I give him up!—his blood shall not be shed
For this bad treason:—let thy private wrong
Pass to oblivion then.

PHILIP.   I think indeed
His blood shall *not* be shed,—at least o' th' instant;—
For,—else my eyes tell false,—he hath made free
To take his exercise, our leave unask'd,
On his black hunter yonder.

ARCHIAS *and* LEON.   Where? where?

PHILIP.   Stay—
Now look!—between yon row of poplars—now—
Just over that thick chesnut—

LEON.   Yes—'tis he.
You can't mistake his seat,—nor the proud lifting
Of his strong hunter's feet.—Well—let him go!—
And, gentlemen,—with most dispassion'd minds
Return we to the Forum,—there to hold
Discourse on what hath happen'd,—and to choose
With wariest circumspection our new path,
That, 'scaping this, we fall not in more snares.

CHARON. It glads me much to find such gentleness
I' th' rear of so much fury. I have friends
In both your parties,—being myself of none;—
And whichsoever shall oppress the other
Inflicts on me a grief.

LEON.   We'll be like bows
After the shafts are shot.—But hark!—The heralds
Make proclamation of our government;—

Let us away!—Charon, a word with you
As we go on.—Lend me your arm, I pray you.
I wrenched my ankle with a fall last night,
And now it stings me.

CHARON.   Have it look'd to, sir.
[*Exeunt* LEONTIDAS *and* CHARON.

PHILIP. Archias—didst thou hear the heralds?
ARCHIAS.   No!—

PHILIP. Nor I. 'Twere best we went to see the ceremony, —were it not? I'll hold you a wager, Archias, that, at the next Pancratium, Polydamus shall keep the ring against all comers.

ARCHIAS (*aside*). I'll employ a surer dagger,—and a more practised arm :—and I'll go about it immediately.

PHILIP. What dost thou mutter, Archias? Shall we not go after, to hear the proclamation? (*Aside*) No answer again? What the plague does he stare at?—Ha! 'tis his new dignity hath closed up his senses thus. It is wonderful how a carved stick, stuck in the hand,—or a robe of a new cut and fashion, should transform a man quite from the shape of his former self, and transmute all his thoughts and faculties,—his carriage, —and his most ordinary and unimportant actions as completely as the magic of Proteus could have done it,—which, in the twinkling of an eye shall change you a good portly man to a wisp of straw,—or the hind leg of a toad to a grave Senator. —I should like now to see a fish-wife suddenly created queen of Persia——

(*Enter* THULIA *in great agitation.*)

THULIA. Oh! Androclides!—have you seen him, sirs?
I heard a voice i' th' street cry he was slain—
For heaven's love—have you seen him?—doth he live?

ARCHIAS. Lady,—but now with most foul scorn you eyed me.

THULIA. Speak! speak! Doth Androclides live? ha? say!
PHILIP. Lady—he *doth* live; and hath 'scaped unhurt;

I saw him on his horse, bound, as I think,
Tow'rds Athens.

(THULIA *shrieks with joy, laughs, and falls backward.*
ARCHIAS *catches her in his arms.*)

PHILIP. She's dead! This is no common swoon, Archias! She's surely dead.

ARCHIAS. Dead! Philip? Thou'rt a raw physician! She knows better than to die, I'll warrant thee. Women never die o' this fashion. The world hath not seen such a folly. They die decently and solemnly; after distributing their trinkets,— their embroideries,—their infinite gew-gaws to their sobbing friends, whom, with a most breathless voice and trembling hand, they awfully warn against the follies and vanities of life.

PHILIP. But, Archias—I do truly think she is dead.

ARCHIAS. Art thou a mushroom, Philip?—Didst hear her make her will? Talk no more of it,—but turn the corner and summon my servants—and bid them bring the litter with them. —(*Exit* PHILIP) Which in truth was intended for a different burthen; but the exchange will be a rich one. Now, my little proud-crested dove, we shall see if thou wilt peck at me, and flutter thy disdainful plumes as before;—or if a close cage shall not bring down that haughty humour of thine to a more obsequious humility. Come, fellows! despatch! But stay—set down the litter there, i' th' shade. The sun burns here unbearably. Now, pretty dove! I'll lay thee in thy nest: and, as thy old mate hath left thee, why, it will be but charity to find thee another, and a better perhaps. (*He carries her off.*)

END OF THE SECOND ACT.

ACT III.

Scene I.—*A room in the house of* Archias.

(Archias *and* Philip *are seated at a table with* Philidas, *the secretary to the tyrants.*)

Philip. Come, Archias; now break off. I think we've wrought
Enough for one day's labor. How's the morning?

Archias. Philip, 'tis yet two hours of noon.

Philip. So late?
I cannot stay then, for the games begin
Betimes to-day,—and I've a heavy stake
On my new Spartan wrestler.

Archias. But a heavier
On that we have in hand. Wait but an hour,
And I'll go with you. We'll send word to stay
The games till we shall come.—

(*Enter a* Servant.)

Well—what's thy errand?

Servant. A messenger, my lord, is here to say
His master, the lord Leontiades,
From Sparta is arriv'd; and, in brief space,
Will call upon you.

Archias. Say we wait his pleasure:—
Philip and I.

Philip. And that our zealous love
Makes us impatient to behold him soon.

Serv. I will, my lords.—There's one below who waits
Your pleasure touching certain state affairs
Of moment,—so he says.

Philip. We will not hear him.
Bid him attend to-morrow.

Archias. Stay—who is he?

Serv. 'Tis an old man who has before been here;
A thin, quick-motion'd, hasty-speaking man.—

Archias. 'Tis our old tailor, Philip :—we must see him.

Philip. Well—show him up.

Serv.   I will, my lord.

Archias.   And stay.
Let some one go, and bid them stop the games
Till Philip shall arrive.

Serv.   It shall be done.   [*Exit.*

Archias. I think 'twere, Philidas, the better course,—
Our colleague being come,—that you pen down
Of our proceedings, since his going hence,
A brief report :—together with a scroll
Of such whose names, as traitors to the state,
We have this morning noted.

Philidas.   Good, my lord—
I know the Archon's temper,—and, even now,
Am busied as you wish.

                (*Enter* Abas.)

Philip.   Well, Abas—well—
What brings thee here this morning? Hast thou found
New game for us to strike?

Abas. In good sooth have I, my lords. Here be six names of men whose evil dispositions, as I find on most trustless evidence,—might inflame the best-rooted government,—bring death, and foul distemperation to its purest strongholds,—yea! and cause it to suffer shipwreck to its lowest foundations—as I have heard your lordships say many a time and oft.

Philip. Hast thou, good Abas? Thou grow'st eloquent.
Mark, Archias, this great danger! Here be men
That shall inflame the roots of government—
Its strongholds kill,—and shipwreck its foundations!—
Was't not so, Abas?

Abas.   Yes, my lord.

Philip.   Thou'lt come
Erelong to th' Archonship. Such minds as thine

Are the great lights of earth,—and must be placed
Where men can gaze upon them.

ARCHIAS.   Are they rich?

ABAS. Yes—yes, my lord,—trust me there, my lord. I know all that befits a good traitor :—all rich but one, who is a tailor; and, I can affirm to your lordships, a most dangerous and treason-begetting fellow,—and his name is Borus.

ARCHIAS.   Then, Philidas, take down the other five,
And let this Borus 'scape ;—or be reprov'd
And, after, pardon'd.   Such a lenience shews
A justice in our measures, which some tongues
Have tax'd for harshness.

ABAS. Pardon me, my lord!   Rather than this one should escape, 'twere better you let go all the others.   If you would not trust a wolf in your sheepfold, or a lion in your nursery—trust not such a villain in Thebes.   I don't know this varlet's fellow.—Would you believe it, lords, that I have now scarce three thimbles at work,—for honesty and loyalty are but ill-liked in this undutiful city,—whereas this most foul and disloyal knave——

PHILIP. Well,—well, good Abas—give us now their names,
With what offence 'gainst each you have to shew,—
And we'll consider it.

ABAS. Here, my lords, be their fair names foully written down,—with their abodes ;—and I'll beseech your lordships to look well after them, for they threaten instruction to the state.

ARCHIAS. Here, Philidas ; take thou the scroll, and read,
One after one the names ;—and then, 'gainst each,
Note down, as they shall come, th' offences charged.

PHILIDAS.   The first i' th' scroll is Acamus—is't not?

ABAS.   It is.   And after it you shall find that he dwelleth beside the temple of Vulcan.

PHILIDAS.   Tem-ple—of Vul-can.   So it is, I think.

ABAS. Oh yes, sir.   You shall find it, anon, a very audible hand: and, thank God, I hope the geography is pretty incorrect : the circumlocution is all my own.

PHILIDAS. I make no doubt on't. Now, sir—the offence?

ABAS. Why, my lords, for a particular offence,—I do suspect him indefinitely of treasonable distentions :—but my more distracted, and general charge, shall be that he did traitorously, and feloniously, aid and assist in counsel, and money, a certain traitorous and condemn'd wretch, who, by your wise and merciful reward, was fined and thereafter banished.—This, my lords, I take to be a traitorous and felonious flying in face of all ill-regulated governments, and leading to the——

ARCHIAS. Stay—stay: we must be brief. Against that name Write '*traitor*'—'tis but short,—yet long enough
To make him shorter.—Go on, Philidas.

PHILIDAS. The next is Maris, of the Athens' gate. What charge 'gainst him?

ABAS. Why, my lords, to save you time and trouble, I should wish to make against these five, briefly, and tediously, the same particular charge of *treason;* which, as I take it, reprehends in itself all others. I did begin, most indubitably, to suspicion their loyalty and sound principles when,—forsaking me,—I found them, to the best of their power, comforting and encouraging that most traitorous and vile, and disloyal, and evil-minded Borus;—that disgrace to our calling—whom I beseech you, as you love the wicked, and hate the virtuous, to banish from this city,—yea, rather to destroy from off the face of this goodly earth.

PHILIDAS. Your charge seems somewhat loose. Have you no act
That more directly, and precisely points
At this great guilt?

ABAS. Why really, sir, and my lords,—if to be disloyal and treasonable be not to be traitorous, I know of nothing else that is so. If to call a man 'traitor' and 'traitorous' be not an indirect and precise way of pointing him out for a treasonable person, I must be content, having no looser charge to make :—would to God I had, if I might thereby pleasure your lordships. But what, my lords, is to be thought of persons that bear about them, in the very cut and fashion of their garments, the proof of their being assisting to, and connected with foul, and disloyal, and traitorous enemies to law and peaceable government,—but that they are themselves foul, and disloyal, and traitorous persons?—and for such, my lords, do I here inscribe them. If this proof do not satisfy you, my lords, —why, let them go,—and take note of the consequence.

ARCHIAS. They are rich,—you say?

ABAS. Rich as Phœnician merchants!

ARCHIAS. Then mark them, Philidas. We cannot stand
In things like these too nicely upon proof.—
'Tis sworn against them ;—that's enough.—And Abas,
If, in the picking, they should prove as fat
As you have weigh'd them to us,—you shall pick
This Borus for yourself.

ABAS. I expected no less, my lords, from your love of justice, and merciless ministration to your humble friends and followers. My lords, I do thank you, and humbly take my leave :—and I hope I shall seem presuming in that I take it upon me to advise that you summon and seize before the goose cools. I have always found a stitch afore breakfast worth an hour's elbowing after dinner.—My lords, your humble slave.

(*About to leave, but lingers.*)

(*Enter a* SERVANT.)

SERVANT. Three handicrafts men of Thebes, my lords, demand admittance to your presence on important matters.

PHILIP. Let them come in. [*Exit* SERVANT.
More accusations, I suppose. Our hives this morning will yield store of honey. . . . Archias,—a word. (*They whisper.*)

ABAS (*aside*). What three men be these, I marvel ;—three handicrafts fellows, he said. What can be their business here, —meddling with government matters? I'll stay and amuse myself with their ignorant appurtenance.

(*He retires to the side of the room.*)

(*Enter three* ARTISANS.)

ARCHIAS. Well, my masters :—what is your pleasure with us?

1ST ARTISAN. Oh, my lord !—no pleasure at all, my lord :—

only we're come to give your lordships items concerning certain treasons and traitorous persons.

Alas (*aside*). Why, what in the name of all the infernal deities, and the convocation of the immortal gods above us, —can those two rascals have to do here?—I left them three under-garments to finish afore noon. I'll prick the villains for this.

Archias. Well, my friends,—who are these traitors?—give us their names, and abodes. But, first, who are you?—what are your names and employments?

1st Artisan. My lord, if you will allow me to speak for myself in such a matter, why truly my name is Telamon ;— and I cannot confess to deny that I am more than a cobbler by trade ;—though it may be, if the fates had thought indifferently, I might have been unfit for something better.

Philip. Telamon is thy name?

Telamon. At your lordship's pleasure.

Philip. Aught of kin to Ajax Telamon think'st thou?

Telamon. My lord, I do not know the man. What manner of man is he?

Philip. Why, he was a great hero, and fought at Troy : and his exploits are recorded in the Iliad of the wondrous Homer.

Telamon. Why then, my lord, I think it's like enough I may be of kin to him, tho' I don't remember that Ajax,—for I am myself somewhat given to be a hero, and have had many a tough fight in my time ; though I don't know that they have been anywhere recorded as yet, unless, maybe, in the judgment-books of the magistrates ;—but I suppose, my lord, that's not the same thing as the wondrosomo you talked of in his eyelid.

Philip. Not precisely. Now, Telamon, what is your charge?

Telamon. Why, my lord, in the second place I'll tell you first of all right how things fell out.

Archias. Do so,—but briefly.

Telamon. Thank you, my lord ; but I hope I know my

duty better than to be brief afore your lordships. When I grow brief, I trust your lordships will disdain to correct me.

PHILIP. Come then, Telamon,—despatch.

TELAMON. Then to conclude. First of all, my lords, you shall understand that I owe certain sums of money to one Palmus, a bad traitor, and a leather-seller.

PHILIP. Good!

TELAMON. By your favour, my lord, I think *not*. I misdoubt it to be good, forasmuch as I owe it to this bad traitor, and moreover disafflicted person. But that's as your lordship pleases: it's not for men like me to say what's good, and what isn't good,—except in the matter of a shoe or so. Mark you now the upshot. Says Talmus to me, 'Pay me the money you owe me;—pay me the money—you idle, drunken rascal.' —I'm not calling your lordship such foul libations;—God forbid I should have so much decency!—that's what Palmus says to me. 'Pay me the money,' says he,—'pay me the money,— you idle, drunken rascal,'—meaning me, my lord.

PHILIP. Hard words, Telamon! hard words! and very unmerited, I don't doubt.

TELAMON. Just as your lordship says: hard words and very unmelodious. And so I thought,—and with that, up gets I with my hammer in my hand, and says I—'Palmus'—says I— 'I suspect you,' says I, 'to be a traitor,' says I, 'and a treasonable person,' says I, 'and a disafflicted,' says I,—and, says I, 'I'll import you to the Archons,' says I :—and with that I knocked him down with my hammer, and he had not a word to say for himself; he was somehow clean conscience-struck with the way in which I defended myself.

PHILIP. I don't wonder at it. You must certainly have descended from Ajax,—for he was a great dealer in the same kind of argument. Did you not also throw your lapstone at him in imitation of your great ancestor?

TELAMON. No, my lord. It appear'd unreasonable to think there was no necessity for that,—for he never stirred more. The Fates had cut his thread, and a rotten one it must have been, and very badly waxed to snap with such a touch, for I ha' given and taken hundreds of such keepsakes, and never the worse for them.

PHILIP. Then I suppose, Telamon, you have come to deliver yourself up to justice, and to meet your reward?

TELAMON. Your lordship's very kind,—and that's just it. For, says I to myself,—'Here's a great traitor killed,—and who did the job?—Why, who should have done it but thee, Telamon, thyself. Pluck up heart therefore'—says I to myself, —'pluck up heart, Telamon, and get thee before the merciless and ungrateful Archons, and ask of them the reward of thy virtue in killing and slaying a bad and treasonable traitor.' And what reward will they give thee, Telamon?' says I to myself — 'what reward will they give thee? — Why, to be sure,' says I to myself, 'what *can* they do less than give thee the traitor's goods and chattels,—house, garden, and stock in trade,—whatsoever that may be?—Thou hast killed a traitor, hast thou not?' says I to myself,—'and what less *can* they give thee?' And so, my lords, here I am, and I trust your lordships will receive me to be an honest and peaceful and loyal subject, and worthy of discouragement and just reward.

PHILIP. Why, truly, Telamon, thou *art* worthy of reward.

TELAMON. Thank your lordship. I'll go and seize in the turning of an awl.

PHILIP. Stay, Telamon, I have not told thee *what* reward. We have a law which saith; 'he that killeth another shall himself be put to death.' How shouldst thou approve of that reward?

TELAMON. Odsbodikins! my lord, that's a good joke! Hang a man for killing a traitor? Then what would become of you, my lords, that have killed scores? But I like to see you merry, my lord. Ha—ha—: hanged for killing a traitor! Ha—ha!

ARCHIAS. Fellow!—remember before whom you stand! The awful throne of justice must not be
A place for fools and jesters. If thou 'scape

With life, esteem thyself too happy. Hence !
Black-muzzled dog !—and learn more reverence.
                                    [*Exit* TELAMON.
Now, fellows—what's your errand ? Speak !

2ND ARTISAN (*after a pause*). Truly, my lord, I have no speech for myself.

ARCHIAS. Then who speaks for thee, fellow ? Answer me, Or get you hence.

(*The two* ARTISANS *bow low, and are going away.*)

PHILIP. Stay—stay, my masters. Archias, you're too rough; Let me examine them.

ARCHIAS.   Just as you please.

PHILIP. Come here, my little men, and pluck up heart : No harm is meant you, Now speak up, and freely. What would you with us ?

1ST ARTISAN (*after a pause*). Truly, my lord, I have no speech for myself.

PHILIP. Why, I am sure thou hast a great soul lodged in that little body. Thou hast a hero's dimensions compressed into a space of four foot by one. Nature designed thee for a warrior, and a leader of armies, and thou know'st it not. So the diamond sees not its own splendour, while the world beside gazes upon it.—Dost thou not feel great aspirations within thee ?—Speak. Art thou not ambitious ? Hast thou not a noble and untamable spirit ?—Speak boldly,—Would'st thou not delight to make the desert lions thy playfellows ?—and the Rhinoceros and the Leviathan of the great deep, the companions of thy leisure hours ?—Speak—speak—I wait for thee.

1ST ARTISAN. I think I should, my lord. But truly, my lord, I have no speech for myself.

PHILIP. Why, there it is. Thus doth Nature compensate for the richness of one faculty by the poverty of another. Thy valour hath swallowed up thy tongue ! Thy soul is in thy right arm. Thou only livest when dealing death about thee. What is thy name ?

1ST ARTISAN. Agamemnon, my lord.

PHILIP. Did I not tell thee thou wert a hero, and a leader of armies? Was not Agamemnon king of kings?—the head of all Greece?—the soul of all her warriors?—Thy name becometh thee, and thou it. Methinks I could have known thy name untold,—had I but given thought to it,—so doth its majesty correspond to the nobleness of thy qualities.—Agamemnon!—Why, the very sound is breathed, as it were from the arch of thy forehead!—The angles of thy elbows point it to the eye! Thou art little less than a demi-god;—would thou hadst a tongue!—But come thou, the second, and scarce less august.—*Thou* wilt bless our years with the mellifluence of thy accents. What is it you would with us? Speak!—

2ND ARTISAN (*after a pause*). Truly, my lord, I have no speech for myself.

PHILIP. Come, come:—deceive me not.—I see by the curve of thy leg,—thy brawny calf,—and the intolerable flashing of thine eye, that thou art an orator, and a law-giver by nature,—and, withal, vindictive and terrible in battle.—What is thy name?

2ND ARTISAN. Achilles, my lord. My father's name is Nestor,—and I have a little brother called Hector.

PHILIP. I should think so. It cannot be otherwise. Why, thou must have in thee the united virtues and greatnesses of all thy illustrious namesakes. Agamemnon is thy elder brother, is he not?

ACHILLES. Yes, my lord : and Telamon is my cousin;—and I have a little sister called Diomed.

PHILIP. Indeed! But it might be expected:—for what should such a band of heroes and demi-gods care for gender, when they set number at defiance ; and only laugh at their pitiful case! Your cousin Telamon is a bold and resolute man I think ;—is he not?

TELAMON (*peeping in at the door*). As bold and deliverant a fellow, my lord, though I infirm it, as ever hammered leather: and if your lordships would but give me a dismission to come in, I would tack the whole matter together for you in the splitting of a bristle.

PHILIP. Hath he your *dismission*, Archias?

ARCHIAS. So he remember in what place he stands,
He may advance. Till Leontidas come,
The time is ours to fool it as we will.

PHILIP. Advance then, Telamon: but hold thy peace
Till I shall question thee.

TELAMON. Thank your lordship. I never make it a rule to open my mouth to no man till he opens his mouth to me, and then——

PHILIP. Telamon! I bade thee to keep silent.

TELAMON. I crave your lordship's pardon; and will be as quiet as a lapstone.

PHILIP. When it is well hammered, I suppose. Come now, Achilles:—thou terror of battlefields! thou who, invulnerable thyself, save on the heel,—carriest wounds and death to thousands! But stay: hast thou not been, perchance, a second time dipped in Styx?—and art thou not now from crown to toe impenetrable as adamant? Shew me thy heel.—In truth thy armour there is none of the best; it gapeth horribly! Thou *must* be conscious of impassibility. Let us put it to the proof.

(*He pricks the* ARTISAN'S *heel with the point of his sword.*)

ACHILLES. Oh!—oh!—oh! my lord!

TELAMON. For shame, Achilles! My lord's only going to lacerate you a bit! for shame, man! for shame!

ACHILLES. Truly, Telamon, I like not such macerations. I will depart.

TELAMON. Then will I strap thee till thou forget thy name, and the son that bore thee. Listen to my lord—thou needle's-eye; and answer as he shall forbid thee.

PHILIP. Telamon—Telamon! Thy ancestor was a mighty man, but spare of speech. Copy him in that, I beseech thee.

TELAMON. Indeed, my lord, I also am a mighty man, and I trust, at most times, have a speech to spare as well as he.— I've done, my lord!—

PHILIP. Now Agamemnon, and Achilles, speak; what is it you would have of us?

ACHILLES. So please your lordship, Telamon shall tell.

PHILIP. Nay—but I'd rather hear it from yourselves. What is't you fear?

ACHILLES. We come, my lord, to speak against our master, and if we should speak ourselves he would prick us for it.

AJAX (*aside*). Oh! you vermin! you are come to speak against me, are you? And truly I *will* prick you, and sharply too.

PHILIP. What! Achilles and Agamemnon fear to be pricked! You are tailors—are you not?

AGAM. No, my lord,—only tailor's men.

PHILIP. Well then! be men as well as tailors. Speak but boldly, and I will protect you.

ACHILLES. In sooth, my lord?

PHILIP. Yea, most magnanimous! in very sooth!

ACHILLES. Then, my lord, I announce my master to be a traitor to this government,—and a hard master to boot!

TELAMON. Well done, Achilles! thou'rt a brave fellow:—let them hear a bit of thy mind.

PHILIP. Silence, Ajax!

TELAMON. Telamon, so please you, my lord.

PHILIP. Go on, Achilles:—you need not fear your master. But you often uncage your fierce thoughts upon him, I dare say.

ACHILLES. My lord, we don't value him a button. 'Tisn't more than three years since we told him, if he didn't advance us two-pence a week wages, we'd dismiss him.

PHILIP. Ha!—you are men of mettle, I perceive. And did he advance you the two pence?

ACHILLES. No, my lord.

PHILIP. And what did you then?

ACHILLES. Why, we told him, my lord—or at least we got Telamon to tell him—that we thought he might be ashamed of himself.

PHILIP. Bless us! That must have been about the time of the great earthquake. But now go on. Your master is a traitor, you say. What hath he done—or said—or contemplated to do?

ACHILLES. Why, my lord, he hath said two or three times in my hearing, and in Agamemnon's to boot, that your lordship, and Archias, and Leontidas were worthy men—and that he had good cause to respect you—and he called you, moreover, true parrots.

AGAM. No, Achilles—it was worse than that! he called them 'true patriots!' and we've hardly been able to sleep since for thinking of such villainy!

ACHILLES. And besides that, my lord, he keeps down our wages—and that shows affection to the state.

ARCHIAS. Come, Philip—end this foolery: I see Leontidas coming up the street.

PHILIP. Well, my little heroes—depart now, and come again to-morrow—and bring your master with you, and we'll try to compromise matters.

ABAS (*coming forward*). Their master is here, my lord—and ready to answer all questions.

PHILIP. What! art thou the traitor? But not now, Abas—our time is pressing; get you hence. Have you the scroll drawn out for the Archon, Philidas?

PHILIDAS. Just finished, my lord.

ABAS. You shall sing for this, my mighty men.

ACHILLES. We don't care a thread for you! Philip will compromise matters, and then you'll hang, you naughty old tyrant!

AGAM. And if Philip doesn't, Telamon says if you offer to prick us any more he'll strap you,—he will!

[*Exeunt the* TAILORS *and* TELAMON.

ARCHIAS. Philip, you too much sink from your high sphere
To bandy jokes with dirty knaves like these.
You're talk'd of for it.

PHILIP.   Grave, and reverend Greek !
Heav'n's grace assisting, we will mend that fault.
You also, solemn sir, are somewhat talk'd of
For sundry jokes that from your lofty sphere
Do make you bend ;—though not with dirty knaves
But fair, clean ladies ;—mend you also that !

ARCHIAS. That sin's a flower grows in your garden too.
But you are still a wag.

(*Enter* LEONTIDAS.)

ARCHIAS AND PHILIP. Good-morrow, Leontidas.

LEON.   Friends, good-morrow.

ARCHIAS. What news from Sparta? Are our friends all well?

PHILIP. How is the hero Phœbidas ? poor fool !
I fear his welcome home was somewhat hot :
He look'd to have a warm one.

LEON.   In few words
If you will listen, I'll unfold you all.
But do not ask me now for argument
Why this was thus, or thus :—nor question put
Of unessential things, which, when time serves,
I'll answer to the utmost ; but not now :
My horses wait below,—and my great haste
Brooks no unheeded stop.

ARCHIAS.   We are dumb statues.

LEON. In brief then, Phœbidas, for having fixed
In Sparta's crown so rich a gem as Thebes,
Must pay, for fine, a hundred thousand drachms.

PHILIP. Why, that's most excellent !

LEON.   Ismenias —
This is good news—hath ended his bad life
Upon the scaffold.

ARCHIAS.   Pluto comfort him!

LEON. Touching the Exiles,—day by day have I
Made it my theme at Sparta,—that no hope
Of an enduring quietness can live
But in their death.   And, ere I came away,
My strong solicitings had wrought so far,
That Sparta hath to Athens sent demand
To drive,—as enemies to all the states—
The Exiles from her walls.   How this shall be,
Time must make seen.   Now, since my going hence
Hath aught of such importanacy chanced,
It cannot wait my leisure?

PHILIP.   No, my lord.
Here's a brief scroll, drawn out by Philidas,
In which you may behold the course we've taken:
What traitors have been fined;—whom put to death;
Whom hold in prison yet:—and many names
Of men, on whom suspicion keeps close watch,
To spring upon their treasons.   Philidas,—
If you would hear it, will run swiftly through,
Giving the general scope.

LEON.   Not now, good Philip.

ARCHIAS. I'll shew you in two words.   Three hundred fined;
Two hundred put to death;—in prison still
Four hundred, and four score.—You have it all.

LEON. You have been active, gentlemen: and still
Must toil on in your course.   There is no law
That binds down the fierce Democrat, but that
Which holds him in his grave.   The prison bars
May let him forth;—the longest banishment
May have an end;—his stripes may be repaid
On us who gave them.—Lay him in the earth,
And he's your true and loyal slave for aye.
Adieu—adieu!

ARCHIAS *and* PHILIP. Good-morrow, Leontidas.

LEON. Philip, if you should pass my house to-night,

Or in the morning,—call on me, I pray you :
I've something for your private ear.   [*Exit* LEON.
    PHILIP.   I will.
Now, Archias,—let's away. The populace
Will grow impatient if we stay the games
Much past the wonted time.
    ARCHIAS.   Come then, at once.
Will you go with us, Philidas?
    PHILIDAS.   No, sirs.
And yet I will. You have a wager, Philip ;—
I'll go to see you lose it.
    PHILIP.   Thank you—thank you.
                                        [*Exeunt.*

        SCENE II.—*A Street in Thebes.*
      (*Enter* CHARON *and* EPAMINONDAS.)

    EPAM. Stay here a moment, where the space is free.
If I were sure what course the fire would take,
I'd help to kindle it. But oft it chances
That, putting flame unto the rotten wood
And choking brambles, the whole healthful forest
Shall catch the blaze, and perish with the rest.
Yet, in forbearance, there's a point to pause at,
Where to *endure*, is to *deserve* the wrong,
And I but ask, is this it?
    CHARON.   No! that point
Is past already. Not to strike at this,
Were to demand from Heaven a thousand whips
To scourge us hourly. For myself I speak not ;—
Their policy,—or fear,—or else pure shame
To strike a neutral,—long and oft confess'd,—
Hath left me yet untouch'd. But, can I see
My friends—my neighbours,—plunder'd—fetter'd—scourg'd—
Put to a felon's death ;—their children driven
Helpless to the rude world ;—and all for sins
So fine to our dull sense, that, to behold them, '
We must look at them through the tyrants' glass :—

Can I, Epaminondas, see these things,
And not risk all to mend them?

EPAM.   Or make worse,—
That's the true question. Yet, so bad they are,—
I bid you not forbear :—and, if I still
Keep free of your designs,—'tis but to hold
A power to mediate 'twixt you, should you fail ;—
Or, if the struggle waver, bring my sword
And life to help you on. 'Tis the last grain
That bows the strong-knee'd camel ;—and one sword
Alighting on an even balanc'd fight,
Shall make the scale go down—— What noise is this?
                              (*Shouts are heard.*)

CHARON. The Games are going on :—no—they are done ;
The people flock this way. There's a new wrestler
From Sparta, who three days hath challeng'd all,
And been the victor. Philip brought him here,
And backs him 'gainst all comers.—Well, my friends,
How has the wrestling ended?

(*Enter and pass over the stage several* THEBAN YOUTHS.)

Several voices (*shouting*). Thebes! Thebes! Thebes!

CHARON. What! has the Spartan been thrown down? Stay, friend—
How has the wrestling ended?

THEBAN YOUTH. Charon,—did'st ever see a child in anger dash down the toy it had been playing with? Just so our Theban champion, after amusing himself awhile with his proud adversary, lifted him up from the earth, and then hurl'd him to it again.—Such a fall hath not been seen. The Spartan will never wrestle more :—Philip rages like a whirlwind.

CHARON. Who is this Theban champion?

THEBAN YOUTH. No one knows; some rustic from the mountains it is thought. There he is, turning the street; he'll pass this way anon.   [*Exit.*

(*Enter, and pass over, more* THEBAN YOUTHS.)
Several voices (*shouting*). Thebes—Thebes—Thebes—
EPAM. Which is the victor?—let me speak with him.
THEBAN YOUTH. Epaminondas, this is he.

(*Enter more* THEBANS, *with the victor, his head crowned with flowers.*)

EPAM.   And thou
Hast foil'd the boastful Spartan ! Thank thee, youth,
For teaching Thebans that they *may* be foiled ;
And in a harder struggle, would they try it.
Come this way, youth, I would a word with thee.
    WRESTLER. Go on, my gallant lads,—I'll follow you.
    [*Exeunt* THEBAN YOUTHS, *crying*, ' *Thebes—Thebes.*'
    EPAM. Thou art Pelopidas—deny it not —
    WRESTLER. Not I !—no more than thou'rt Epaminondas !
What hath Pelopidas to do in Thebes ?
    CHARON. Great Jove be merciful ! What dost thou here ?
    PELOP. Walk through a charnel-house,—and see the tyrants
Make mockery with the bones. 'Tis pleasant, Charon—
We'll jest with theirs anon.
    EPAM.   Pelopidas !
Art thou gone mad ?—Into a public show
To bring thyself,—even in thine enemy's eye.—
Beneath his very beard,—for the poor pride
Of victory o'er a wrestler !
    PELOP.   But a Spartan !
'Twas Thebes 'gainst Sparta ;—not Pelopidas
Against Opites.—Could I, tamely, hear
In Athens that a fourth time this proud bully,
With Philip at his back, had held the ring—
Defying Thebans in the heart of Thebes ?
No—no ! I'd gladly reason with thy head,--
But will not break my heart.—There is beside
A greater business on my hand than this.

Charon, I'll call upon you in an hour :—
Be thou there too,—for much I long to clasp
My dear friend to my heart.

  Epam.   I fear some eye
May pierce, like mine, through thy disguise.

  Pelop.   No—no—
'Tis but to cast this bauble from my head,
   (*Throws away the crown of flowers*)
And I'm a noteless clown.—Were the black snake
To scan me now, he should not know me thus,
Were I resolv'd on't. I threw off disguise,
Looking upon thy face—or even thou
Hadst given, perchance, some oboli for drink
To the stout wrestler.

     (*Enter* Philidas.)

  Philidas.   Gentlemen, good-day.
Where be your colours, Charon?

  Charon.   We wear none :—
Philip hath curs, and his—more than he likes—
Upon his champion's ribs.

  Philidas. By Jupiter, it was a glorious fling!
Philip hath lost five talents on that throw.
He's in a fever.

  Pelop. Let him lose some blood.

  Epam. (*to* Pelop.). Come here, I pray you. (*They whisper.*)

  Philidas.   Charon, who is yon clown
That talks so free of letting Philip blood?

  Charon. You do not know him?

  Philidas.   No—and yet, I think—
Is't not the Theban wrestler?—Yea, by Jove!
I'm sure 'tis he. Good Charon, for that fling,
Give him a purse of gold—a heavy one ;—
I'll be your debtor for it till to-night—
But name me not :—such gift, in Philip's ear,
Would sound but oddly.

CHARON.   I'll remember you.
What!—are you going?

PHILIDAS.   Philip waits for me.
Their bloody scroll still lengthens every day.
Eight more were prick'd for death, but yester-morn;
To-day are four;—and twenty mark'd for fines,
Will crush them to the earth. My heart drops blood
While my unwilling pen records their dooms.
Dolops is mark'd for death : I've given him note,
And he is gone. If you see Merion,
Tell him, his gold, his jewels, and himself,
Were safer in the desert than at Thebes.
I'll call on you at night.

CHARON.   Is there aught new?
You were at Athens since I saw you last.

PHILIDAS. I came back yesterday; and shall unload
My treasures to your ear anon. Take this
For present use.—I saw Pelopidas,
Melon, and Androclides, and the rest.
Their purpose is resolv'd;—their hearts are firm;
They wait but for the time. Another month
Will ripen thought to action. Fare you well.
Commend me to your friend. He seems intent
To learn a fall of that same bone-breaker.

CHARON. Adieu, good Philidas.—Don't fail to-night.

PHILIDAS. Depend on me.—I' faith an iron fellow!
I've seen him somewhere.   [*Exit.*

PELOP.   Well:—he knew me not.

CHARON. He says he saw you yesterday.

PELOP.   He did.

EPAM. Pelopidas, you have amaz'd me much.
Let's go with Charon now, and hear the rest.

PELOP. Go on before then. I'll take this way round
And be with you anon.

EPAM.   Walk heedfully.
Remember you're a clown.—

PELOP.   And clowns must walk
With sober step where lords may play the fool.
The clown shall stick to me, fear not.   Adieu!

CHARON *and* EPAM.   Farewell—farewell!

[CHARON *and* EPAM. *go out on one side*, PELOPIDAS *on the other.*

SCENE III.—*A room in the house of* ARCHIAS.

(*Enter* ARCHIAS, *followed by* MENON.)

ARCHIAS. Tell Philip I'll be with him in an hour.
I'm wearied, and must rest ere I go forth.
And bring more lights;—and throw some cedar-wood
Upon the fire:—the night is wet and dark.

MENON. Lights ho!   It is, my lord, an awful night!
Did you see aught i' th' street, my lord?

ARCHIAS.   No, Menon.
What should I see?

MENON.   Some of our fellows tell
Of ghastly things abroad.

ARCHIAS.   What things?

MENON—   My lord—
You'll laugh, or else be angry.

ARCHIAS.   Tell thy tale;
Or I'll be angry now.

MENON.   They say, my lord,
That many, long since dead, were seen to-night:
Bodies that wanted heads:—and some with throats
Pinch'd where the cord had strangled them: and some . . .

ARCHIAS. Peace, fool!   Thou hast a body, but no head:
Yet no one makes a wonder of thee.—Here—

(*Lights and fuel are brought in*).

Bring round the couch before the fire.   And Menon—
I'll taste the Cretan wine that came to-day
From Bias.   Let me have the crystal bowl;
It shows the sparkling best: (*aside*) and minds me too

Of Thoön's wife—who thought that price enough
To buy her husband's safety—till she learn'd
To pay in better coin. (*Aloud*) Actor is dead.

  MENON. I thought, my lord, his sentence had been changed.

  ARCHIAS. It was. His wife and niece both sued to me,
And I had sworn to save him: but too late;
He was found dead in prison—starved to death.
Hath any one been here from Chromius?

  MENON. There's one, my lord, hath waited these four hours.

  ARCHIAS. Who is he?

  MENON.   'Tis an aged man, my lord;
Grey-headed,—a tall man, but bent with years,
And very feeble. He's done nought but weep.

  ARCHIAS. And you've wept, too, for sympathy, no doubt!
Sweet, tender-hearted chick! 'Tis his old father,—
A proper messenger!—Bid him get home.
Say Chromius dies to-morrow, before noon;
Such is the law:—but let his daughter come
Betimes i' th' morning, and I'll talk with her
Touching her father's pardon.—Now get hence,
And let me alone.   [*Exit* MENON.
    Come, little dove,—
I'll ope thy cage, and let thee forth awhile,
To strut and flutter till thy plumes are pluck'd;
And that shall be erelong. (*He unlocks and opens a door.*)
     Dear Thulia—
Sweet lady,—I would speak with you.—She sleeps;
Or will not answer me.—How the winds shriek!
And Jove is thundering overhead!—What now!
  (MENON *enters with wine, etc.*)

  MENON. My lord, you call'd for wine.

  ARCHIAS.   Then set it down.
And come no more till I shall summon you.

  MENON. There is a man below, my lord, who asks
To see you instantly.

ARCHIAS. I'll see no man!
This is the plague of office;—night and day,
To be the bell for every fool to ring.
To-morrow let him call.

MENON. I told him so,
And said you were abroad: at which he laugh'd,
And swore I lied with a right modest face,
For he had seen you enter.

ARCHIAS. What's his name?
Whence is he?—what's his business?

MENON. He'll say nought,
But that he comes from Athens, and goes back
By day-break.

ARCHIAS. Ha! from Athens? A low man
Is he?—broad-shoulder'd?—beetle-brow'd?

MENON. The same.
A most ill-favoured man. You will not see him?

ARCHIAS. Yes, Menon. Bring him in. He comes with news
From certain friends, and must be seen to-night.
[*Exit* MENON.

Now, Androclides—dost thou walk the earth?—
Or glide amid the shades? Oh! what small line
Divides the *now*, from the *hereafter!*—Hark!—
His foot is on the stair:—ere I count nine
It will be told me he is dead—or lives:—
Yet 'twixt the healthful breath, and the last sigh,
Perhaps was scantier space.—Well—well—what news?

(*Enter a* MURDERER.)

MURDERER. 'Tis done;—look here!—up to the handle red!
(*Shewing a dagger.*)

ARCHIAS. Ha!—yes—it is so—put it by——

MURDERER. My lord,
You do not fear to look at——

ARCHIAS. Is he dead?

MURDERER. Dead as my dagger's handle.

ARCHIAS. Did he die
At once? or linger from the stroke?

MURDERER. Why, hark—
'Twas in the night I struck him; at his door.
He fell against it, and the noise brought forth
His servants in alarm. I could not stay
To ask them if the job were to my mind,—
But from the stroke—'twas somewhere nigh the heart—
He must have died o' th' instant—aye, my lord,
Before the blade came out.

ARCHIAS. Here—here—thy wages—
There are a thousand drachms:—leave off this trade,
And get a better.—Quit the house at once,
And speak to no one.

MURDERER. It would please me well
To have a better trade; yet this should do,—
Full work'd,—and at such wages. Thanks, my lord—
I will obey your wish. My lord, good-night.
A thousand drachms! [*Exit.*

ARCHIAS. Well!—how is't with me now?—I have sought this!
Why should I shake to hear it?—I'm a fool!—
What's in *his* death that it should scare me more
Than that of scores each day?—Yon murderer,—
Fresh from the deed,—and with the gory steel
Wrapp'd in his bosom,—gave me a 'good-night'
As calm as the just man who leaves his child,
Bidding it trust in Heaven.—I'll shake off this.
What if I call his wife, and tell it her,—
And so get rid on't?—I will do't—Great Jove!

(*He goes towards the door. Loud thunder is heard, and the room is bright with the lightning.*)

Why art thou angry? (*He looks out.*) All the heaven is fire!
And the winds howl and shriek as they were mad.
I cannot do't to-night: and yet I will;—
For she *must* hear it; and, the sooner told,

The sooner shall it work to my intents.—
What noise is that?—By heav'ns! 'tis she—she sings—
Oh! God! it is the song her husband loved
Of his first wooing her by the sea-shore,—
And on the way to Corinth.—Not to-night:—
I cannot tell it her to-night!—Yet must:
The ill that we put off doth ever grow,
Like an untended wound, to worse disease.
I would this thing were yet to do.—'Tis done!—
I cannot turn time back,—or I would be
An infant now; and free of this.—Menon——

(*Enter* MENON.)

The door is barr'd within;—she will not speak.
Let her be told that I have news from Athens,
If she will come to hear it.

MENON.   There have been
Two messengers from Philip,—whom I told
You were retir'd,—but would be with him soon.
And now, my lord, he hath sent Philidas,
With positive command to bring you off.
He feasts to-night, and hath some Georgian nymphs
Just come—and you must see them.

ARCHIAS.   I'm not well,
But yet I'll visit him. Where's Philidas?

MENON. In the gilt chamber.

ARCHIAS.   Beg him wait awhile
And I'll attend him.   [*Exit* MENON.
   Philip's in a roar
Of jollity,—and yet to-day he lost
Five talents at the games;—and two old friends
Hath he impeach'd, to make those talents good
Out of their broken fortunes.
And Leontidas,—a strict, sober man,—
That worshippeth the Gods—and keepeth free
From wine, and women, and all sweet excess—
He's in his quiet bed,—his prayers put up—

His conscience easy:—yet *his* word to-day,
Sent to their death three aged harmless men,
Whom we had wish'd to spare! Why then shall I,
Who have but slain the enemy that stood
'Tween me and Heaven, be thus remorseful?—Hence!
Thou idle idiot Conscience! I will be
Thy fool no longer.—Hark!—she comes!—Good wine,
Give me thy potent spirit,—for my own
Is weaker than an infant's.   (*He drinks eagerly.*)
                            'Twas not she—
She will not come.—I do not feel this wine,—
My heart is cold, and trembling.—Here is some
Of fiercer ardour,—I will rouse this coward
Or burn him in his hole.—
                    (*He drinks again, long and eagerly.*)
                            Ha!—now I feel it.
Beautiful liquor! how thy nimble spirit
Glances through every vein and nerve!—Brave wine!
Thou'rt the soul's sunshine!—All, but now, was dark,
Dark as the grave!—I could have slunk away,
And hid in charnel-houses.—Now, I'm bold—
Light-hearted,—jovial—fit for Philip's rouse—
What care I if he's murder'd?   (*Loud thunder.*)
                            Roar away—
Big, blust'ring Jove,—till thou art hoarse—I care not:

            (*Enter* THULIA.)

He said he struck him to the heart——
    THULIA.   Who's murder'd?
    ARCHIAS. Ha! lady—are you come?—'Tis very kind!—
                            (*Pours out wine.*)
Sit now, I pray you.
    THULIA.   Sir, you sent for me,
To tell some news from Athens. How's my lord?—
    ARCHIAS. Lady—I pledge you.   (*Drinks.*)
    THULIA.   For soft pity's sake
Tell me—I beg you,—is my lord in health?

I heard you, as I enter'd, talk of murder—
For God's love, speak!—Why do you look so wild?
(He drinks again.)

ARCHIAS. Who heard me talk of murder?

THULIA.   I, my lord.
You said 'he struck him to the heart.'

ARCHIAS.   'Tis false!
I had no hand in't.—Pour me out some wine,
And we'll be merry.—What's a murder now?—
Why, everybody's murder'd!—Sweet-lipp'd wench!
Thou'lt have a better husband soon than he—
Ha—ha—I pledge thee——

    (*He raises the bowl to drink.* THULIA *starts forward, and grasps his arm.*)

THULIA.   Monster! hell dog!—speak,
Who has been murder'd?—Say it is not he——

ARCHIAS. Why—who is murder'd now?—Give me some wine.

THULIA. Beast! thou shalt drink no more till thou hast spoke.
Doth Androclides live?

ARCHIAS.   Ha—ha—you jest—
Why—he's been dead this month!—stabb'd to the heart,—
I' th' street——I saw the dagger——

    (THULIA *starts back, in speechless horror.* ARCHIAS *reels, and throws himself on a couch.*)

                              Give me wine.—
Philip—I will not drink again.—Ha—ha—
Thou'lt tell his wife on't :—'twas at his own door—
Where be the Georgians?—Fill another bowl—
Dost know where he was buried?—Ha—ha—ha—
(To THULIA)
Philip's a changeful wag,—thou shalt be mine—
Aye—aye—that pleases thee.—But listen here.—
There's been a horrid murder somewhere——
[THULIA returns to her chamber.
                                     Menon!
Menon—I say—I will go home.

(Enter MENON.*)*

MENON. My lord?

ARCHIAS. I will go home this instant.—Philip's drunk,
And gone to bed—and all his Georgians too—
I will not stay——

MENON. My lord, you are not well.—
Philip hath not been here,—nor you with him :—
But he expects you. Philidas is come,
And waits to take you.—Shall I put him off—
And say you are not well?

ARCHIAS. Ha!—is it so?—
Then I've been dreaming.—Go—call Philidas,
And I'll to Philip's revel—and we'll roar   [*Exit* MENON.
Till we fright back that thunder.—Philidas
(Enter PHILIDAS.*)*
Come—we'll be merry.—Is the litter there?—
I cannot walk in such a burning sun—
Where are we going?—

PHILIDAS. Why, to Philip's revel.
But, Archias, you've been revelling already.

ARCHIAS. I think so.—Is it common, when we're dead,
To ask our friends to drink with us?

PHILIDAS. How? how?—

ARCHIAS. Why, Philip's murder'd :—here's been one to tell
me.—
And now he bids me sup with him.—Mad wag!

PHILIDAS (*going to the door*). Menon, call your fellows—get
your lord
To bed, and let him rest an hour.—My lord,
Philip, o' th' sudden, is unwell,—and begs
You will not come to-night.—

ARCHIAS. Ha—ha!—mad fellow!
He knows they stabb'd him to the heart!—Ha—ha—
Will Androclides ask me too,—I wonder :—
Pah!—I'll not sup with *him!*—Leave me to sleep.

PHILIDAS (*to* MENON). Get him to bed.

MENON. He will not now be moved :—
He often slumbers thus.

PHILIDAS. Then leave him here. [*Exit* MENON.
A cobbler had been fined for getting drunk ;—
Aye, by a drunken magistrate—I've seen it.
And now for Philip. How he'll stare to hear
That he is stabb'd to th' heart !—Heav'ns !—what a beast !
[*Exit.*

(THULIA *enters, wildly, with a dagger in her hand. She stands over the couch ready to strike.*)

THULIA. Foul murderer !—tyrant !—'tis thy latest sleep !
Thou wilt awake in hell !—

(*She attempts to strike,—but starts back in horror.*)
Oh ! horrible !
Am I not mad ?—Is this the gentle breast
That would have wept to see a sparrow die,—
And now with murtherous weapon comes to sink
A soul to endless tortures ?—Androclides—
Thou'rt in Elysium—*he* sent thee there.—
Monster ! fiend ! miscreant !—But I will not curse ;
Nor foul me with his blood—Sweet Heaven ! have pity !
And let me not be mad !—He may repent :——
I'll pray for him and me.

(*She throws away the dagger, and kneels down.*)
The Scene drops.

END OF THE THIRD ACT.

ACT IV.

SCENE I.—*A room in the house of* CHARON.

(CHARON *sits by a table, on which are many papers. His wife*, CLYMENE, *employed in embroidering, sits at the opposite end.*)

CHARON. So, dear Clymene, train our little flower,
And he shall flourish;—shelter'd from the frosts
Of avarice,—ambition's feverish heats,—
Anger's fierce tempests;—free from all the blights
And sore diseases that false culturing
Brings on the pretty flowerets that we breed.—
And, for his pattern in all virtuous deeds,
His guide to wisdom,—often only reached
Thro' error's mazes, and misfortune's glooms,—
Still to Epaminondas turn his eye.
As on the dial's face we look, to know
How the blest sun is journeying through heaven,
So, on that noble Theban let him gaze,
To find bright Virtue's path. He will not err.

CLYMENE. Dear Charon, let it be so.

CHARON. Briefly, *thus*
I'd have him fashion'd: gentle—but not tame;—
Wise—and yet modest;—firm—but never harsh;
Bold—but not violent;—of cheerful mind,—
Yet never heartless in his levity.—
Patient, to bear Heav'n's judgments—but like fire,
To snap the tyrant's bonds. Dost heed me, love?

CLYMENE. Yes, Charon. Are you ill?

CHARON. No—

CLYMENE. Is there aught
Of such a doubtful issue soon to be—
That you forecast the worst?

CHARON.   Why ask you that?

CLYMENE. Nay, Charon—answer me.—Who are these guests—
Coming so secretly, and unawares?—
Why arms, and armour, in the dead of night
Brought, with a thief's soft foot-tread, to your house?—
I know it, Charon—and right well I know
'Tis for no boyish sport,—but some great act
Whose mightiness and scope you think too vast
For my poor mind to grapple with.—Dear Charon,
When have you found me weak like common wives?
When have I blabb'd the thing you would conceal?
When have I shrunk to bear what must be borne?
When have I fled the danger should be met?
If I deserve your trust——then give it me:—
If not—I ask no more.

CHARON.   I would have spared
Thy bosom, dear Clymene, to the last,—
But thou wilt force me on.—Dost think this Thebes
Can writhe for ever underneath the lash,
And not essay to snatch the bloody scourge
From out the tyrants' hands?

CLYMENE.   I thought 'twas this.

CHARON. My story shall be brief. Twelve Theban Exiles—
Pelopidas the head, and heart of all—
Have sworn the tyrants' overthrow.—With them,
For life, or death,—for weal, or woe, I join.
To-day they come;—for *them* the meal's prepar'd;—
To-night they rest:—to-morrow will they strike.—
To-morrow Thebes shall live,—or we must die.

CLYMENE. A fearful throw, dear Charon,—when the dice
Must turn up life, or death.

CHARON.   We choose the risk.
See that your bearing in this exigence,
Belov'd Clymene!—hang no signal out
Of fear, or coming danger:—on your slaves
Impose no charge of secrecy:—be calm;
Yet rather gay, than grave. Our looks, and tones

Are Nature's language, which the infant knows
Ere it can lisp;—a universal book
In which all ages, and all countries read:—
Dissimulation turns the leaf,—and points
The page it would have read. In this must we
Play false for our true end:—yet, with a look——
Remember this——as though we heeded not
If any read at all;—lest, anxiously
Pointing *one* page,—a wary eye take note,
And turn the leaf to read.

  CLYMENE.   Hypocrisy,
Dear Charon, is a garment I've not worn,
And 'twill not fit me well. Yet I will try it.
When the storm comes, our robes are well enough
So they will keep the rain out.

  CHARON.   'Tis a cloak
Of magic web, that, on the giant's back,
Fits easily as on the smallest dwarf.—
Old age, and infancy;—the mean—the proud,—
The beggar—and the king;—the grave—the gay!—
The vestal,—and the prostitute!—the judge
O'er his furr'd robes,—the felon o'er his chains;—
The lawyer—and the client,—the smooth priest,—
And the rough soldier;—the wise-faced physician,
And his expiring patient—all—all wear it!
The father puts it on, when he exhorts
His son to temperance and chastity,
Unpractised by himself:—the son, too, wears it,
Hoping his sire shall reach a good old age,
That keeps him from his money, and his lands:—
Daughters and mothers:—brothers, sisters, wear it:—
'Tis worn in hovels, and in palaces:—
At the bright altar—in the fulsome stews,—
By day—by night—in sunshine, and in frost:—
We wrap it round the infant at its birth,—
We shroud the corpse beneath it;—and the grave
Hath it to deck its tombstone!

CLYMENE.   I could laugh,
But for far graver matter; to hear this.
Count all the slanders of thy life before,
And they will not match this one railing fit.
Thou art infected from thy natural health
By some tart snarler.—Talk no more of this;
But tell me how your friends shall pass the gates,
And walk the streets unknown.—Hath a calm eye
Read your design, and found it well cohere?—
It is a fearful game!

CHARON.   But 'tis begun.—
And must be play'd to th' end. The stake is down,
And cannot be withdrawn.

CLYMENE.   And if it could,
I would not say—'withdraw it.'—But, your friends——

CHARON. All is foreseen. They come not in a group;
But separate, at different gates;—with nets,
And hunting-poles, like sportsmen:—so you'll call them,
If any ask. With this disguise, and night,
Or evening's duskiness to wrap them in,
They will be safe.—Well now,—my pretty boy—

(*Enter their little son*)

Why have you left your play? Go—get thee gone;
But come and kiss me first.—What want you now?

BOY. Oh, Papa! I saw little Polydarus this morning upon such a beautiful little horse—and he says it's all his own—and he's only six years old—and I shall be six next year—and I should so like to have such a pretty little horse to gallop about—and I'm sure you're a deal richer than Polydarus's papa—and I shall never like to ride my nasty little wooden horse any more, for it only jumps up and down and doesn't gallop a bit.

CHARON. Well—well—my pretty horseman!—wait awhile:
The roads are rough and dangerous:—wait till spring;
Thou'lt then be older; and the mornings warm;
And, if I live, I'll buy thee such a horse:

Wait till the spring, my boy. How wouldst thou ride
In such a snow as this?—Go—get thy ways. —
They'd take thee for a snow-ball on thy horse.

    Boy (*as he goes out*). Thank you, dear papa. I wish it was
        spring now.   [*Exit.*

    CLYMENE. I wish so, too, my boy;—then this fierce strife
Would one way have an end. Is there no port,
Dear Charon, where this little boat might lie,
While we ride out the storm? That prattling tongue
Hath done what orators had fail'd to do,—
Made me a trembling coward.

    CHARON.   Dear Clymene—
O'er anxious to *avoid*, we oft *make* danger.
The hare, in starting, draws the greyhound's eye,
Who had been safe, close sitting on her form.
Let him abide at home. Now, my dear wife,
For some two hours I must go forth. Look gay:
Let no one, from the clouds upon your brow,
Say there's a tempest near. All will go well.—
If Philidas return, say I am gone
On that we spake of last.

    CLYMENE.   Is *that* staff sound?
Or, too much lean'd on, may it not break short,
And throw you headlong?

    CHARON.   There are many men
Whose fair exterior shews like firmest rock,
Whereon the hills might their foundations have;—
Yet hollow are within;—and at the last,
When all yon pile is rear'd, will sink away,
And whelm it in a gulf: but a true arch,
Beneath the heaviest load still firmest stands:—
And such is Philidas.

    CLYMENE.   I say no more.
You are not rash, dear Charon,—choleric,—
Revengeful,—nor o'erfond to mix in broils;—
And therefore with a cold and wary thought
Would weigh the chances, ere for life, or death,

You drew the bloody sword.—Here I give up
All doubts,—and trembling fears,—and do resign
Myself, and all that's dearer, to the Gods,—
To be as they decree.—Now shall your friends
See if my weakness shame your confidence.

    CHARON. Belov'd Clymene, thanks.—A cheerful heart
Soars like an eagle o'er the precipice,
Where poor despair falls headlong.—The spear, thrown,
Will fall where it *must* fall, altho' with prayers
We deaf all heaven to turn its point aside :—
Our spear is thrown :—let's calmly watch it light.
And so, for two short hours,—sweet love, adieu !
                              (*He embraces her.*)

    CLYMENE. Adieu—adieu—dear Charon !   [*Exit* CHARON.
I'm on a narrow plank,—above a gulf—
And must not look below,—or I shall fall.
Oh ! my dear Charon !—and my sweetest boy !—
I cannot read what Time hath not yet written ;
But the blank page doth blind me as I gaze,—
Fill'd thick with shadowy horrors !—I'll not look !—
Great Jove ! into thy hand I give them up !   [*Exit.*

    SCENE II.—*A room in the house of* ARCHIAS.

        (*Enter* PHILIDAS *and a* SERVANT.)

    PHILIDAS. Not risen yet ! . . . you say ? Why, 'tis past noon.
Is he not well ?

    SERVANT.   He revell'd late last night.
Philip was here, with several Theban lords,
That loved their liquor better than their beds.
'Twas day-break ere they left it.

    PHILIDAS.   Is he stirring ?

    SERVANT. I think not, sir,—for Menon is not up.
He stays his master's hours :—my services
Are to the lady Thulia.

    PHILIDAS.   Is she well ?

    SERVANT. She takes no physic, sir.

PHILIDAS.   How in her mind?

SERVANT. She seldom weeps,—and never makes complaint.
Indeed she talks to no one,—save to give
Her quiet thanks for our poor services:—
Scarce eats at all,—and is most pale and wasted.

PHILIDAS. Unhappy lady!—Go—let Archias know,
That I have spurr'd from Athens since the morning,
And wait him here.

SERVANT.   From Athens did you say?

PHILIDAS. From Athens.—And, good fellow, bring some wine;
I've had a bitter ride.

SERVANT.   'Tis very cold, sir.
                    (*He places wine on the table.*)

PHILIDAS. Why dost thou linger?

SERVANT. Oh! forgive me, sir!
You know not who I am: but you I know
To be the friend of my dear master's friends,
And of his wretched widow.

PHILIDAS.   What's thy name?

SERVANT. My name is Clonius. On that dreadful day
When Leontidas, with his faction, drove
Pelopidas, and his, from Thebes——

PHILIDAS.   I know it.—
Thou art the youth whom Androclides saved
From prison,—art thou not?

CLONIUS.   I am;—and oft
From this worse prison have I hoped to save
My most unhappy lady:—but, alas! . . .

PHILIDAS. I've heard of all thy faithfulness. Be sure
It shall have more than thanks. Go—tell her now
The sky is brightening;—bid her have good cheer;
The clouds will quickly pass.

CLONIUS.   'Twould please her, sir,
To hear it from yourself. I'll call her here,
And guard the door without.

PHILIDAS.   Good Clonius—haste,—
Implore her come. Let Archias, too, be told
Of my arrival. (*Exit* CLONIUS.) How the news I bring
Will make her heart leap up! And Thebes—Oh! Thebes!
Thine, too, must rouse,—or be for ever still!
                          (*He pours out wine.*)

(THULIA *enters, attired in black.*)

PHILIDAS (*aside*). Oh! what a blight hath fallen on that flower!
(*Aloud*) Dear lady!

THULIA.   Sir, you wish'd to speak to me.
You are from Athens :—have you seen our friends?

PHILIDAS. Dear lady!—sit.

THULIA.   I thank you, sir ;—my strength
Shall bear me up through our short conference.
I pray you, sir, go on.

PHILIDAS.   Our friends, dear lady—
Are well,—and full of hope :—and I have news
Shall comfort even you.

THULIA.   Tell the cold corpse
To wrap its grave-clothes round, to keep it warm,—
And then bid me take comfort!—But, go on :—
I feel for others ;—for myself, am dead.

PHILIDAS. And yet the news I bring *shall* comfort you.

THULIA. Go on, sir—pray you.

PHILIDAS.   Lady—a great blow
Will fall erelong, whose consequence may be
Deliverance to yourself—and to all Thebes——

THULIA. Oh God! be merciful! and speed that blow,—
So it be just!

PHILIDAS.   I may not more declare,
How this shall be. Heaven, in its mercy, keeps
The future from our eyes,--or our great dooms
Would madden us to see them. And in this,
If in nought else, I'll copy the kind Gods.

Knowledge is good, but as it works to good ;—
Beyond that,—evil merely. Not to know
The ill *may* visit us,—is, not to see
The sharpening knife may cut us to the bone :—
Not to foreknow the good may chance to us—
Is—not to crave a fruit may be most sweet ;—
Or may conceal a scorpion :—therefore, lady——

    THULIA. You are most kind, sir, and I thank you much.
If you have aught of moment else to say
I pray you tell it ; for this conference stands
On a gulf's brink.

    PHILIDAS.   No, lady ;—Clonius waits—
Our guard without the door. There *is* a thing
I have to tell ;—that I would not but tell
For half this city's wealth :—and yet, when told,
'Twill shake you like a plague fit.

    THULIA.   Pray, sir, tell it :
And see how harmless will your tempest blow
Upon my icy bosom.—Oh ! you know not—
But, pray you, on sir.

    PHILIDAS.   When the sun is set,
Then come the freezing cold, and the black darkness,
And all the world seems dead.—But, when again
From the clear east he throws his golden fires,—
Darkness is gone ;—the dead earth lives anew—
Dost thou conceive me, lady ?

    THULIA.   I know not
What thought you'd have me fashion from these words :
But you mean kindly, sir. *My* sun is set—
In the dark grave ;—but never more shall rise
To bid me live !—Such settings have no dawn !

    PHILIDAS. Yet, dearest lady—it hath sometimes chanced,
That, when we thought the bright orb gone below,
It hath but shrouded in some ebon cloud,
From which to burst in glory.—

    THULIA (*after an earnest pause*). Either, sir,
With most false judgment, you would seek to rouse

My torpid heart by touch of cruel fire,—
Which were a grievous sin—or—tell me, sir—
I have a thought—Great God!—it cannot be—
(*She seizes his hand.*)
Tell—tell me—doth he—doth he——

PHILIDAS. Lady, pause.
Go not too far. Joy hath its drowning depths
As well as grief.

THULIA.   Speak—speak—my heart—my heart—
Mercy—for mercy speak—doth he——

PHILIDAS.   He doth!

THULIA. Ha!—speak his name——

PHILIDAS.   Thy lord!—is—not—yet—dead—

THULIA. Ha! ha!—not dead?—not dead?—did'st say not dead?

PHILIDAS. Yes, dearest lady: I *did* say not dead.

THULIA. Art thou awake?—Am I not lunatic?—
Oh! burn me—cut me to the quick—not dead?—
My Androclides—is it he?

PHILIDAS.   Yes—*he*.
I say he's not yet dead.

THULIA.   Not *yet?* not *yet?*
Where is he?—where?—Oh let me fly—where? where?

PHILIDAS. Lady—be calm!

THULIA.   Where is he?—I must go—

PHILIDAS. Be patient, dearest lady.

THULIA.   Where's my lord?
My heart will burst——

PHILIDAS.   In Athens is your lord—
And there you must not,—cannot go.

THULIA.   Oh God!
And he will die!—I will not be withheld——
(*She rushes to the door.*)

PHILIDAS. He will *not* die,—unless you go to kill him.

THULIA. How's that?—speak—speak—

PHILIDAS.   I say he will not die
If this wild rashness slay him not. Be calm—
He is not ill—now start not, lady—force
Thy frenzied brain to reason.—Hear—and speak not.
The murderer's blow——

THULIA.   Ha!

PHILIDAS.   Touch'd no vital part (*a pause*).
The wound is heal'd (*a pause*)—his strength is come again (*a pause*)—
Thou wilt behold him—

(*During this last speech* THULIA *looks with a wild eagerness at* PHILIDAS—*and remains silent and motionless after he has done;—and at last sinks upon the couch.*)

(*Enter* CLONIUS.)

CLONIUS. Menon is stirring, sir;—and comes, I fear,
This way.

PHILIDAS. Dear lady—haste you to your chamber;
Your tyrant will be here—for heav'n's sake——
                    (*He endeavours in vain to rouse her.*)
                                        Clonius—
Open the door—I'll bear her to her room——
Wait you a moment here.

(*He carries her off through the door at which she had entered.*)

CLONIUS. Poor lady! thou wilt soon go to thy rest!
Then Archias—then—look for thy punishment—

(*Enter* PHILIDAS.)

PHILIDAS. Is it not strange how joy should mimic grief?
She's like a statue,—cold and bath'd in tears,
I've laid her on a couch. Go—send her women—
But speak no word of this.—
                    Ha! gentlemen—

(Enter PHILIP *and* LEONTIDAS, *ushered in by* MENON, *who retires.* CLONIUS *goes out.)*

Good-morrow to you both.

LEON. *and* PHILIP.   Good-morrow, sir.

LEON. What news from Athens——gentle Philidas? What of the Exiles?—

PHILIDAS.   Set your minds at rest—
I have so urg'd their speedy banishment,
They'll have no home at Athens.—Nay, I marvel
If even this day they be not driven forth.

LEON. Your zeal deserves our thanks,—and something more
That shall not be forgot.—Come with us now,
And, as we walk, we'll farther question you.

(Enter ARCHIAS, *much disordered.)*

ALL. Good-morrow, Archias.

ARCHIAS.   Gentlemen, good-morrow.
I pray you sit.

PHILIP.   Yes, Archias ;—but not here,
We go to sit in judgment.   There's a crew
Of wealthy traitors for our morning's meal :—
We call to take you with us.

ARCHIAS.   My good friends—
I'm much disorder'd—but will follow you
With what swift haste I may.

LEON.   As your true friend
I tell you, Archias,—leave your midnight cups—
Your spicëd meats,—and perfumed concubines,—
Or you will rue it.

ARCHIAS.   Sir—you are most kind
To charge yourself with my poor private faults :
I know not how to thank you :—but, dear sir—
Let me entreat you,—be less cold, and stern—
Pray less—and offer fewer sacrifices—
And have more charity—and——

LEON.   Ha !—what's this ?—

PHILIP. Ho! gentlemen,—for shame.—Nay—touch not
steel :—
If, of our goodly tripod, two o' th' legs
Should break each other,—why the third must fall,
And all be shatter'd.—Speak no further word—
And think nought hath been spoken.—Archias—
You'll follow with all haste. Come—let's away—

ARCHIAS. Leave Philidas an instant.
                              [*Exeunt* LEON. *and* PHILIP.
                          That proud lord
Misdeems himself a giant,—standing up
On his high self-conceit !—Oh Philidas !
I am made wretched with distemper'd dreams.
For ever at my bed there seems to stand
Pale Androclides, with his gaping heart
Spouting a flood.—I wake—and he is gone—
I sleep—he's there again.—What may it mean?
How came he by his death ? hast ever heard ?

PHILIDAS. Now by my faith ! this is mere foolery.
Take physic, sir :—it is the body's ail
That thus infects the mind ;—and, purging one,
You shall make sound the other.

ARCHIAS.   I do think
'Tis as thou say'st.—Here's for my physic then ;
                              (*Pouring out wine*)
'Tis th' only drug. Is't not to-morrow night
We revel at your house ?

PHILIDAS.   To-morrow night—
Fail me,—and you shall miss such curious fare
As you shall marvel at.—

ARCHIAS.   What,—women ?—ha—
You'll keep your secret still ?—

PHILIDAS.   Yes, Archias—
But take this of them.—Thebes hath had none such
Since she was Thebes.

ARCHIAS.   Ha-ha—good friend ! Come, come—
Away—away—my excellent good friend !   [*Exeunt.*

Scene III.—*A room in the house of* Charon.

(*Enter* Charon, *with a* Servant.)

Charon. Where is your lady?

Servant. In the dining hall.

Charon. Go, let her know I'm here. [*Exit* Servant.

(*Enter* Clymene.)

Ha! here she comes.

Clymene. Oh! my dear Charon,—what a long two hours!
My heart has been, as in a battle-field,
Where fear and hope were killing one the other;
And rising still to fight, and kill again.

Charon. And no blood shed at last. I wish our Greeks,—
Since they must squabble—would invent some way
To shew their valour,—and yet keep their limbs
As safe as your two champions.

Clymene. But, dear Charon,
Hath aught untoward chanc'd?

Charon. No, dearest wife,
Our chariot glides, as on a crystal road.—
Think not of harm. Hath Philidas been here?

Clymene. No, Charon. (*A knocking at the gate.*)

Charon. Hark!—There's someone at the gate.

Clymene. 'Tis he, perchance.

Charon. His is a quicker rap,
Like one in haste.—'Tis our conspirators—
But no—'tis still broad daylight. Yet this storm
Might serve as well as darkness for their screen.
The earth is thick with snow,—and not a man
Walks through the streets.

(*Enter* Epaminondas.)

Ha! my dear friend. I did not think this storm
Would let our sun come out.

EPAM.   But—being forth—
You'd wrap him in your clouds.—No—I'm no sun,
For I cannot suck up your flattering mists.

CHARON. I would you were,—that you might then condense
Your burning rays into one point,—and scorch
Our tyrants on their thrones.

EPAM.   Their guilt deserves
Scarce less a stroke.—Fair lady—a good-morrow—
I saw you not through your good Charon's fogs.
Give me your pardon.

CLYMENE.   Sir, I've none to spare:
I am a daily beggar for't myself.
But I'll give 'good welcome' for 'good-morrow.'
Yet why *good-morrow*, when 'tis almost night?
For that give reason,—then I'll pardon give.

EPAM. And in these times 'tis no unwonted thing
For reason to need pardon.—Folly, king—
Reason's a rebel, whom each loyal fool
Thinks glory to hunt down.—For your *good-morrow*
'Twere no hard task, methinks, to carve quaint reasons
Through an Olympiad.

CLYMENE.   Cut us but one,
And let it be fantastical.

EPAM.   As thus,
Is't not that we would lengthen the day's youth,
Even as our own? We like not that age steal
Upon our brows, to draw his ugly curves
O'er the smooth, shining forehead;—and the hair,
Glossy, and curling, and luxuriant, change
To thin—straight—dull, and grizzled—or vile grey:—
So still we put off, year by year, the curse:—
At twenty, but mere boys;—at thirty, men,—
But young men still;—at forty, nothing more:—
For what is the stiff beard,—the wiry hair—
The hard, firm muscle,—the full-rounded form—
The stern eye,—the strong feature?—merely youth,
Just where the blossom hardens into fruit.

CLYMENE. But fifty comes.

EPAM.   Oh! then 'tis just man's prime
Till now, the nerves were slack,—the reason crude—
The passions merely mad,—wild colts, unbroke :—
Life, till this moment, was scarce worth the gift!
A turbulent dream, from indigestion bred :—
Just now he is awak'd—and feels his strength—
And looks on real things,—not hollow shapes,—
As through his life before ;—and thinks 'tis pity
But man were born just on his fiftieth year.
Oh! what a world 'twere then to revel in!

CLYMENE. Suppose him sixty.

EPAM.   Well,—and what is that?
If not so swift his foot, 'tis yet more sure ;—
His voice is strong,—his appetite as keen
As shallow-headed thirty.—For white hairs,
Who, but a fool, would care if white, or black?
Or—caring—not prefer the virgin snow
To the red clay, or brown, or sooty earth?
Why, Jove himself is painted hoary-lock'd!
And 'tis the mind that makes the man :—all else
Is but the cavern where the diamond lies.
Sixty is merely fifty at its best!
Happy who lengthens out a long three-score!

CLYMENE. But he is seventy now ;—or good four-score.

EPAM. Blest time! Oh! what soft calm is all about!
Life's fever is burnt down :—and the mild pulse
Vibrates *so* quietly!—'Tis wisdom's hour!
And wisdom is *true* strength :—not that brute force
That lies in the full arm, or nervous thigh :—
The ox, in that, is greater than the man.
Oh! this, at last, is the true wine of life!
All, past before, was merely pulp, and rind,
In a long fermentation. The shrunk limbs—
The palsied hand—the hairless crown—the voice—
Thin, and as frequent as the grasshopper's—
Why—what are these?—Merely the lengthening shades

That mark the evening coming that *must* come ;—
And comes more oft to fifteen, than four-score !—
Be happy then !—The sun is just as bright,
About to set, as when 'twas newly risen :—
Nay, brighter,—for the morning's fogs are gone.
So talks th' old man :—old to the world alone ;
But, to himself, an everlasting youth ;—
Less beauteous *perhaps*,—but better, and more wise.
I have known many such.—And so't may be
We like to lengthen out the youth o'th' day,
And bid—' good-morrow '—till the sun hath set.
At least, fair lady—that's my first quaint guess.
                    (*A knocking at the gate.*)

CLYMENE. I'll tax you for a better at fit hour.
I could make such myself, to my wheel's hum.

EPAM. If 'twere not to waste time, that house-affairs
Might better use.—But now, my noble friend,—
What news from Athens?

CHARON.   You shall hear, anon.
(*A* SERVANT *enters, ushering in* PELOPIDAS *and* MELON, *dressed
            like hunters.*)
Right welcome, gentlemen,—I fear your sport
Hath little prosper'd in so rough a day.
Where have you left your friends?

PELOP.   They are below,
Shaking their garments. 'Tis a pelting snow :
But we're not empty quite :—we've left without
A three days' feast for half a score sharp stomachs ;
Our own as sharp as any.

CHARON. (*to the* SERVANT). Let the meal
Be placed with all good speed :—and see the fire
Roar up with plenteous logs.

SERVANT.   I will, my lord.   [*Exit.*

CHARON. Now, my dear friends,—again,—right welcome
    home ! (*Looking at* EPAMINONDAS)
He knows you not, Pelopidas ;—nor yet
Partakes our plot. Shall we withhold it still? (*They whisper.*)

Epam. I take my leave, dear lady. These are birds
With whom I would not wish to share the nest.
Commend me to your lord.

Clymene. You shall not go :—
They're not all vultures. They're from Athens, too ;
Will tell you of your friends.

Epam. For that I'll wait.

Pelop. No, Charon ;—he *must* join us. His sole voice
Will call a thousand young and ardent spirits,
Proud to encounter death for any straw
He flings in honour's stream.—His word shall give
A stamp on that we do, shall prove it gold,—
Which else might seem but brass.—I'll find a time
To urge him to it.—Lady, my ill manners,
More than my garb, I fear, betray the rustic.
Your pardon, pray. This is my trusty friend,
And fellow-sportsman, Melon.

Melon. Proud to hunt
Such game with such a huntsman.

Clymene. Gentlemen—
You are most welcome.—Be your horses swift,—
Your boar-spears sharp and strong !— [*Exit.*

Pelop. (*to* Epam.). Sir, you have friends
In Athens, as I hear. We now come thence,
And may have tidings, did we know their names.

Epam. I thank you, sir. I've many dear friends there,
'Twould glad me much to hear of. Know you aught
Of young Pelopidas ?

Pelop. He's lately dead.

Epam. Dead ?—dead ?— (*A pause.*)
Why, thou tormenting wag !—what madness now ?

Pelop. (*embracing him*). Madness of joy, to clasp thee once
    again,
Dear—dear Epaminondas !

Epam. Dear Pelopidas !
I wish thee here,—yet hence.—What ! some new wrestler

To be tripp'd up at venture of thy head?
Or what strange folly else?—

PELOP. Oh no! The game
Is for a higher stake :—with greater players.
Come this way.—I must have thine ear awhile.
(*They go to the back of the stage.*)

(*Enter* GORGIDAS—PHERENICUS -THEOPOMPUS—DEMOCLIDES
—*and* CEPHISIDORUS, *in the garb of hunters.*)

CHARON. Welcome, my friends!—right welcome, every one!
(*They embrace.*)

ALL. We thank you, noble Charon.

GORGIDAS. Oh, this Thebes!
How changëd is her aspect!—She seems dull
And lonely, and grief-worn,—like some poor widow
Above her husband's grave.

CHARON. We have a cordial
Shall make her laugh anon.—Oh!—from the dead

(*Enter* ANDROCLIDES)

Given back,—dear Androclides,—welcome,—welcome!
(*They embrace.*)

ANDRO. Dear Charon, thank you. Know'st thou of my
 wife?

CHARON. She lives—she lives;—and lives in hope again,
For she has heard thou livest. Philidas
This morning saw her. Till to-morrow night,
Dear friend, forget her;—or but think of her
To make thy sword the keener.

ANDRO. Speed thee, sun!
Leap over this long night to the new day :—
Then flog thy fiery horses through the sky—
And leave glad night again!—I pass'd his house;
The monster's house!—Oh! Charon—had I met
That hated form—thy namesake at the Styx
Had greeted him erenow. Foul, bloody villain!

(*Enter* PHILIDAS.)

PHILIDAS. Friends,—all of you well met.—Welcome to Thebes! (*They embrace.*)

SEVERAL TOGETHER. Thanks, Philidas.

PHILIDAS. Ha! dear Androclides—
Think of to-morrow night——

ANDRO. Nay, Philidas,—
Tell me not so: I think of nothing else.

PHILIDAS. Charon, a word with you. (*They retire.*)

EPAM. (*coming forward with* PELOP.) Then be it so!
With hand and heart I join in your emprise:
Freely,—though much unwilling: hating war,—
Yet, for the smaller evil, choosing it;—
To choose compell'd:—as, of two horrid deaths,
I'd take the quicker and less terrible,—
Approving neither.—Yet, forget not this;—
I join no faction 'gainst its opposite:—
I make no private feud of man 'gainst man:—
'Tis 'gainst th' oppressor, and the murderer,
I league with the oppressëd.—Beyond this
I go not with you.

PELOP. Nor shall we go first.
The three *must* die; and there the sword shall stop——

EPAM. If you *can* stop it.—"Tis a furious hound
That, once broke loose, is hardly whistled back
'Till he have fill'd his maw.—If they *must* die,—
Why, be it so! I cannot give my hand
To any private slaughter;—but my voice
Shall not be raised too harshly to denounce
A crime forced on by fate.

PELOP. We ask no more.
Give us your voice—and we've a thousand arms
Ready for any danger.—For your sword,
Why—spare it if you will:—but time hath been
That, sparing it, you had not spared your friend.

EPAM. Spare *your* friend now. But we've no time for words.
What is to do,—must speedily be done.
Against the hour I'll bring what aid I can,
And may the good Gods guide us !

PELOP. Here are some
You have not seen.

EPAM. Ha ! my belovëd friends !
Give me your hands : our hearts are join'd already.
(*They embrace.*)
Dear Androclides !—coming from the grave,
Thou'rt so *most* welcome,—'twere almost a sin
Not to have sent thee there !

ANDRO. I think so too.
And do intend my thanks to the kind sender.

EPAM. Well, gentlemen ;—I pray Heaven prosper you,
As you deserve to prosper ; but not more.
With a pure heart, unto this enterprise
I bring my aid ;—and so I hope do all.

SEVERAL. All—all !

EPAM. If, for revenge, or wantonness,
One drop of blood be shed,—your cause is foul'd,—
And freedom's champions will be faction's slaves !
With this I leave you. So farewell to all. [*Exit.*

ALL. Farewell, Epaminondas.

CHARON. Come, gentlemen: the board is spread: the meats
Send up rich incense : let's away—

PELOP. Stay, Charon !
A dinner waiting is a serious thing—
So is our plot. Briefly, before we go,
Let's hear once more the order of the act,
That all may understand.—Speak, Philidas.

CHARON. But who will listen ?—When a dinner beckons,
Who stops to hug a speech ?

PHILIDAS. 'Tis even so :—
The brain's small whisper is but little heard,

When empty stomachs shout.   Go in, go in.
I'll see you on the morrow.
    PELOP.   As you please.
Give me one word before you go.   (*They whisper.*)
    CHARON.   Come, sirs,
No ceremony :—your hot compliments
Will make your dinner cold.
            [*Exeunt all but* PELOP. *and* PHILIDAS.
    PHILIDAS.   You need not fear.
Charon knows every signal.—When they come,
I shall withdraw—throw wide the prison gates—
For there's no key but turns at my command—
Arm our good friends,—and to the market-place
Bring them to wait your bidding.   If your dragon
Escape you not,—fear nothing for our wolves.
He goes to rest betimes,—and will not stir
When he is in his den.
    PELOP.   And *shall* not stir,
When I have found him there; fear not for him.
Good-night.
    PHILIDAS.   Good-night, Pelopidas.
                  [*Exeunt at opposite doors.*

END OF THE FOURTH ACT.

ACT V.

SCENE I.—*A room in the house of* LEONTIDAS.

(*Enter* LEONTIDAS; *and a* BOY *carrying lights.*)

LEON.   Here,—bear these things into my chamber, boy :
Place them beside the door : then come again.
Art sure 'tis Philidas that gives this feast ?
Dost know his house ?—or who hath told thee so ?

BOY.   Oh yes, my lord ; I know the house well.   My brother
lives with Philidas ; and, several days back, he told me of this

feast being toward :—and, but now, in passing, I saw great lights there, and heard music and rejoicing.

LEON. Go now, and come again. [*Exit* BOY.
What fopperies
Are these for men on whom a state depends !
How can the brain that every night is steep'd
In wine,—and whipp'd to froth by the smart lash
Of hare-brain'd witlings,—be fit counsellor
Where great state interests plead !—This Philidas
Grows hateful to me,—thrusting his soft pity
Between the traitor, and the threaten'd blow :—
He shall be crush'd erelong.—Turn'd reveller too !
And rich,—'tis said. Whence come his funds ? And Philip
Hath lost at play thrice his paternal wealth,—
And yet hath princely means.—So Archias hath :
Yet his rare wines,—his ceaseless revellings—
His Tyrian-vested concubines—his jewels—
His gorgeous tapestries,—his gilded halls—
Great Jove !—why 'tis a monarch's state he keeps !
And still he's rich ! Oh ! I do much suspect
The iron sword of justice hath glanc'd off—
Touching on golden armour !

(*Enter the* BOY.)
Take these next :—
Dost know what other guests are there to-night ?

BOY. I have not heard their names, my lord. Some dozen nobles of the city :—and also some ladies of marvellous beauty, later in the evening, are expected.

LEON. Women—didst say ? What !—women at the feast ?

BOY. Yes, my lord.

LEON. Here,—take away the rest. Then get thee gone.
Lie like a watchful cat before his door ;—
And, when these women enter, bring me word.
I will reward thee. (*Exit* BOY.) What ! all decency
Laugh'd in the face !—What would the Spartan say,
To hear of women where the Archons feast ?

Oh heavens! 'tis monstrous! Is it fit such men
Should fill with me the awful justice seat?—
What do I need of them?—Let them heed well,
Or I will shake them to the dust!—Great Jove!—
But they shall blush,—for, at their folly's height
I'll stand before them, and rebuke them all. [*Exit.*

SCENE II.—*A hall in the house of* CHARON. *Arms and armour are strewed about the floor.*

(PELOPIDAS—ANDROCLIDES—GORGIDAS—THEOPOMPUS —MELON—CEPHISIDORUS—*and* DEMOCLIDES *are busied putting on their armour.* CHARON *and* CLYMENE *are assisting.*)

PELOP. This breast-plate is too small.

MELON. Try this.

CHARON. Here's one
Might clip a giant in. But use good haste:
The signal is put up that all goes well,
And we must hold us ready.—Will that fit?

PELOP. Somewhat too wide:—but 'tis the better fault.

ANDRO. Thank you, dear lady.

CLYMENE. Wherefore do you shake?

ANDRO. Oh! ask me not: I have no tongue to-night.
My soul seems coiled up for one desperate spring,
And likes no motion else. If I do shake,
'Tis as some burning mountain, when the fires
Are gathering for a burst.—Thanks, lady—thanks.

PELOP. And this, you say, the sword Ismenias wore. —

CHARON. The same.

PELOP. 'Tis a rare blade,—and fits my hand.
He still shall wear it,—for his deadliest foe
This night shall be its sheath.

(*A loud knocking at the outward gate.*)

CEPHISI. What noise is that?
(*They pause, and look toward the door.*)

CLYMENE. Fear nothing, gentlemen : 'tis but some gossip
Who comes to tell me of her morning's head-ache :—
Or that her daughter lost a tooth last night—
Or that her lap-dog's ailing.

   (*Enter* PHERENICUS *in haste. He stands silent.*)
 PELOP.   What's amiss?
Why dost not speak?
 PHEREN.   I fear we are undone!
 PELOP. Then tell us how.—We have our armour on,
And will do something.
 PHEREN.   Here's a messenger,
Puffing with hot haste—sent from the Polemarchs,
With stern demand that Charon instantly
Do go before them.
   (*A pause. They look anxiously at one another.*)
 PELOP. Does he say the business?
 PHEREN. No—and I ask'd him not,—for he look'd strange.
 CHARON. Bid him return, and I will follow him.
 PHEREN. His order is, he says, most peremptory
Not to return without you. (*A pause*).
 PELOP.   Charon, go—
If we're discover'd—dash the signal-light,
As you pass by it, to the ground.—We're arm'd,
And, seeing that, will forth at once,—and do
What fate will let us.
 GORGIDAS.   But he may be seiz'd—
Tortur'd—or threaten'd with an instant death
If he reveal not :—what awaits us then?
I would not have him go at all.—Send word
That he is ill, and in his bed.
 CHARON.   No—no—
Then would they seek me here,—and that were worse.
Suspicion often is a coward cur
That, fairly met—turns tail and slinks away :—
But—run from—may become a furious beast,

And worry you to death.   I'll go at once.
The business may be foreign to our fear;—
But, should the worst be true,—my voice in this
Is with Pelopidas,—that, on the instant,
Ere they are well awak'd, ye sally forth,
And strike the tyrants down.—Behold this glass—
                          (*Taking up an hour-glass*)
I turn it now.—If, half its sands run out,
I come not back,—delay no moment more :—
Unsheathe your swords, and get about your work.
If I return there needs no signal else.—
Hath this your sanctions?—

    PELOP.   I am well content.

    ANDRO.   And I.

    MELON.   And I.

    PELOP.   Why are you silent, sirs?
                  (*The others whisper.   Exit* CLYMENE.)

    THEOPOMPUS.   It is not, Charon, that we aught misdoubt
Your perfect truth, and zeal——

    CHARON.   Go on, sir, pray.

    GORGIDAS.   We all esteem you, sir, most honorable.

    SEVERAL VOICES.   All—all—

    CEPHIS.   And shall be ever bound to you,
As a most noble gentleman.

    CHARON.   Well, sirs—
I see what scares you.   Should they threaten death,
Or show the torture,—I'm too soft a plant
To live in such a tempest,—*that's* your thought.   (*A pause.*)
I blame you not;—for 'tis well known to all
That I'm no soldier;—never saw a battle :—
And 'tis, too oft, the noise and strut of war
That goes for bravery :—but I have known
As firm a heart in a soft woman's breast
As ever heav'd up mail.—Come to the proof—
He that misdoubts me :—let him thrust his hand

Into this fire with me,—and, if I start,
Or snatch away the first, then trust me not.

PELOP. No—no—it shall not be—
SEVERAL. We want no proof.

(*Enter* CLYMENE *hastily, with her little son in her arms.*)

CLYMENE. You doubt my Charon!—here are hostages,
Myself—and this far dearer—(*puts down the child*)
When *he's* false,
Let *us* not live.—You'll have your vengeance so,—
And we shall 'scape our shame!—Here—take him, sirs—
Take both—and spare us not!—

CHARON (*embracing her*). Belov'd Clymene!—
Here, gentlemen,—you have your hostages.

PELOP. If there's that man in all this company
So vile to take this gage—I cast him off—
And hold him in my hatred!

ANDRO. There's no wretch,
Even the worst in Thebes, would stoop to this!

ALL. We'll have no hostages.

SEVERAL (*together and in succession*). Dear Charon, go.—

THEOPOMPUS. Charon, forgive me if I knew you not.

CHARON. Then, sirs, I have your confidence again?—

ALL. For ever, Charon!

CHARON. For these hostages,
They shall remain with you.

PELOP. No, Charon, no!
Do not degrade us. I'd as soon take pawn
For money lent to my most honor'd friend,
As take your pledge in this.

ANDRO. It shall not be—
Remove them, rather, from all reach of harm:—
So, if you perish, may your son yet live
T'avenge his country's wrongs.

CHARON. I thank you—No!
Let us together live, or die. What fate

More glorious could I wish him, than to fall
In such a struggle, where his father falls,
And such a band of friends.—My pretty boy!
Farewell—(*embracing him*) farewell!

BOY. Where are you going, father?

CHARON. Not far, dear boy. I shall be back anon.
Belov'd Clymene! (*embracing her*) as the breath to life—
So art thou to my soul! The Gods protect thee! (*He kneels.*)
Immortal Jove! oh! hear us now!—Our foes
Are tyrannous, and strong;—and bow us down
With misery to the earth!—but let them fall
By our just hands,—and send our country peace!—
Hear us—and give the sign! (*A loud burst of thunder.*)

ALL. Our prayer is heard!
The Gods are for us!—

CHARON. Oh! all ruling Jove
Our hearts do thank thee! (*He rises.*)

PELOP. Charon—get thee hence—
Or I cannot abide.

CHARON. Kind friends—adieu—
Look to the hour-glass. Give one parting grasp—
(*He shakes hands with all.*)
Clymene!—one fond kiss—My boy—ah! rogue!
The spring will soon be here, and thou shalt ride.
Now get thee to thy bed. Adieu—adieu! [*Exit.*

PELOP. Are we all arm'd?

SEVERAL VOICES. Yes—all—

PELOP. Let every sword
Leap freely from the scabbard:—every dagger
Be ready for the grasp.—Come, dear Clymene,—
Thou hast a hero for thy lord. Be gay—
All shall go well.—Come, where's our woman's gear?
Time is a race-horse now, and near the goal.
Show us the way.

CLYMENE. Bear you the hour-glass, sir,—
And warily—for every dropping sand

May tell a brave man's life.—Come, gentlemen—
A woman fitly may lead warriors on,
Who go to play the woman.

PELOP. Lead the way.
Bring Charon's armour :—he will need it soon.

GORGIDAS. I have it here, Pelopidas.
[*Exeunt omnes.*

SCENE III.—*A room adjoining the feasting-hall in the house of*
PHILIDAS.

(*Two* SERVANTS *in waiting enter on the same side.*)

1ST SERVT. They are coming now. I heard a knocking at the gate.

2ND SERVT. No—'tis not they. Our master said they were not expected till much later.

1ST SERVT. Then will Archias be so drunk, he will never be able to look through his brimstone loopholes upon them. His eyelids will be as heavy as the city-gates ; and his strength to uplift them as if a child should try to shoulder away the citadel.

2ND SERVT. Faith ! 'twixt him and Philip, there will not be the difference of a drachm's weight. In truth they are all rascally drunk already.

(*Enter* CHARON *with the* MESSENGER.)

CHARON. Go, tell the Archons I await their pleasure.
[*Exit a* SERVANT.
You're jovial here to-night. How's Philidas ?

SERVT. I thank you, sir—exceeding well.

(*Enter, from the feasting-hall,* PHILIP, ARCHIAS, *and* PHILIDAS,
followed by the SERVANT.)

PHILIDAS (*to the* SERVANT). Go—get you hence,—and wait
till you are called. [*Exeunt* SERVANTS.

CHARON. Good-even to you, lords ;— you find me prompt
T'obey your summons.

PHILIP (*to* MESSENGER). Sir, you may retire. [*Exit* MESSENGER.

ARCHIAS. Charon,—who are these strangers, lately come
Into the city,—and somewhere conceal'd,—
And countenanc'd by certain citizens?
Philip—I'll not be prompted ;—'tis the way :—
If you can question better, so—I've done.

PHILIP. Who are these strangers, Charon?

CHARON. Good my lords—
I cannot answer you. I know none such.
I'm an unfrequent stirrer from my home,
And pick up news oft when all Thebes hath lost it.
Who are the men you speak of?—and whence come?
And by whom harbour'd?

PHILIP. Nay—We ask you that—
A rumour is abroad that such are here,—
And your name coupled with it.

CHARON. My good lords—
Be not your minds disturb'd with such vain talk.—
Rumour's a subtle wizard, who, from straws,
Or very atoms that our eye scarce notes,
Will pile you up a fortress, mountain-high,
Shall seem to threaten heav'n :—yet—do but touch—
And all is gone !—A word, dropt by a beggar,
He catches up, and multiplies to seem
The shoutings of a host. There is no knave
That lies like Rumour :—for he's like the wind,
Whispering at once into ten thousand chinks,
All glad to catch the whisper : through he glides,
And hastens on,—and to ten thousand more
Whispers the lie ten thousand different ways ;—
Oh ! trust him not, my lords :—when he speaks *truth*
He is no longer Rumour.

ARCHIAS. Art thou drunk,
Most noble Charon—that thou talk'st so well?

CHARON. No, Archias,—I'm not drunk.

ARCHIAS. Then, by the Gods!
Thou shalt be :—for I'd love to hear thee speak,

Strengthen'd by liquor;—seeing that, all cold
And dull in sober sense, thou talk'st so well.—
Come in—and get thee drunk.—Didst mark him, Philip?
Rumour—and fortress—beggar—mountain high—
Ten million chinks—and whispers—and what not?
I call that speaking.—Come, and get thee drunk.—
Charon—I'll have thee drunk.

  CHARON.   Excuse me, sir.
My health is frail. I am forbidden wine.
For those same strangers that you talk about,
'Twere better perhaps not disregarded quite ;—
I'll make enquiry—and return anon,
If so 'twill pleasure you.

  PHILIDAS.   I'd wager now
'Tis some low fellow that hath got this up
To vex you at the banquet.

  PHILIP.   Very like!
Good Charon, see about it.—Very like!
With this small sting t'avenge the good we did
His brother, friend, or father,—sending him
By a short cut to Pluto's pleasure-ground.
No, Charon—heed it not.—If we should chase
Each gnat that buzzes round us, we should kill
Ourselves with killing.

  ARCHIAS.   Philip—Philip—hark!
They've struck up a new tune.—I love that tune
Better than wine.—Come in—I will not miss it.
Charon, return—and be a God with us.
We shall be drunk anon.—'Oh! love and wine.'
           (*Goes out, singing.*)

  PHILIP. *Anon* he will be drunk.—Now I *am* drunk;
And, knowing it, do prove me partly sober.
Charon, good-night.—*Anon* he will be drunk.
Ha—ha—I like the wag.—*Anon*—ha—ha—   [*Exit.*

  PHILIDAS. Charon,—get quickly home, and arm thyself.
Pelopidas must wait some half-hour still.
Bid him take Melon with him. With the rest

Return upon the spur. I'll single out
Some six for the first blow ;—'twill be enough.
The others will be near for every chance.—
Thou'st play'd thy part most bravely.—Speak not now,—
But haste away.

  CHARON. My sword shall be my tongue.

(CHARON *goes out, and* PHILIDAS *returns to the banqueting-room.*)

  The foregoing scene draws away, and discovers

   SCENE IV.—*The Banqueting-room.*

  (ARCHIAS— PHILIP — PHILIDAS — *and many* THEBAN
   LORDS *lie upon couches beside tables covered with
   wines and fruits. Two* BOYS *are in waiting to pour
   out the wine. Music is heard.*)

  ARCHIAS. Once more—once more.—By Jupiter! once more—
Come—come—again—'Oh! love and wine.' (*Sings*).

  PHILIP. Are you all sleeping, lords?

  SEVERAL VOICES.   No, Philip—why?

  PHILIP. Then Archias disturbs you. For my part,—
I'm so well season'd to them,—his best songs
Still set me snoring for a harmony.

  ARCHIAS. Thou hast no harmony about thee, Philip.—
Thou'dst rather hear a traitor's wind-pipe squeak,
Pinch'd by a cord,—than hear Apollo sing.

  PHILIP. If he sings aught like thee. Take off thy wine
In pity to our ears.

  PHILIDAS. Come, my good lords—
You're sluggards at your drink. Here is a wine
Ye have not tasted ;—'tis a drink for Gods.
Their nectar's physic to it.

  ARCHIAS.   Pour it out—
Brim up the goblets :—Fill,—thou rosy knave !
Thou Ganymede to me thy Jupiter !—
Fill to the brim, thou blushing peony !
Leave space but for a fly to stand and sip,

I'll fling a lightning at thee.—Lords—I drink
To the bright goddesses, who from their heaven
Shall visit us to-night.—Are you prepar'd?
    PHILIDAS. The goblets are all crown'd.
    ARCHIAS.   Then off with them.
    ALL. To the bright goddesses!—
    PHILIP.   Ah! Philidas!
This is indeed a nectar-mocking drink!
It is not Greek?
    PHILIDAS.   No—'tis from Italy.
I've but a stinted measure,—yet enough
For this night's rouse.—Fill up the cups again—
We'll sleep in heav'n to-night.
    PHILIP.   Oh, Jupiter!
Methinks I see thee on thy golden throne!
    ARCHIAS. Where—Philip—where?
    PHILIP.   There, Archias—dost not see?
And Juno stands beside;—and Mercury
Holding his cup:—all Thebes might lie within it
Like a huge pearl. Dost not behold?—there—there—
    ARCHIAS. No—no!—'tis thou that liest in Thebes—thou'rt drunk. . . . .
Where are the goddesses? Dear Philidas,
Why tarry their bright wings?—Bring round the cups.
Who gives a health?
    PHILIP.   I'll give one, Archias.—
A health to Lentulus, and his three sons!
    ARCHIAS (*lifting the cup*). To Lentulus and his—— Why, they are hang'd!
Were hang'd this morning,—were they not, wise wag?
    PHILIP. No:—tumbled headlong from the citadel.
But drink their health the same: they were good fellows
To you and me;—come,—drink to the kind friends
Whose *talents* we inherit.
    ARCHIAS.   Hold thy tongue!
Thou brainless drunkard!—Dost thou think the rose

Will keep such secrets safe?—Where are the girls?
The goddesses?—Go—fetch them, Philidas—
I drink to them again.

PHILIP.　　　　　　And I.

PHILIDAS.　　　　　　　　And all. (*All drink.*)

(*A knocking at the outer gate.*)

PHILIDAS. Hark! they are here. I go to welcome them,
And bring them to you. Fill your cups again:
Be jovial, lords.—What, Archias—thou'rt awake
At such a sunrise. I'll be back anon.
See that the cups be fill'd (*to the boys*).　　　　[*Exit.*

ARCHIAS.　　　　　　I'll drink no more.
Lords—do not drink again.—'Tis drunkenness
To drink till you are drunk.—'Oh! love and wine.' (*Sings.*)

1ST LORD. 'Tis a marvellous piece doubtless. That stag's head looks almost more natural than Nature herself. And for the dog close behind his haunches, I will take it on my oath that I can hear him bark.

2ND LORD. Now art thou more natural than Nature made thee, to say thou canst hear a picture bark. But 'tis past controversy, a most choice work. Methinks I can see the eyes of that black steed flashing like a torch in a gusty night. Whose is the work?

3RD LORD. 'Tis done by one Apollo,—a native of Cos,—so Philidas reports.

1ST LORD. Apelles—Apelles—not Apollo.—What! is all the world drunken?—Apelles, I tell thee:—a lad of some eighteen years.—I saw him at work upon that very picture, and offered him money for it.

2ND LORD. How much?

1ST LORD. Nay,—that's a secret. But in truth 'twas fifty drachmas, and yet he refused it.

2ND LORD. And, had he been dead a few Olympiads, thou wouldst have offer'd another,—fifty times that sum,—though, maybe, the picture should be the worse for age and ill-using.—I see thou art a true patron. Your true patrons let living artists starve,—and almost starve themselves to encourage those that are dead. A painting shall never get the true mellowness till the painter be rotten.

3RD LORD. And faith, that's partly true!—

2ND LORD. I have known your staunch patrons to refuse, at a small price, a new picture that would do honour to any country,—and yet, almost on the same day, to give a princely sum for one that had little to recommend it but that the painter died three hundred years before. This they call 'patronizing of the art'—but in truth they should call it 'the art of patronizing'—Eh—lords?

3RD LORD. Thou'st hit it on the head. I've seen it oft.

(*Enter* PHILIDAS.)

ARCHIAS. What! are they not yet here?

PHILIDAS. Yes—they are come.
But being ladies of true modesty,
They like not that their looks be pored upon
By curious servants—nor their talk o'er-heard.

PHILIP (*to the* SERVANTS). Get everyone of you away.

[*Exeunt* SERVANTS *and* BOYS.

PHILIDAS. And more:—
They make demand that, till themselves consent,
They shall not be uncover'd—nor required
To speak but in a whisper.

ARCHIAS. Show them in,
And let's proceed to judgment.

PHILIP. None shall harm them.
I'll be their champion. All of you take heed;—
If any touches them but by their leave,
I'll trip his heels up.

PHILIDAS. Then I'll bring them in. [*Exit.*

ARCHIAS. Wilt thou trip me up?

PHILIP. You,—or any man.

ARCHIAS. They are more likely, Philip, to trip thee.
Why, thou'rt so drunk a straw might knock thee down.

PHILIP. A straw?—why that's a giant's club, to what
Would serve to lay thee flat.—See that no fly
Be on the wing before thou dare to walk,—
For, if it light on thee, thou canst not stand.
A kitten sneezing in thy face should be
A hurricane to thy top-heavy boat
Would turn keel upmost. Why a mustard seed,
Shot from a baby's dimpled thumb, would knock
Thy drunken head down like a battering-ram!

(*Enter* PHILIDAS, *leading in* ANDROCLIDES — GORGIDAS — CHARON — THEOPOMPUS — CEPHISIDORUS — DEMOCLIDES —*and* PHERENICUS, *disguised like women, with long cloaks, and their heads covered and overshadowed with garlands.* —*The* LORDS *all rise, and offer seats to them.* PHILIDAS *takes* ANDROCLIDES *to the couch of* ARCHIAS, *which is in the front.*)

PHILIDAS. Now lords, I pray you, of your courtesy,
Be gentle, and not rude. For a short space
I leave you to yourselves. [*Exit.*

ARCHIAS. Why, thou art sweeter than a citron grove;
But there's no breath comes through thy perfum'd leaves.

PHILIP. Now, lords—fair play.—What would I give to see
That beauteous face in the broad light of day!
That ugly garland sits like night upon it.

(*Enter a* SERVANT.)

ARCHIAS. Fellow! what dost thou here?

SERVANT. My lord, there is just arrived from Athens a messenger who hath brought this packet—from your kinsman and namesake, Archias the High Priest,—and he demands most importunately that it be instantly read, for that it contains business of the utmost importance.

ARCHIAS (*putting the packet under his pillow*). 'Business to-morrow!' see the fellow fed,
And bid him come to-morrow. [*Exit* SERVANT.
              Loveliest lady—
If that thy voice be sweet as is thy breath,
'Twill drown our ears with heavenly melody.
    PHILIP. Why dost not answer me? I swear by Jove!

(*Re-enter the* SERVANT.)

    ARCHIAS. Why—what again?—

    SERVANT. My lord, the messenger most vehemently demands that you read the packet without delay; for that a report is therein given of some dreadful conspiracy. He says 'tis a most awful business.

    ARCHIAS. 'Business to-morrow.'—He's a merry fellow;—
I'm sure he is,—and so commend me to him.—
Tell him I'll make his fortune;—but not now—
'Business to-morrow!'—What's the fellow's name?

    SERVT. 'Tis Abas, my lord,—the tailor,—and he entreats that you will read the packet.—He has spurred all the way from Athens within these three hours.

    ARCHIAS. He's a good fellow—make him drunk as Bacchus.
'Business to-morrow!'—Tell my worthy friend
The night was made for sleep and jollity.
'Business to-morrow!' [*Exit* SERVANT.
              Is't not so, sweet girl?

(*The* SERVANT *re-enters, forcibly holding back* ABAS.)

    SERVT. My lord, he *will* come in—I cannot hold him.

    ABAS (*without*). My lord—my lord!—your life—the life o' th' state!—

    ARCHIAS (*staggering up*). Where is my sword?—Thou curs'd ill-manner'd slave!
Bind him, I tell you!—whip him well—old fool!
Drag him to prison!—

    (ABAS *is dragged away—crying out—*'*Dreadful plot*'—
      '*Murderous conspiracy*'—*etc.*)

ARCHIAS (*reeling to his couch*). The outrageous ass !—
How he hath flush'd me !—Come, my loveliest,
Take off this odious garland, that shuts up,
Like a dull fog, the beauteous lamps of Heaven.
I am not drunk.—Come—let me see thy face—
I swear to thee I think I know thee—Come—
I' faith I am not drunk !—

  (ANDROCLIDES *slowly uncovers his face, and looks on him.*)

 ARCHIAS (*in a terrified, but suppressed tone*). Ha !—who art
  thou ?
What is thy name ?—I do not like thy face——
Speak—what's thy name ?——

  (ANDROCLIDES *shows him a dagger, and points to his own heart.*)

       Art thou his sister then ?—
I did not slay him !—Put thy garland on—
And go away.—Why look'st thou at me so ?—
Art thou alive ?—or from the charnel-house ?
Thou horrid thing !—take off thy burning eyes—
What would'st thou have ?—What would'st thou do ?—
       (*Shouting in an agony of terror.*)
Help, Philip !—He is come !—Oh ! help !

 ANDRO. (*throwing off his cloak and leaping up*). Strike ! strike !

  (*He stabs* ARCHIAS, *who falls dead. At the same moment
  all the* EXILES *fling off their garlands and cloaks,
  and cry* ' *Strike !*' PHILIP *is stabbed by* GORGIDAS
  —*and falls.*)

  (*The* EXILES *then draw their swords.* CHARON *runs to
  one door, and* DEMOCLIDES *to the other. Cries of
  'Treason !' 'Murder !'*)

 CHARON. Silence, a moment—silence !—hear me speak !

 SEVERAL VOICES. 'Tis Charon—listen to him—

 CHARON. Your lives are safe—so you resist us not—
We want no blood.—For this night must you be
Our prisoners :—on the morrow we'll talk more.
Friends—take them hence.
    (*The* LORDS *are led out by some of the* EXILES.)

                    Now to the market-place !
Epaminondas, with a thousand youths,
Is there already ;—and Pelopidas
Hath ere this question'd Leontidas.—
Leave that dead brute, dear Androclides,—come,—
We must away.

    ANDRO.   Oh ! thou foul homicide !
I hate thee—for thou'st made me hate myself !—
Would thou hadst died of dropsy—or of plague—
And left my hand unfoul'd !

                (*Enter* PELOPIDAS, *in haste.*)

    PELOP.   Hath he been here ?
The tyrant was gone forth—and hath escap'd me——

    CHARON. Escaped ?—That must not be !—

    PELOP.   I'll hunt him out;
If any hole in Thebes do give him room.
Farewell at present.—To the market-place !—
Ho ! gentle Archons—are you there ?—I' faith
You seem to love that carrion, Androclides.

    The voice of LEONTIDAS *is heard without, exclaiming:*
Refuse me not—I will go instantly——
Where are these lords—and their vile paramours ?
Stand back—I tell ye.

    PELOP. By the great Gods ! 'tis he !—Let him come in—
Then guard the door :—but drag these out of sight.
                          (*The bodies are drawn back.*)

    LEON. (*without*). By heav'ns ! I'll cleave thee to the earth !
    Give room !   (*He enters.*)
Shame on you, Archons ! feasters with loose women !—
What's this ?—Where are the Archons ?—Who are ye ?
Why are ye silent ?—

    PELOP.   Your best friends are so—
Why should *we* talk ?—Call Archias,—or Philip,—
They'll answer you from hell—and bid you down.
Look there— (*pointing to the bodies.*)

Leon. Ha!—murder?—treason?—What's thy name?—
Villain!—I know thee now!—Foul Democrat!
Is this thy bloody work?—

Pelop.   No—no—'tis theirs—
Mine is with thee.—Black dragon!—'tis thy hour!—
I told thee it should come!—Look at this blade—
Ismenias wore it——

Leon.   Then it was a villain's!—
And doth become thee—coward that thou art!
Thou dar'st not meet me in the open field,
Sword against sword!

Pelop.   As thou Ismenias met'st?—
But thou'rt brave now.—Friends,—to the market-place!
Make proclamation of the tyrants' deaths.—
These take with you,—and bid them wait the third.—
Charon, I'll have no *nay:*—that man who stirs
To meddle here, shall be no friend of mine.
Get hence—and quick!—

Charon.   Come, Androclides—come—
He'll have his humour.—To the market-place!

(*The* Exiles *go out, with the bodies, leaving* Leontidas
and Pelopidas *alone.* Pelopidas *locks the doors,
and throws the keys out of the window.*)

Pelop. Now, bloody dragon!—sword to sword we meet.
Thy reign is past; thy punishment to come—
Thy grave, or mine, is here——

Leon. (*attacking him*).   Then be it thine!

Pelop. Ha!—what so quick?-- (*They fight.*)
A loud knocking is heard at the door, and the voice of
Epaminondas *exclaims:*
Pelopidas,—I charge thee ope the door—
Or I will force it—

Leon.   Let thy good friends in—
Valiant Pelopidas,—they come to help thee.

PELOP. Dost think so?—Then I'll ope the door. But first
Answer me this—
*They fight again. The noise continues, and the door is just
giving way, when* PELOPIDAS *exclaims:*
Nay then—the sport must close.—Take that—and this—
And get thee to thy friends—

(LEONTIDAS *falls dead. At that instant the door is
burst open, and* EPAMINONDAS, *with* ANDROCLIDES,
CHARON, *many of the* EXILES, *and others, rush in.*)

EPAM. Madman!—what frenzy's this?—

PELOP. Not worse than thine
At Mantinea, when I lay for dead,
And thou, against a score of glittering blades,
Didst guard me—

EPAM. Tush! no more of this!—Come on—
The market-place is like a sea of heads,
And, if we speed not, there may come a storm.

ANDRO. Pelopidas,—the people call for you.
(*Shouts are heard without.*)

PELOP. Then some of you bear off this tyrant's corse,
And I'll go with you.—Ha! good Philidas!

(*Enter* PHILIDAS, *and many others.*)
Our work has thriven, you see—
(*Pointing to the body as it is carried out.*)
How have *you* sped?

PHILIDAS. Stay not to talk.—I come to fetch you hence.
The prisons are thrown wide—our friends are free—
The city's in a roar—the people call
For their deliverers.—Go, all of you
Link'd in a body, to the market-place.—
Come—come—away—

PELOP. And, as you go, still shout,
'The tyrants are o'erthrown—and Thebes is free!'
(*Shouts heard without.*)

Epam. Hark! hark! They call for you—Yet list one word.
Three tyrants ye have slain!—see that for these
Ye do not make a thousand!—Now—away—
> (*As they are going out*, Philidas *detains* Androclides.)

Philidas. Stay, Androclides.—When they've all pass'd out,
I have a word for thee.

Andro.   They are all gone—
What is it you would say?

Philidas.   There is a friend
Here in the house, whom I would bring to you.
Wait but a moment.   [*Exit.*

Andro. Friend?—Oh heav'ns! what friend,
Thou thoughtless Philidas, can move me now
Till I behold my Thulia!—I'll not stay.

> (*He goes to the door. At that instant the opposite door opens, and* Thulia *enters. Both stand for a moment motionless: then walk slowly till they meet. They gaze, each in the other's face—then rush together—and the curtain drops.*)

PHILIP.
A Tragedy.
IN FIVE ACTS.

Persons Represented.

PHILIP—*The last King of Macedon.*
PERSEUS ⎫
DEMETRIUS ⎬ *His Sons.*
ANTIGONUS ⎭
DYMAS.
MEGES.
LYSIUS—*Prince of the Bastarnæ.*
ORONASTES.
LYSIMACHUS.
MARCIUS ⎫ *Roman Ambassadors.*
CECILIUS ⎭
APELLES.
PHILOCLES.
CALLIGENES—*A Physician.*
ARATUS.
JANIRA—*Sister to Lysius.*
THEOXANA.
ARCHO.

MACEDONIAN LORDS, GUARDS, SOLDIERS, ATTENDANTS, JAILOR.

The Scene lies chiefly at Pella, in Macedon, and partly in Thessalonica.

ACT I.

Scene I.—*A street in Pella.*

(*Enter* Dymas *and* Meges.)

Dymas. Assure thyself of this,—Demetrius
Will never,—and I'll give thee reasons for't,—
Sit on his father's throne.

Meges.   But is he not
The idol of the people, and the . . .

Dymas.   Pshaw!
You were the people's idol—so were I—
So any slave, that look'd to wear the crown—
So Cerberus himself, if his foul paws
Were clambering up the throne.

Meges.   But of the troops
He is as much beloved—

Dymas.   The troops?—Oh yes—
They think he'll be their paymaster: no doubt
They love him fiercely,—and would charge hell-gate
If he but winked that way, to prove their love.
But so they will for Perseus, finding *him*
The treasure-holder; and with love as fierce
To pleasure him, would cut Demetrius
Into invisible atoms.

Meges.   But the king
Loves young Demetrius better.

Dymas.   Not a jot!
Kings have no natural love. He hates them both.
He never loved aught, save his concubines,

Each for a week or so.—He loves himself,—
And power, and what supports his power; and hates
All that might wrest it from him :—of all men,
That man he hates, who, in expectance, sits
Upon *his* throne, and counts the lingering years
Till the bright crown and sceptre shall change hands.

  MEGES.   Then his birth
Is of a wedded wife; while Perseus
Springs from a lawless bed.

  DYMAS.   Tush!—lawless bed!
Will that make dull the sword that Perseus hires?
Or when he pays his soldiers, will the coin
Be worse, or better, that the head it bears
Is bastard, or legitimate? Mark me now:
Demetrius is of heedless, open soul;
Calls things by their right names,—and speaks his mind
On all occasions frankly; tells a knave
He is not virtuous;—praises a good deed,
Tho' done by one on whom the king hath frowned;
Speaks openly of whom he likes, or hates;
Cares not t'offend, so he but *take* offence,
Whoever be the mark on't: and, with this,
He hath a haughtiness he brought from Rome,—
Whose flatterers blew him up to high conceit
Of his own excellence, that will gender hate
In all he shews it on.

  MEGES.   But there again,—
Will not the Romans——

  DYMAS.   Pray you, give me leave—
I'll hear you speak anon. You know me well
To be your friend;—you know me—do you not?

  MEGES. In truth I've thought you such.

  DYMAS.   Be sure I am.
And what I'd move you to, is your own good;
Nought to my profit. That Demetrius
Can never fill the throne, is to my mind
As palpable as is the earth we tread.

If you then to his fortunes tie yourself,
His fall will drag you down.—Why, leave him then,
And pay your court to Perseus, in whose shine
You shall be glorious. You've example for't;
Each day some favourer of Demetrius comes
To stand on Perseus' side: they see the cloud
Peeping above the hills,—and hear the wind
That soon shall blow a storm; and so they run
To speedy shelter under Perseus' roof;
Where you must haste too, or abide its rage;—
And that would grieve me. But I know you wise—
Delay no moment,—come along with me;—
I'll show you to the prince, and——

MEGES.   Stay awhile.
That you do mean me well, I will not doubt—

DYMAS. Be sure I do.

MEGES.   But yet you counsel ill.

DYMAS. Make that appear, and I'll come o'er to you.

MEGES. Then, first, Demetrius has the people's love.

DYMAS. Ay! for a week,—or four-and-twenty hours.
I've answered that before.

MEGES.   The army's too——

DYMAS. Till Perseus shake the gold—I show'd that also.

MEGES. And, of a surety, Philip loves him best;
However you deny it: and, his birth
Being legitimate——

DYMAS.   Nay, nay;—all this
Is, like a last year's story, proved a lie.
If you have nothing else but chaff like this,
One breath will scatter it.

MEGES.   But hear me, then.
What's Philip's will, or what the people's love,
The army's too,—tho' all were on your side,—
Opposed to haughty Rome? Demetrius
Is loved at Rome, where Philip is despised,
And Perseus hated:—and, rest sure of this—

Rome will have whom she chooses king, or none.
Look here (*showing a letter*), I know that Perseus, in his wiles,
Is tortuous as a serpent; in revenge,
Cool and unhesitating; and goes on
Right to his mark, tho' o'er his father's neck
He tread to reach it :—but, to strive 'gainst Rome,
He lacks the lion's daring, and his strength—
Which would far better stead him. . . . Well, sir—now
What think you of it?

   DYMAS.   Lend me this scroll,
To use as I think fit,—and your fond hopes
For poor Demetrius are not worth a straw :—
This, shown to Philip, will incense him so
That he'll give instant order for his death,
Or banishment,—or use such other means,
That the reversion of Demetrius' crown
Were, at a drachm, too dear.

   MEGES.   If that were sure—

   DYMAS. 'Tis sure as Fate. You owe Demetrius nought—
Let him go down at once : why should *you* drown
To help a man that cannot keep afloat ?
What hath he done for you?

   MEGES.   Why, that's most true—
Yet he's a noble and frank-hearted prince—
And, if he should succeed——

   DYMAS.   If—if—why if?
The man that builds his fortunes on that *if*
Might, for his wisdom, go to batter down
A bulwark'd town with pebbles. Come along ;
The king is now in court : he hears to-day
Th' ambassadors from Rome. You'll see anon
On what a ticklish base Demetrius stands ;
And how firm-rooted Perseus. As we go,
I'll give you farther reasons——

   MEGES.   Which I'll weigh ;
And afterwards resolve on.

   DYMAS.   Let's despatch,
For the morn wears.   [*Exeunt.*

SCENE II.—*A Room of State in* PHILIP'S *Palace.* PHILIP *sits on his throne, surrounded by* PERSEUS, DEMETRIUS, ANTIGONUS, DYMAS, *and other* LORDS. MARCIUS *and* CECILIUS, *the* ROMAN AMBASSADORS, *stand together and somewhat apart from the rest.*

MARCIUS. Here, Philip, we conclude. Rome will not stand
An idle looker-on, while her allies
Are trampled under foot.—You know her will:—
Recall your forces from Bithynia,—
Your garrisons from every Thracian fort;—
And, nor by open, nor by covert means,
Oppress her friends, or aid her enemies—
Then Rome remains at peace. If you refuse,
She bids you think of Cynocephalæ;
And tells you, the good swords that conquered there
Have not been blunted. Think upon't we pray you:
And so we take our leave.—Philip, farewell. (*Going.*)

PHILIP. Stay, Marcius and Cecilius;—we *have* thought:
And you shall bear our answer. Rome's commands
Shall be obeyed. Would they had been more just!
Or we more strong to cross them!—But, to Heaven
We trust th' event!—Tell it to haughty Rome,
Philip forgets not Cynocephalæ,—
But Rome forgets her greatness, when she stoops
To listen every pitiful complaint
That comes 'gainst Philip.—And, with this, my lords,
We do dismiss you.

CECILIUS.   As your truest friends,
We caution you to such a course in this,
That in broad day your deeds may bear the eye
That pries the closest.

PHILIP.   Thank you for your pains.

MARCIUS. And, to your private ear, I'd whisper this.
When Philip needs ambassadors to Rome,
Whom he'd have listened to,—he would do well
Sending his son Demetrius. So adieu.

CECILIUS. Philip, adieu.

MARCIUS *and* CECILIUS. Lords, all of you farewell.
MACEDONIAN LORDS. Farewell.
DEMETRIUS.   Marcius,—a word with you.
  [*Exeunt* DEMETRIUS *and* ROMAN AMBASSADORS.

PHILIP (*descending hastily from his throne*).
Insufferable arrogance!—Proud Rome—
Look to thyself erelong—thou den of thieves!
For I will strike thee yet,—or lower fall.—
Bearded upon my throne!—and not a hand
To strike the upstarts down!—Demetrius—
Where is the Roman minion?—

PERSEUS.   Sir, my brother,
Your duteous and right loyal son . . .

PHILIP.   Speak on—
A forthright tale,—thou everlasting sneerer.
Whate'er Demetrius be,—thou art his mate
In all his worst.—Recall my garrisons!
Give up my fortresses! Deny my aid
To my oldest friends!—and threatened on my throne
By fellows such as I can tread upon
Each hour i' th' day! Which of you witnessed this?

PERSEUS *and several* LORDS. We all, my liege, beheld it.

PHILIP.   Loyal souls!
(*To* PERSEUS) What *you*—our eldest son, and heir to the throne,
You heard,—and saw,—and had nor tongue nor hand,
To tame their insolence;—not even an eye
That dared to wink reproof.—And you sir, too—
And you—and you—and, old Antigonus, you—

ANTIG. Philip, reprove me not, for I can show—

PHILIP. Peace! on thy life, old man! I'll hear no prating.
Where is Demetrius?—Bring him to my sight.
Better a beggar free—than fettered king!
But Rome shall echo yet to Philip's shout,—
And her grave senators shall duck the head
To Philip's veriest slaves;—and her proud dames
Shall wait on Philip's concubines.—Oh Gods!

Let me have vengeance—full—full—full to the brim.
Vengeance,—let me have vengeance.—Carthage will aid,
And Sicily—and many Grecian states,
That hate the Roman, while they hug him hard—
And gold—and golden promises—ha—ha—
I'll fee them well—I'll——

(*Enter* DEMETRIUS.)

ANTIG. (*to* DEM.). He's incensed to the height,—
Do not speak to him now.

DEMETRIUS. Nay, give me leave :
I'm guiltless,—therefore bold. Behold me, father ;
You summoned me—I haste at your command.

PHILIP. They say, from Hæmus, all th' Italian plains
Lie like a map.—The war shall try new fields.
I'll fight no more, like to a baited beast,
In my own den,—the lion shall go forth.
For Italy—for Italy !—
(*To* DEM.) Oh sir—
I crave your pardon that I saw you not :
We missed you from the presence. Please you, prince,
If so an old and humbled king may crave
Of his young, haughty son, Rome's favourite—
Why went you hence with Marcius, even now?
With Marcius, who had held his finger up,
In impudent rebuke to your throned sire,
And school'd him like a boy?—Was't well? Was't well?

DEM. I knew not, father, that he uttered more
Than, as the Senate's organ, he was bid :
In doing which he had no greater guilt
Than the mute parchment that upon it bears
The words of mortal quarrel. For myself . . .

PHILIP. Despatch !—Few words, and weightier matter, sir.

DEM. I did but beg that Marcius, reaching Rome,
Would to some dearest friends remember me.

PHILIP. Ay—ay !—Thy dearest friends — and our worst
foes !

Look to't, Demetrius!—He's no friend of mine
That's linked to my black enemy. Look to't!
I say look to't!—Foul whispers are abroad——

DEM. If any whisper that Demetrius
In anything's disloyal to his king,
Or to his country,— here Demetrius says,
And loudly, he's a villain that so whispers,—
A liar, and a coward!

PHILIP.   Words—brave words!—

DEM. Which with my sword I gladly will maintain
On him who dares dispute them.

PHILIP.   Boast no more
Of what you'll do,—but look your course be clear.
Sharp eyes are on you. There's the taint of Rome
Upon your very brow,—your gait,—your speech;—
Your every motion is Rome-spotted, prince.

DEM. Till, at some happier moment, I may plead
To him who is at once my judge and father;
And set forth truly all my love to him,
And to my country,—now a vain attempt,
In this assembly, where stand counsellors
Who have poured poison in that father's ear
Against his son,—for which forgive them, Heaven!—
Humbly I take my leave.

[*Exeunt* DEMETRIUS *and* LORDS *of his party.*

PERSEUS.   Thy humbleness
Is prouder than another's arrogance.

PHILIP. Oh! for one moment to stand up in Rome
Her victor—but one moment!—all that's yet
Of life to come, I'd toss away unprized
For that one instant!—see—and hear—and die!

(*Enter* LYSIUS.)

LYSIUS. Health unto Philip! To his arms success!

PHILIP. Philip returns thy greeting. By thy mien,
And free discourse, some prince I hold thee, youth:
Please you go on.

LYSIUS.   To Philip, the great king,
The strong Bastarnæ proffer amity,
And close alliance. Philip's wars be theirs,—
And theirs be Philip's.—For a farther tie,
A princess of the royal blood I bring,—
My sister—for my name is Lysius,—
Whom, so he please, to one of Philip's sons
I give in marriage.

PHILIP.   And in happy hour
Thou com'st, young prince. This amity I hail,
And straight will seal the bond. And, for the maid
Thy sister, she already is my child;
For, with a fond contention, my two sons
Will strive who wins her first. For thee, young Lysius,
Come to my arms, and let me call thee son.
Thy fame hath gone before thee.

LYSIUS.   Royal sir,—
You bend me with the burthen of your love.
Permit me, I beseech you, to haste now,
And with this joyful news to bless the ear
Of my loved sister, who . . .

PHILIP.   Nay—go at once,
And bring her to me, that upon her cheek
I may bestow a father's blessing kiss,
And show her to my sons. Stand on no form.

LYSIUS. Your majesty will bind me ever yours.
I take my leave.

PHILIP.   What forces now in field?
Are your horse numerous?—and your infantry,—
How stand they for the push, dear Lysius—ha?

LYSIUS. Full thirty thousand are our foot, pick'd men;
Our horse ten thousand. Never better steeds
Gallop'd o'er battle-field.

PHILIP.   Dear Lysius, haste.
Bring me my future daughter to my arms.
Ten thousand horse,—and thirty thousand foot—
Said you not so?

LYSIUS.   Even so.

PHILIP.   Picked men—strong steeds—
Haste—haste, dear Lysius, haste.—Yet, stay awhile,
We hold, to-day, a solemn festival;
The rites performed,—our army in review
Passes before us :—after that, divides
Into two bodies, each beneath the lead
Of Perseus, or Demetrius, our two sons,—
And so, in friendly strife, mock battle wages
With blunted weapons. There thy sister bring;
Where she shall see our royal sons contend,
And take her choice of them.

LYSIUS.   I haste to her.   [*Exit.*

PHILIP. Ten thousand horse,—and thrice ten thousand foot!
What, lords,—all mute?—Is there no tongue let loose
For joy of such a fortune?—'Tis at Rome
This should be heard in silence.

PERSEUS.   Royal sir!
Our hopes are by our fears for-ever checked :
From foreign aids we cannot so much hope,
As from domestic enemies we fear.

PHILIP. What is't you mean?

PERSEUS.   We in our bosoms hold,
If not a traitor, yet at least a spy.
The Romans, since he was a hostage there,
Have sent his body back,—but keep his heart.
On him the Macedonians fix their eyes,
Persuaded that they never shall have king,
Save him that Rome shall choose.

PHILIP.   I like not this!
But I see through you. For my throne and power
Ye are contending, ere I give them up :
And each of you would deal his brother death,
To make succession sure.—In time beware;
Lest, in my wrath, I sweep you both away,
And choose a stranger heir.

PERSEUS.   So please you read
This letter: then condemn me if, too soon,
I call Demetrius spy.

PHILIP (*reading at intervals aloud*). 'And, moreover, I can satisfy you'—'Philip suspected'—ha! ha!—he will give you cause anon, 'Perseus hated by the Senate'—'the determination that Demetrius shall succeed'—Indeed! indeed! 'For, if Philip should again compel Rome to war, his throne will be declared forfeit.' (*Folds up the letter.*)
Ha! shall it so?—How say you,—forfeited?
Is Rome become the mansion of the Gods?
What think you lords? Have they the Thunderer's bolts
Stored in their Capitol?—Yes, sure! and we
Must go and do them humble reverence.
On his old knees your king must humbly bend,
And beg his fate and yours of godlike Rome.—
Yes—yes—it shall be so :—and, for more pomp
Of worship, with our golden armour on
Will we our lowly pilgrimage begin :—
And in Rome's temples will we offer up
Rich sacrifice :—each soldier shall be priest,
And his sharp sword the knife of sacrifice !—
Oh Gods! immortal Gods!—what a rich steam
Of bloody incense shall your nostrils quaff!
Take back your letter, sir.—Demetrius king?
So—so.—This eaglet would soar up betimes;
He shall fly lower,—or his wings I'll break,
And hurl him to the earth.

(*Enter a* MESSENGER.)
                Speak out at once
Thy business, and begone.

MESSENGER.   My gracious liege!
From Marcius I am come, who, in his haste,—
For which he craves forgiveness—took not thought
Of that wherewith he was intrusted to you—
This packet.

PHILIP.   Whence?—from Rome?

MESSENGER.   From Titus Quintius.

PHILIP. Go now.   [*Exit* MESS.
What have we here? 'From Titus Quintius
To Philip, King of Macedon.'—Proud worm!
Titus to Jupiter were next.—These knaves
Think kings and deities their playfellows;
And men the baubles only for their sport. (*He reads in silence.*)

    DYMAS (*to* 1ST LORD). There's wormwood there. Look how
he bites his lip.

    1ST LORD. Will it be war?

    DYMAS.   Not yet. We must not stir
Till we be stronger; or Rome lose her strength.

    1ST LORD. He's pale with rage.

    PHILIP (*stamping furiously*). Damnation!—'Tis too much!

    PERSEUS. What ill afflicts my father?

    PHILIP.   Look you here.—
But no! I trust you not. My sons are traitors.
I'll take no counsel; but I'll have revenge:—
I'll have revenge, and deep.—Perseus, the troops
By this are in the field. Betake you thither;
And whisper in the ears of all your friends
That they to-day must do their best. Remember
The princess sees you: and I'd have you win her;—
But you must toil for't.—When the tourney's done,
To him that best delights her, she shall send
Her ring,—or other token that her choice
Fixes on him. And 'tis an honour, prince,
Worthy your striving for.—The trumpets—hark!
Let us away.—Ride thou at my right hand;
So shall be seen how in thy father's sight
Thou art held worthiest.

    PERSEUS.   Prouder so to be
Than sitting on the throne of Macedon!

    PHILIP. Too flowery, prince! No more! Antigonus!
After the tourney come to me again.
Thoughts are within me that to deeds must grow,

Such as the weak will start at. But the act
By the strange time is fashioned. Strongest kings,
No more than weakest hinds, their way can hold
Direct to th' point,—and *do* but what they *would.*
A seeming crime makes oft a real good—
The guilt is Fate's—forced on us—but our own
The good that follows it. But now no more.
Lords, to the field,—we meet again anon.

LORDS. Our humblest duties to your majesty.
[*Exeunt* KING *and* LORDS *on opposite sides.*

ANTIGONUS. What dreadful thing is brooding in thee now,
That needs this dark concealment? Crime enough,
Fate's, or thine own, already hast thou dared:
Yet doubtful still the after coming good—
If evil not the rather. Doctrine false!
And policy most foul and dangerous,
That *wickedly* would seek to work forth *good!*
Soundness, from rottenness, doth never grow;
Nor, from distemper, health. From evil, good
As little can be born. Beware, O king!
Lest the fair seeming path beneath thy feet
Do gape, and in a fathomless abyss
Headlong precipitate thee,—wise too late!
[*Exit.*

SCENE III.—*A Plain.*

(*Shouts heard from a distance; alarums, and the clattering of arms.*)

(*Enter* LYSIUS *and* JANIRA.)

LYSIUS. Stand here, Janira: they'll not pass this way.

JANIRA. Oh brother! Is it not a splendid sight?

LYSIUS. Yes,—for a mimicry.—Look—look!—they fly!
Perseus the first to run;—Demetrius
The foremost to pursue. By Jupiter!
It waxes almost to a real strife,—
Wanting but real weapons,

JANIRA. Glorious youth!
How beautiful he looks!

LYSIUS. Ha! see—the king
Makes signal to desist—— (*Shouts are heard.*)

JANIRA. How rapidly
The storm is hushed!—I saw Demetrius,
With arm uplifted for a sudden blow,—
Yet, on the instant, did he check himself,
And let his sword fall dead.

LYSIUS. He seems incensed.

JANIRA. Dear brother,—to Demetrius bear my ring:
He must my husband be,—or I'll have none.

LYSIUS. The king's against him. If you'd wear a crown
Send me to Perseus.

JANIRA. Were that crown more rich
Than Jove's own diadem of living light,
With Perseus I'd not share it. Scarce a word,
A look with each I've changed,—yet inly feel
That life with one were bliss,—with th' other woe.

LYSIUS. So fixed?

JAN. Even so. Whether for good, or ill,
My lot is cast!

LYSIUS. Then will I bear your ring. [*Exit.*

JAN. One hath my love,—the other my contempt,—
Almost my hatred. Is not this a fault?
I know not that;—but 'twere, I'm sure, a fault
To give my heart to one; my hand to th' other.
He has received the ring.—He kisses it—
He comes—Oh heavens! what shall I say?

(*Enter* DEMETRIUS *and* LYSIUS.)

DEM. (*kneeling*). Bright princess!
When the sun shines upon us, then we bless
His cheering beams,—as now your dearer rays

I worship, that have cast a golden light,
Where darkness was before,—in this poor heart.

    JAN. Nay, prince—this glittering flattery . . .

    DEM.   'Tis truth!

    JAN. Bespeaks more show than worth.

    DEM.   By heavens 'tis truth!

    JAN. By heavens 'tis flattery! How can you love
What, till a few hours past, you had not seen?
There is no reason in such love methinks.

    DEM. Oh! ask me not a *reason* why I love:
Ask why I like the perfume of the rose;—
The singing of the pensive nightingale;—
Ask why the gorgeous canopy of Heaven
Is glorious to my eyes;—or the great voice
Of the vast ocean music to my ears;—
I cannot tell you:—neither can I tell
Why I do love you:—yet I so do love
That, to express it, I can find no words
But what seem laboured, forced,—beyond the mark—
Yet are, indeed, far tamer than my thoughts.
I pray you deem me not that worthless thing,
A common flatterer.

    JAN.   You make amends.
But pray you rise, for frowning looks are on us.
The king and Perseus stand in talk together,
And we're the matter of it.—Pray you, sir.

    DEM. First on that hand let me a kiss impress,
And seal it mine,—thus—thus.—Now, king or prince
May smile or frown, 'tis one. (*He rises.*)

    LYSIUS.   The king comes here.
Let's meet him.

    JAN.   But his face, methinks, is dark.

    DEM. Midnight itself would brighten like the morn,
Shone on by thee. Come on,—and have no fear. [*Exeunt.*

SCENE IV.—*A room in the Palace.*

(*Enter* PHILIP *and* ANTIGONUS.)

PHILIP. It matters little—she hath made her choice—
Nor will I cross it. Listen to me now.

ANTIG. Most anxiously do I your words attend.

PHILIP. The axe hath felled the old and gnarlëd trunk:
But there are shoots, that soon will grow to trees
As poisonous as the first. They must be cared for.

ANTIG. What means your majesty?

PHILIP.   That Philip's throne
Shall not be a mere stool for Rome to raise,
Or kick down at her pleasure.—Mark this man;
This haughty Titus. My own son he sets
My opposite;—rash fool! my prudence lauds
In that I sent this flashy boy to Rome,
Ambassador;—says, roundly, that, to *him*
Was granted what, to me, had been refused,—
So much the Senate loved him! Yes, by Heaven!
And then exhorts me, as a friend—a friend!
Oh! ye great Gods! for every friend like this
Give me a keen sword, and a giant's arm!—
As my *true* friend exhorts me, once again
To send Demetrius, with a larger train
Of nobles and ambassadors, to Rome;—
Who may our present troubles set at rest,
And spare a war might—hell and furies!—end
With forfeit of my empire!—

ANTIG.   Dares he so?

PHILIP. 'Tis written here;—and written on my heart,
In letters all of fire. But, mark me now.
Against the pride and tyranny of Rome
To my last gasp I'll fight:—her foes my friends;
Her friends my foes. All natural ties I'll break
Rather than this new bond. Were my right hand
Grown friend to Rome, I'd have it hewn away.—
Antigonus—Demetrius loves you well.

Antic. I think he doth.

Philip. Advise him ;—caution him :—
He is my son ;—but—if I prove him false—
I'll crush him like an adder.

Antic. Good my liege !

Philip. By the Eternal Deities I'll do it !
For less I love my sons, my crown, my life,
Than I hate Rome, and every friend of Rome.

Antic. Your ear is poisoned 'gainst a noble son,
Who loves you well, and is right true and faithful.
My life upon his loyalty !

Philip. Enough !
Heaven grant he prove so !—Meantime, that the bed
Where treasons spring, may not o'er-rank become,
I'll have it weeded.—When my just decree
Brought to the death those traitors, I yet left,
In foolish pity, their young rebel broods :—
And they are now eternal orators,
Pleading against me their false fathers' deaths,
When rather, for their own lives,—forfeited,
Yet spared,—should their hourly thanks be mine.
I'll play the fool no longer :—they shall die.—

Antic. My gracious liege—I pray you . . .

Philip. Peace—old man !—
I'll have no tiger-cubs, for their smooth skins,
And pretty playful tricks, preserved and reared
Till the grown monsters turn and rend their rearer—
They shall not live !—I've said it.

Antic. Philip—pause——

Philip. Old man ! I will not hear thee. They shall die !
Give order for't—and presently.

Antic. No ! never !
I say't again,—I will not lend my breath
To such foul guilt ! Nay, more,—while I can speak,
I'll tell it to the world,—and point at thee,—

And call thee monster! Yea, by Jove I will!
Rave as thou mayst!

PHILIP. Art thou gone mad?—Hence!—fly!
Lest I forget thy grey hairs and long toils.

ANTIG. Forget them all, when thou thyself forget'st
To wade again in blood.

PHILIP. Thou prating fool!
If I stay longer thine may be the first.
Away—away!—I would not take thy life.
Speak not a word—or I may turn again—
Thou foolish dotard! [*Exit* PHILIP.

ANTIG. Thou unhappy—king! [*Exit.*

END OF THE FIRST ACT.

ACT II.

SCENE I.—*A garden belonging to the Palace of* ANTIGONUS.

(*Enter* JANIRA *and* ARCHO.)

JAN. 'Tis late i' th' morn I think. The dew's all gone.

ARCHO. The sun has risen this hour.

JAN. Demetrius said
He'd meet me here by sunrise; and then ride
Among the mountains to enjoy the morning.
'Tis his first promise,—yet he keeps it not.

ARCHO. Heaven bless you, madam! don't believe a word
Of what he promises. A lover's word
Is less than nothing, for his oaths are nothing.

(DEMETRIUS *enters behind.*)

Why they will swear by all the eternal Gods,
That you are lovelier than a nymph o' th' woods;
That violets are poison to your breath;—
That—I have heard them say it——

JAN.   What,—to thee?

ARCHO. To me? Why not to me? To me they've said it;
And to a million, and a million more :—
That your sweet eyes are bluer than the sky—
When they, perhaps, are jaundiced ;—that your skin
Is smooth as marble,—purer than fresh snow,—
Tho' it, in truth, be dingy, freckled, rough :—
They'll swear—I know not what they'll swear ;—and may,
Ere I again believe them.

JAN.   Prithee, peace!
I did not think thou'dst been so forward, girl.
Demetrius would not swear, or say, I'm sure,
Other than truth,—or,—if I thought he would—
I'd . . .

DEM. What, Janira?

JAN.   Tear him from my heart.

DEM. Stay till you find him false. But, my sweet love,
No more of this. And let not this light wench
Sully your better thoughts of holy love.
Pure love is as a fire that shoots from Heaven
Into the human heart ;—where all that's gross,
Selfish, or false,—it burns and melts away ;—
But all that's true, and generous, and pure,—
That doth it brighten still, and glorify,
Till the poor earthly breast becomes a shrine
For thoughts and passions pure as those of Heaven !

JAN. I do believe it.

DEM.   He who slanders love,—
Hath never felt it :—who calls woman false,
Hath never been beloved :—who rails at lovers—
Hath never known, or not deservëd one.

JAN. My dear Demetrius !—But, I pray you now,
Why have you failed your promise ?—I've been here
This hour or more.

DEM.   In sooth my purest plea
Is but a soiled one.

(*Enter* ANTIGONUS *hastily.*)

ANTIG. Pardon me, fair lady.
(*Then to* DEMETRIUS)
A word with you.

DEM. A moment give me leave.

ANTIG. The king demands your presence instantly.
Three messengers upon each other's heels,
Came breathless.

DEM. What's the business?—say it quick.

ANTIG. One that, alas! will little pleasure you.
What, last night, passed between you,—I know not :
But Perseus to the king accuses you
Of an intended fratricide.—

DEM. Of what ?

ANTIG. That at the tournament you sought his life,
Which he but saved by flight;—that to your feast
You asked him, there to stab, or poison him——

DEM. Oh Gods! is't possible ?—

ANTIG. That, failing so,
You went unto his palace at dead night,
Pretending jollity, and generous love,—
But seeking murder.—

DEM. Am I in a dream?
Is this a brother ?—Oh Antigonus!
I am aweary of this wretched life.
Day after day some petty lie :—some word,
Dropt as by chance ;—some brotherly excuse,
That is in truth, a slander ;—some head-shake ;—
Some half-checked sigh, as though the loving breast
Groaned, to breathe forth my guilt ;—all odious arts
That cunning can devise, and malice act,
Are practised to my ruin :—and, at last,—
The crown of all,—this bold and hellish charge
Strikes at my life,—and from a brother's hand !
Oh Gods !

Jan. (*coming forward*). My dear Demetrius,—what's amiss?

Dem. Nothing, Janira;—nothing—nothing, love.

Jan. Nay, say not that. Why strike upon your breast,
And clench your hands, and . . .

Dem.   Listen to me, love.
I must away unto the king. A charge
Most black and false hath been against me brought;
Which, like foul smoke, I can at once blow off;—
But I must speak for't. Pray you stay not now.
When I return I will unburthen all
My griefs unto you; which will thus grow light.
Go, and fear nothing.

Jan.   Dear Demetrius—
Lysius hath left me. Make no longer stay
Than need demands;—and, pray you, think of me.

Dem. Sweet love! I will—I will.
                    [*Exeunt* Janira *and* Archo.
            Of fratricide?

Antig. Were you at strife, my lord?

Dem.   At strife? Oh no!
The mounting lark is not in merrier mood
Than I last night. In sooth too merry mood.

Antig. What—flushed with wine?

Dem. Even so. Yet nothing more
Than might th' occasion, and such friends excuse.
I never had a humour less disposed
To aught unkind:—but—to a brother's death?
Oh Heavens!

Antig.   That you are innocent, my lord,
I'd pledge my life:—but yet I hope your proofs
Are such, would laugh at question;—for the king
Is stirred against you; and, when passion storms,
The strongest reason's a weak citadel.

Dem. Oh! when suspicion sits beside the scales,
A thing too light to bow the snowdrop's head,

Shall crack the beam. But let us to the king.
You will plead for me when my words are vain :
He'll lean to you.

  Antig.   Yes—as a madman leans
To him that would control him.—Never raged
A fiercer madman than . . .

  Dem.   Antigonus!

  Antig. Take not offence that I plain truth speak out.
What are our passions, uncontrolled and fierce,
But a mere madness?—You are Philip's son,—
Yet were as safe within your enemy's reach.
He bids me warn you. Look, Demetrius—
Thus did he stamp his heel into the earth;
And thus to crush you, like a venomous snake,
Should he but prove you false—swore horribly.

  Dem. So let him!

  Antig.   Let him?—Ay! and let him, too
Put boys, and girls, and infants to the death,
By hundreds! He's their king:—what claim have such
To life, when Philip wills their death?

  Dem.   What mean you?

  Antig. That you're not safe ;—that none of us are safe.
Me—spite of my grey hairs, and years of toil,
He has cast off—I heed not for myself,—
But for my country. The wild beast is loosed ;
And I, who tamed him, trodden to the earth.

  Dem. I have heard nought of this.

  Antig.   But yesterday,—
Burning with fury against Rome, and all
That favoured Rome,—and most against yourself—

  Dem. Alas! my father!

  Antig.   To complete the crime
Begun on those, whom his suspicious dread
Sent,—for their love to Rome,—to violent death,
Upon their children he resolved to seize ;
Of age, or sex unheeding,—yes—by Heaven !

DEM. Oh! say it not.

ANTIG.   'I'll weed this treason-bed—
'They shall all die'—he cries :—'give order for it'—
'I'll have no tiger-cubs, for their bright skins,
'Preserved till the grown monsters tear their feeder.
'Give order for their seizure :—they shall die.'

DEM. Oh! horrible!

ANTIG.   Even to his face I told him
I would not do it. He went off in wrath;
And threatening me. Yet would I not there cease;
But to the palace, at the evening hour,
Went to have speech with him.

DEM.   How sped you then?

ANTIG. He would not hear me :—called me doting fool :—
Bade me away,—and in my presence, signed
The fatal mandate.

DEM.   Will he shed their blood?

ANTIG. In sooth I fear it.

DEM.   Good Antigonus,—
There is a lady whom, for all that's loved,—
Beauty—and dignity—and heavenly grace—
All men might worship. Somewhat past her bloom,
Even like the rose full blown,—she yet hath charms
Might tempt the sickliest taste :—yet not for these
I love her, but for that fine majesty,
And purity, and nobleness of soul,
Which make her, more than woman, great and good;
Yet leave all woman's best and loveliest gifts
In all their tenderness.

ANTIG.   There is but one
Upon whose head this diadem will sit,—
The noble Theoxana.

DEM.   Even she.—
When her brave husband to the scaffold went,—
He was my friend; gay, strong, and beautiful.

Oh! to my soul I loved him!—his last words,
Embracing me, were these—' Protect my wife—
Protect my children.'—In my soul I swore,—
And have not failed them. Good Antigonus,
Advise her instantly;—bid her depart
Ere on her tender young the tiger spring.—
Her means are ample,—and her spirit high.
She needs not gold—nor other aid than this
Timely advisement. Not a moment lose,
Or all may then be lost. I'll to the king,
And trust my own defence. Adieu, dear friend.

 ANTIG. Dear prince, farewell. The time is sore diseased,
And we must bleed for't.—Ere the sun go down,
My messenger shall bear the warning voice.
Heaven guard her;—and you, prince, not less. Heed well—
Snares are about you;—swords are bared against you,—
And daggers in men's tongues. Jove shield you well!

 DEM. And thee, kind friend!—I have no fears. Adieu.
         [*Exeunt at opposite sides.*

    SCENE II.—*A room in the Palace.*

  (PHILIP, *seated upon the throne; with* LYSIMACHUS *and*
   ONOMASTES *upon lower seats at either hand.*
   PERSEUS *and* DEMETRIUS *stand on opposite sides,*
   attended by their respective friends.)

 ONOMASTES. Under submission, my dread liege,—thus
  read,—
And truth-like most it seems,—the blacker stain
Flies from the charge,—and leaves upon the prince
No spot save such as . . .

 PHILIP.   Truth-like may it *seem*,
And yet be false as hell!

 DEM.   'Tis true as heaven!
And the foul charge as foolish, as 'tis foul!
My true offence is that I'm loved at Rome:—
With this you taunt me, father; and call crime,
What ought to be my glory. I sought not,

Either as hostage, or ambassador,
To be sent thither. When you gave command,
I but obeyed ;—and such my conduct there
As, humbly do I hope, reflected not
Upon yourself, your crown, or country, aught
That honour censures. 'Tis yourself, my father,
That have my friendship with the Romans caused :
While you're at peace, that friendship will subsist :
But, at the war's first signal, it will die,
And I'll proclaim our enmity. Our love
In peace was born, and cannot live in war.
If, father, towards yourself I lack respect ;
Or, if against my brother . . .
  PHILIP.   Stay,—enough !
Who'd be a father, seeing sons like mine,
That should be staffs whereon his age might lean,
Turned into rods to bruise him !—Brothers ? Asps !
A false accuser *this*, or *that* a wretch
Unfit to live, who would his brother's life
Have taken from him ! But I know you now.
Upon my throne both turn your guilty eyes,
And just so long would suffer me to live,
That, by surviving one of you, I hold
The crown for th' other . . .
  DEM.   Never such a thought . . .
  PHILIP. Silence, presumptuous boy ! May the king speak ?
Demetrius, and Perseus,—not from words,
Or from such hasty trial, will I pass
On this affair my sentence, but from all
Your other actions, small as well as great,
And from your general carriage, which shall be
O'erlooked with keenest scrutiny. Go now,
And, if you can, in heart, as well as name,
Be brothers.
  PERSEUS. I would be so.
  DEM.   Would you were !
  [*Exeunt, on opposite sides*, PERSEUS *and* DEMETRIUS, *and
   their partisans.*

PHILIP. He's clear of this ;—yet fouled with what is worse :
His heart's a traitor, for it clings to Rome.
Oh wretched Philip! cursed with sons like these!—
My reverend friends, I thank you,—ere the night
I'll farther speak with you. As you pass hence,
Bid the lord Dymas here.

  ONOM.   Our love and duty
Are ever at your bidding.

  LYSIM.   And our prayers
Are for your good success.

  PHILIP.   Farewell. I thank you.
     [*Exeunt* LYSIMACHUS *and* ONOMASTES.
He shall not live, if I do prove him false.
By heaven! I'd pluck my heart from out my breast,
Could it conspire with Rome ;—and shall my son
Be dearer than the very seat of life?

    (*Enter* DYMAS.)

Come hither, Dymas. I believe thee true ;—
Single of heart,—and with no party leagued
To warp thy judgment, or thy virtue taint.

  DYMAS. Your majesty too deeply honours me.

  PHILIP. Not more than thy deserts. I have a task,
That, for its proper execution, asks
A pure and upright soul ; a wary eye,
Observing all things,—and a judgment ripe.
These qualities are thine.

  DYMAS.   My gracious liege!

  PHILIP. Speak not ; but hear me. For some certain end,—
Not now to be disclosed,—I would make proof
If, from the top of Hæmus, all that stretch,
Incredible, of prospect may be seen.
'Tis said, the Black Sea, and the Adriatic—
The Danube, and the cloud-surmounting Alps,
And the vast, beauteous plains of Italy,—
All lie within the scope of that hill's ken.

DYMAS. I've heard 'tis so, my liege.

PHILIP.   That will I prove:
And, to that end, to-morrow shall set forth.
With me goes Perseus; but Demetrius stays:
Him to thy special charge do I consign.
Watch every motion;—dive into his soul;—
Hear his discourse;—and lead him on to speak
His unrestricted mind;—and, when he halts,
And looks suspicious,—then do thou speak first,
What he would seem to ponder.—When he grieves,
Do thou be sorrowful;—and, when he laughs,
Be thou his echo.—If he talk of Rome,
Do thou out-go him when he praises most:
If of his brother, let his deepest hate
Find thine yet deeper;—so his very heart
Shall lie for us to read;—and, of his guilt,
Or innocence, assured,—our future course
Shall, with unhesitating step, be trod,
Acquitting, or condemning.

DYMAS.   My dread liege!
The subject lives but in his monarch's smile:—
And every sense and faculty he owns
Is his but as an instrument to use
In his great master's service.—Your command
Truly will I obey:—yet in such fear,
Knowing my weakness,—and this mighty task,—
As that I'd gladly to some stronger back
Have left the valued burthen. But 'tis mine;
And I will labour in it.

PHILIP.   Be a spy—
Not a seducer. Tell the guilt thou seest—
But, make none.—'Tis a fearful trust thou hast:
A prince's life,—a monarch's happiness,
Lie in thy hand. If other than the truth
Thy tongue shall tell:—if bribe, or party zeal,—
Or any base advantage of thine own,
Sway thee to falsehood,—there's no plague in hell
Horrid enough to pay thee.—Look well to't.

Dymas. My gracious liege . . .

Philip.   No, no; I doubt thee not,
I do but warn thee.   On the strongest bridge
We tread with caution when a gulf's below.
Were I to doubt thee,—doubt must quickly change
To strong assurance.   Monarchs do not toy
With traitors, proved, or dreamed of.   Fare thee well—
Yet stay a moment.—Look thou leave not aught
To uncertain memory, that may disguise,
Or alter, or distort what once was plain.—
Keep thou a tablet, where each word and deed,
Fresh in thine ear, or eye, may be fixed down,
For me to ponder on.—He is my son:
Heaven grant he prove not false!—And yet, if true,
His truth makes Perseus false!—Accursed Rome!
All is thy doing.   Oh! Eternal Gods!
Give but one hour of conquest; and, all else,
Refuse me if you will.   [*Exit.*

Dymas.   Demetrius—
Thy fate is in my hands; and thou must fall.
I do not hate thee;—nay, I honor thee:—
But, plucking thee from thy bright eminence,
I may myself uplift even to that height
From which thou fallest.—Power and honor call,
And I must follow them.   Good—I *would* be ;—
Great—*must* be.   So farewell Demetrius.
I'll lead thee to the precipice's brow ;—
Philip shall hurl thee down.   [*Exit.*

Scene III.—*Another room in* Philip's *Palace.*

(*Enter* Perseus *and a* Servant.)

Perseus. Ere Dymas leave the palace, bring him here,
Haste, or you'll miss him.   [*Exit* Servant.
            Let the fool be his!—
I quarrel not with that.   The crown's my bride;

Or shall be,—else my wooing shall be rough for't.

(*Enter* DYMAS.)

Good-morrow, Dymas.

DYMAS.   'Tis to thee good-morrow,
More than to me: yet may to both be good,
So made good use of.

PERSEUS.   Answer me at once,
What sudden journey's this, where I must go,
Dangling among the train of the old king,
Like some smart gewgaw?—And what conference
Held he with you even now?

DYMAS.   That journey's end
May lead you to the throne. That conference
Hath told me so; and pointed out the way.

PERSEUS. Then let us spur upon it. Speak at once.

DYMAS. But,—Perseus on the throne,—will he forget
The hand that helped him there?

PERSEUS.   That hand shall be
Feared as my own. What politic soul is thine
That still distrusts what I a thousand times
Have sworn unto thee!—If, thro' aid of thine,
I climb that eminence where I, by right,
Should sit,—and not thro' favour or intrigue,
I'll hold thee yet as giver of that throne;
And thou shalt use the sceptre when thou wilt,
As 'twere thine own. —By heaven, and by deep hell!
I swear it to thee!

DYMAS.   Philip looks towards Rome.
This new alliance hath blown up the flame
That seemed burnt out. Yet he saith nothing on't.
Lycius, with secret orders, is gone home.
And Philip, on the morrow, will set forth
To look from Hæmus, on th' Italian plains.
And thither must you also.

PERSEUS.   Ha! for what?

That, in our absence, may the traitor leap
Into the empty throne?—Goes he not too?

DYMAS. No—no—he stays behind to lose the throne.
To my especial charge the king hath left him;
To watch him,—read his purposes,—his thoughts.—
So far is your work, prince; the rest is mine.
You've wrought suspicion;—I must forge the proof:
And I will do't—aye! and such blazing proof,
That Philip, looking on it, shall be blind
To all but vengeance.

    PERSEUS.   Thou'rt the best of friends!—

    DYMAS. Let this suffice thee now. It were not well
That we were seen together;—and sharp eyes
Are in the palace. Come to me at night,
And we'll speak farther.

    PERSEUS.   Urge him to the death!—
Remember that. I have no hope to live,
And reign, Demetrius living. He's a drug
That every day I am compelled to drink.
The phial must be broken,—cast away,—
Ere I can breathe in health.

    DYMAS.   If that weak clay
That's called Demetrius be not iron proof,
He *shall* be broken,—and his poison spilt.
So up to Hæmus, prince, and draw free breath;
For Macedon is thine.

    PERSEUS.   And Perseus thine,
To use in what thou wilt.—The idiot's caught
With this new toy,—this princess.

    DYMAS.   Heed her not.

    PERSEUS. Oh no! The pretty butterfly may light
On that flower suits her best. She is no bee
To know where lies the honey. Let her go.
An hour past sunset we shall meet again;—
Till then adieu.

    DYMAS.   Adieu. I'll to my charge.   [*Exeunt.*

SCENE IV.—*Thessalonica.*

A room in the house of THEOXANA.

(*Enter* THEOXANA *with her two* CHILDREN.)

THEOX. No — not to-night, my children! 'Twas this night—
Two long, dark years back—that your noble father
Received the tyrant's summons ;—and the morrow . . .
But no—why should I cloud your sunny brows
Because my own is dark ?—Go to your dance.

ELDEST CHILD. Thank you, dear mother, we'll not dance to-night.

SECOND CHILD. Pray you forgive us.

THEOX. Go—go—take your mirth.
I'll watch you from this window. How the sun
Pours gold upon the lawn,—and steeps the trees
In floods of golden light !—You pretty May-flies,
Go, wanton in his beams !—and, as your feet
Press the green sod, put in them all your soul ;
And for one hour, at least, you shall be happy.

ELDEST CHILD. Come—come away ; — 'twill please our mother so.

(*The* CHILDREN *go out.* THEOXANA *stands looking at them through the window.*)

THEOX. Beautiful children ! How their nimble feet
Spring on the velvet turf !—and their bright faces
Sparkle like sunny waters ! Kind heavens !—
And I was gay as these ;—had foot as light ;—
A glance as quick ;—a heart all merriment !—
And now——what am I ?—

(*Enter a* SERVANT.)

SERVANT. A messenger from Prince Demetrius
Craves instant audience.

THEOX. Bring him hither quick.

[*Exit* SERVANT.

I fear some ill at hand.   His wicked brother
Aims at his life;—or the old tyrant——Well—

(*Enter a* MESSENGER.)
What is thy business?

MESSENGER.   Pray excuse my boldness.
This to the noble lady Theoxana
The Prince Demetrius sends;—and this Antigonus,—
(*Giving letters*)
Whose messenger even at your city gates
I overtook.

THEOX.   What dreadful business needs
This double warning?—Generous prince, thine first. (*She reads.*)

' My father's fury is at its height.   Fly, dear lady:—the lives of your children are threatened.   The bearer of this is trusty, and may aid in your escape.—Yours—DEMETRIUS.'

My children's lives?—Know you, sir, aught of this?

MESSENGER.   Nothing, fair lady.

THEOX.   Good Antigonus
Clear thou this mystery.   (*She reads.*)

MESSENGER (*aside*).   Some dreadful thing
That scroll does tell her.—Heaven have mercy then!

THEOX.   Amen! for man hath none.

MESSENGER (*aside*).   She has o'erheard me
Oh! she is sorely racked.

THEOX.   Thou shalt not, tyrant!
While there's a mother's hand to set them free.
Their father thou hast sent into his grave;
And now—but they shall 'scape thee, if there's steel—
Poison,—or choking water,—or steep rock,
That can their souls, and beauteous bodies part.
Ay! tho' this hand should deal the horrid blow.
What's to be done?—Save them,—or with them die!
Good friend, thy name?

MESSENGER.   Aratus, gentle dame.

THEOX.   Ha! 'tis a name owes Philip little thanks.

His wisest, truest friend, of that same name,
The tyrant poisoned, and *his* son Aratus.

ARATUS. Oh! 'twas a cruel deed!

THEOX. Dost serve the king?

ARATUS. No farther than all subjects serve their king;
My service is to Prince Demetrius.

THEOX. And he reports thee faithful.

ARATUS. The kind prince
Should have none else but such.

THEOX. Wilt serve me truly?

ARATUS. Ay! madam—to the death!

THEOX. I do believe thee;
Thy face is index to a faithful heart.
Then hear, and mark me well. Th' insensate king,
Mad in his hate, hath issued a decree
To seize the children of all those, whose lives
He late took on the scaffold. They will die.
Thus am I now forewarnëd, ere escape
Be hopeless.

ARATUS. Gracious Heavens!

THEOX. Forbear, and hear me.
To Ænéa on the morrow are we bound,
To keep the festival. Go thou with us.
The vessel lies in port, and all's prepared.
There as in wonted sports we pass the day,
Hire thou a bark, as for our home return;
See that 'tis roomy, and provisioned well:—
At deep midnight, when all are locked in sleep,
For some far isle, beyond the tyrant's grasp,
We will put forth. Oh! heaven will fill the sails
To save the innocent.—And yet *he* died,
That was all truth and honour!—My good friend
Wilt thou so serve me?

ARATUS. To my latest breath!

THEOX. Then haste away, and get thee to thy rest:

At daybreak must thou rise. Take this—nay—take it—
A king refuses not the beggar's mite,
That goes to fill th' exchequer. Be not thou
More haughty than a king.

    Aratus.   Most gracious lady—
Command me to the death.   [*Exit.*

    Theox. Thou shalt not have them, tyrant. With these hands
I'll throw them to the waves; or pierce their hearts
Even with their father's dagger, ere to thee,
Black monster! I surrender them.—Oh Gods!
And they are dancing on the sunny grass,
As joyous as the summer flies about them—
Perhaps as soon to die!—Jove! to thy hands
I do commit them.   [*Exit.*

End of the Second Act.

ACT III.

Scene I.—*A mountain-top in the vicinity of Pella.* Demetrius *and* Janira *stand looking forth toward the east.*

    Jan. How long will't be before the sun comes forth?

    Dem. Even now he's at Heaven's portal. Dost not see
How all the eastern sky is touched with fire,—
While overhead, and westward is deep blue?
And there's one cloud,—the only one in th' heaven,
Floating upon the golden atmosphere
Like a huge rock of ruby.

    Jan.   Beautiful!
Most beautiful!—Oh! have I lived till now,
And ne'er seen this?

    Dem.   How men will haste and crowd
To see a monarch in his tawdry state!—
Yet the great king of light goes daily up
To his resplendent throne; and scarce an eye
Follows his rising.

Jan.   Demetrius—
Where is the glorious stretch of prospect round,
You talked of? All below us is dense mist—
Nought visible but this huge mountain's top,
And one or two below us, that scarce lift
Their bald heads through the fog. Our morning's toil
So far is lost;—yet I repent it not ;—
For, tho' the earth be hid, yet this fair Heaven
Is beautiful, beyond the scope of thought,
To one that hath not known it :—and the air,—
How fresh and sweet !—and this most solemn stillness,
As tho' all life had bowed th' adoring head
In worship of heaven's King !—Demetrius—
Oh ! is it not most beautiful ?

Dem.   Go on
With thy sweet musings. All that's beautiful
In earth, or heaven, seems yet more beautiful
In thy loved praises. What, to man, were earth
With all its pomp of mountain and rich plain?
What ocean, with its ever-varying might?
What the bright ceiling of unbounded space—
The unapproachable glory of the sun,
Or midnight, myriad-starred?—Oh what, to man,
Were all, if woman were not ? Her sweet voice
Gives fragrance to the sweetest breath of morn ;
To noon gives brightness,—calmness to the eve,—
And cheerfulness unto the gloom of night.

Jan. This is the tale you tell a thousand ears,—
And all believe it.

Dem.   Dost not thou ?

Jan.   Be sure on't.
But answer now. Why all this sudden haste ?
Why to this mountain-top,—this very morn,
No hour's delay permitted,—am I brought ?
And what's the business clouds your forehead thus ?
Nay—nay—I read it in your every look,
And hear it in each word. Come—no disguise :

Your joys and sorrows must be mine,—mine yours;
But cannot if we hide them. Speak your grief,
And, in the very utterance, half its pain
Shall pass away.

DEM. Janira—to this hill,
In my young days a hundred times I came
To see yon sun get up. This morn's my last.
And I would take my leave on't ere I go.

JAN. Your last?—What mean you?

DEM. I must fly, my love.
Too well I feel *here* is no home for me:
A brother hates me,—and a father doubts:
One would destroy me,—th' other will not save.
Perseus, to take my life, sets daily snares;
Philip beholds him,—and almost abets.
I have no choice but an ignoble fate,—
And by a brother's hand;—a life ignobler,
Gained by that brother's death;—or else this flight.

JAN. Where would you fly? Oh! is it come to this?

DEM. To Rome, dear girl, where I have powerful friends,
And true ones. Perseus then may hate, and plot;
And my poor father rage and threat, in vain.
We shall be safe; and hear the distant storm,
Unheeding of the bolt.

JAN. But, should your flight
Be intercepted . . .

DEM. Have no fear of that.
The king will not return these four days yet.
Dymas will aid me thro' Pæonia; there
Lies all our difficulty; and his power,
As governor, can make it smooth and safe.

JAN. Is Dymas honest?

DEM. Honest? He's my friend:
Bound to me by a hundred services:—
He can't deceive me.

JAN. But he's Philip's friend:
And high in trust.

PHILIP.

DEM. Yet sees where Philip errs :
And will not aid his crimes. From him I learn
What urges me to this. He counsels me,
For he knows well my danger, and the path
By which to 'scape it.

JAN. Be his counsel good !
I like it not, and do not like the giver.
But I have no experience of man's heart,
And cannot judge,—or I should say—beware ;—
Dymas is hollow.—Do not ask me why ;—
I have no reason. When he speaks to me,
I feel a danger ;—when he looks on me,
I shrink away,—yet have no cause to shew,—
If't be not instinct.

DEM. I do think him true ;
But now will mark him surer. Look, my love,
The mist is clearing off ; and spots of green
Appear like islands in the vapoury flood.
Anon 'twill all pass off ; and then I'll shew thee
A hundred places that are dear to me
From sweet remembrance.

JAN. Look ! Demetrius—look !
The sun is peeping, like a burning eye,
Above the far earth's rim. Oh ! beautiful !
See—up into the sky a thousand rays
Shoot round . . .

DEM. And all the mountain-tops are touched . . .

JAN. And the green forest is all capp'd with gold.
Now he goes up. Oh ! the whole world should wake
To see this majesty——Demetrius,
Let us behold it often ;—for, methinks,
This sight might keep us virtuous more than aught
Philosopher or priest could talk to us.
Who, that saw this, could on that day do ill?
Look ! look ! But now I cannot look.

DEM. Then hear.
This very eve with Dymas I shall sup ;

And in the night set forth. Dost thou so love me,
As,—setting pomp and ceremony by,—
Thou canst in private let our hands be joined;
That so, without a spot on thy fair name,
Thou mayst fly with me? Dost thou so far love?

JAN. Oh! farther much,—or I loved not at all.
But think again before it be too late.
We must confer again, and yet again,
Before this step be taken. Show me now
The places that you spake of, for the mist
Is melting off, and gives to view a world,—
Or what might seem such. How magnificent!

DEM. We'll mount our horses; for a hundred points
Give, each, a different prospect; and all grand.
Come, my beloved;—one happy morn we'll have,
Tho' sorrow come at eve.

JAN.   Oh! do not fear.*   [*Exeunt.*

SCENE II.—*A room in* PHILIP'S *Palace.*

(*Enter* DYMAS, *with a* SERVANT.)

DYMAS. When did the king arrive?

SERVANT. Some half hour back, my lord; and the prince sent immediately to request speech with you. His majesty seems not in his wonted cheer, and forbade all show of rejoicing. But, so please you, my lord, I will announce to the prince your arrival, for he is impatient to have speech with you.   [*Exit.*

DYMAS. Do so, good fellow. Not in wonted cheer?
I've that shall rouse him. This dull melancholy
Is mere stagnation : but in that do breed
A thousand venomous and horrid things,
Which in the cataract, or storm-shook water,
Had never lived. Best life is found in action;
And death—but total rest. The red-eyed soldier,

---

* 'This is a *very* beautiful scene—but I doubt its effect in representation —is a marginal remark I remember seeing in one of my MS. copies of this play, on its being returned by Macready.—M. E. A.

Even in the battle's hurricane, when his sword
With every motion gives, or wards off death,
Is happier yet than he, who, by the fire,
Moans o'er the toothache. Welcome, noble prince.

(*Enter* PERSEUS.)

PERSEUS. Dear friend, I thank thee. Well—what—hast
thou sped?
Hast got him sure?

DYMAS.   When he that lies entombed
In Egypt's broadest pyramid,—the mummy
That, farther back than dim tradition goes,
Hath slept beneath the everlasting load,—
When he shall rise, and shake the burthen off,
And walk into the air,—Demetrius then,
And not till then, shall from his shoulders fling
The fate that waits to sink him.

PERSEUS.   Best of friends!
But how?—how mean you?

(*Enter a* LORD-IN-WAITING.)

LORD.   Let me not seem bold
T' intrude upon you. Twice the king hath asked
For the lord Dymas, and impatient waits.

PERSEUS. He comes o' th' instant. Briefly tell me now.
[*Exit* LORD.

DYMAS. I'll give the pith. Demetrius to Rome
This night will fly,—start not, nor say a word—
All shall be after told thee. Philip's rage
Will rise to madness when I pour the tale
Full in his ear. The tender-hearted boy
To cross his father's vengeance hath conspired
And certain traitors aided in escape.
They will be captured,—but th' attempt not less
His own doom seals. Last news I have to tell,
And at this moment best,—our trusty friends
Philocles and Apelles are returned.

I've spoken with them—they are well prepared—
The lesson that we taught is not forgot ;—
'Twill change each drop of sweet that stays behind
In Philip's bosom to the bitterest gall :·
And, when the scroll from Quintius comes at length,
'Twill turn him all to poison : every word
Will bear Demetrius death,—and every look
Shoot burning arrows thro' him.—
    PERSEUS.   So it will !
But go about it straight. Philip's displeased ;—
'Shamed of his fruitless, and most foolish quest
To look at Italy from Macedon ;—
And 'tis a humour that will keenly bite
On whatsoever it can fix its teeth.
    DYMAS. I'll change his darkness soon to fiery light.
Be not far off ;—you may be wanted too.   [*Exit.*
    PERSEUS. His fate is come at last. He cannot 'scape.
By heavens ! I hate him worse than ugly death ;
And will not long endure to breathe with him
The air of heaven.—He draws on him all eyes ;—
Ensnares all hearts ;—steals all men's expectations ;—
Plots for the throne, which is my proper right ;—
Lures to himself the bride, that should be mine ;—
Stands like a sun to which all eyes are turned :
And leaves me but a shadow.—I must hate him,
Or not be man ;—and I do hate him so
That I would rather feel the pangs of death
Ten times each day I live, than see *him* live
Crowned with his insolent hopes.—To-night—to-night—
Somewhat must be to-night—Ha ! fool ! thou look'st
For this blest night to cover thy foul deed,
And in thy black rebellion set thee safe.—
Fool ! traitor ! Roman minion ! 'tis thy last !   [*Exit.*

    SCENE III.—*Another room in the Palace.*
      (*Enter* PHILIP *and* DYMAS.)

    PHILIP. I blame thee not. It was the task I set thee ;
An arduous one ; and faithfully hast thou

Fulfilled my bidding.—Send the traitor here :—
I'll see him ere I sentence.

    DYMAS.   My dread liege!
Have pity on him :—think it more his fears,
Than treasonous intents that moved him on ;
For truly he had wondrous fantasies,
That haunted him, of snares about him laid,—
False whisperings 'gainst him in your royal ear,—
Foul accusations,—and, I know not what ;—
Things to perplex an older brain than his,—
And drive it on to madness. . . .

    PHILIP.   Or to treason!
Talk on't no more. Thou art too milky blooded,—
Who deals with rebels should have nerves of steel,
And liquid fire within his veins,—and heart
Unthawing as the snows of Caucasus.—

    DYMAS. For Theoxana, and her traitor brood,—
Vex not in vain, my royal liege, your soul.
Eight days the eastern wind right in the bay
Drove furiously, defying all escape.
Our vessels in pursuit were seen from shore,
Visibly gaining on her. (*Shouts heard.*)

    PHILIP.   Why that noise?
The matter of those outcries?

            (*Enter* PERSEUS *and* LORDS.)

    PERSEUS.   Good, my liege,
That which shall glad you. Theoxana's taken,
With her two children. Passing on to prison,—
I stayed the officers to hear your pleasure.

    PHILIP. Bring them before me. This is news indeed!
                        [*Exeunt* PERSEUS *and* LORDS.
I'll hear the furious lioness roar out,
To see her Roman cubs snatched from her sight.
Go call Demetrius too :—I'll have them brought,
The traitor and the traitress, face to face,—
And then to prison both.

DYMAS.   My royal liege
The prince, two hours ere daybreak, was away
Among the mountains.
    PHILIP.   How?—
    DYMAS.   Intending flight,
He had desire to pass one parting day
In scenes that from his boyhood he had loved.
With evening he'll return to sup with me.
Such his intent, and so I did report it
Unto your royal ear.
    PHILIP.   His purposed flight
You told of,—not his absence. But, good Dymas,
He must not hear of this. Ride forth at eve
To meet him;—put what colour on't you will,—
And let no busy tongue inform his ear
Of what hath chanced.—He hath hot friends among us
May make his capture dangerous. More anon——

(*Enter* THEOXANA *and her two* CHILDREN, *conducted by*
    PERSEUS, LORDS, *and two* OFFICERS.)

Ha! traitress! art thou caught?

    DYMAS (*aside*).   Traitress! By heaven!
Imperial Juno rather!
    THEOX.   Art thou Philip?
    PHILIP. Look round thee, woman,—and, if thou see'st here
A head more kinglike, then am I not Philip.
    THEOX. I see none here that might not wear as well
That bauble on thy brow;——but there's no face
On which so legibly is written *tyrant*.
Thou, then, art he.
    PERSEUS.   Bold, shameless woman, peace!
Or I will tear thy insolent tongue away.
    THEOX. Ha! let me look upon thee.—Thou'rt his son;
The very copy of the foulest picture
That ever libell'd man.—Nay—draw thy sword—
Upon a woman!—captive!

PHILIP. Answer me,
And leave thy railing. What dost thou deserve,
The wife of a black traitor, and the . . .

THEOX. False!
He was no traitor. Thou'rt the traitor, tyrant!
Traitor to heaven, and rebel 'gainst mankind.
Ay! stamp thy foot, and rage, I fear thee not.

PHILIP. But thou shalt fear me. By the throne of Jove!
I'll make thee crouch and whine like a whipp'd cur.
Away with them to prison.

CHILDREN. Mercy! mercy!

THEOX. Nay, ask it not, my children.—We must die,—
Let us die nobly, and not cowardly.

PHILIP. Be not too sure thou shalt have leave to die.

THEOX. Then shall I live to curse thee, and bring down
Heaven's wrath the fiercer on thee.

PHILIP. Thou art bold;—
But I have means to tame thee.

THEOX. *Thou* art bold;—
For thou hast lived defying earth and heaven :—
But there are racks more terrible than thine
Awaiting thee in hell to make thee tame,
Thou hoary murderer! Ay! murderer!

PERSEUS. My gracious father,—must I hold my hand
From punishing this insolent?

PHILIP. Keep peace.
The higher she goes up,—the worse her fall.
Let her have room. 'Twill be rare sport anon
To hear these big tones changed to puling cries
For mercy!—mercy!

THEOX. For thyself beg that
Of the incensëd heavens. Of thee, be sure,—
I will not ask it, tho' thy art strain out
The torture to eternity. But, tyrant—
I do defy thee. O'er thy hoary head

My murdered husband's scornful spirit stands
And points in mockery at thee :—but on me
He smiles, and lifts his hand to heaven.

  PHILIP.   No more.
Away with them to prison :—and such freedom
As with a strict security may live,
That let them have, no more. Upon the morrow
Bring them again before me.

  THEOX.   Come, my lambs ;
For one day longer will the butcher spare us.
Let us to prison.

  CHILDREN. Mercy for our mother!
Oh king, have mercy!

  THEOX.   Peace! I charge you—peace!
 [*Exeunt* THEOXANA *and her* CHILDREN *with the* OFFICERS.

 PHILIP. She hath a noble heart. I pity her.

  DYMAS (*aside*). She hath a form divine, and I will woo her.
(*Aloud*) Apelles and Philocles, my dread liege,
Last night returned from Rome,—were it not well
To hear what they may witness of the prince ;
Which, either shall confirm his guiltiness,
Approving so your wrath,—or,—which heaven grant!—
Shall from him wash away those foulest stains
That now disfigure him.

  PHILIP.   Go—call them quick.

  DYMAS. They wait without, my liege. I'll lead them here.
                 [*Exit.*

  PHILIP. That fellow's honest :—loyal to his king,—
Yet loving to his son, that is disloyal ;—
Painting his foul deeds o'er with colors fair,
That yet conceal not all their filthiness,
But show them, like a harlot's rotten cheek,
More ugly for their fineness.—Must he die?
My son—my youngest—once my best beloved?
Oh hard decree!—But he is false—disloyal—
Friended with Rome—accursëd—damnëd Rome!

Ha! if I prove him so,—a father's love,
Tho' it were chain of strength enough to hold
All earth suspended in heaven's glittering hall,
Must crack—and let him sink.   Oh ye good Gods!
Give not to beds of kings fertility,
For they but gender serpents : let the peasant
Increase, and multiply,—and, for old age,
Secure the love of children, and *their* children,—
But make the loins of kings like barren rocks ;
Their issue is a plague.—Ha! then I see it
Writ on your faces.

(*Enter* DYMAS, *and other* LORDS, *with* APELLES *and* PHILOCLES,
the AMBASSADORS.)
                    You need use no words
To tell me he's a traitor.—For yourselves,
I give you welcome, my good lords.   The thing
You have to say,—say freely, and fear not.

   PHILOCLES.   Bad tidings do make hateful those who bring
them.

   PHILIP.   In eyes of fools alone.   I am not one
To fling away in rage the golden cup,
For that the draught it brought was bitterness.—
Without more prelude, to the matter, sirs.
How stands Demetrius with our mortal foe?
How with the Senators and Consuls, first?
The army, and the worshipp'd mob of Rome,
That all are kings?

   PHILOCLES.   Pardon, my gracious liege,—
Hear, and believe me.   Of all ages, ranks,
Conditions, and opinions, is your son
The theme for Roman praises.

   APELLES.   'Tis most true!

   PHILOCLES. Go to the Senate—and you'll hear his name ;
Walk thro' the camp—'tis still 'Demetrius' ;—
Stand in the market-place,—men talk of him ;
Glide thro' the fields, or by old Tiber's banks,—

'Demetrius'—still 'Demetrius' is the word—
Small harm in this, were nothing worse to come:
But I must utter what to speak I dread,
Did not the greater dread lest . . .

  PHILIP.   Falter not!
Out with it!—By the omnipotence of Jove!
If thou dost keep one syllable from my ear,
Thy life shall rue it. Let it have full vent;
They'd have him on my throne—I know they would—
Look not aghast—but say 'this is not so'—
Or say—'this *is* so'—(*a pause*). Staring idiot! speak—
Or with this hand I'll strike thee to the earth.

  PHILOCLES (*kneeling*). Dread majesty! forgive me that I
  say—
This *is* even so (*a pause*).

  PHILIP. Go on. You hear him, lords.

  LORDS. With sorrow, most dread liege.

  PHILIP.   On sir—speak out.
How say the Roman gods our fate shall be?
Let Philip hear, that he betimes may learn
To tremble and obey.—Nay, my good lord—
Stand not on foolish ceremony: speak
Rude matter in plain words. The weakest eye
May boldly look the sinking sun i' th' face;
Take measure of his bulk,—and count the spots
Upon his clouded disc;—tho' at his height,
The strongest shrank to gaze upon his pomp—
So kings, before whose state all eyes were dimm'd,
All tongues were mute; or only heard in praise
Such as men give the Gods,—shall, at their fall,
Become the unfear'd gaze of basest eyes;
The theme of rudest tongues.—Speak, therefore, out,
And tell the manner of our swift deposal,—
As 'tis at Rome decreed;——and, with what state,
And what permitted power, our loyal son
Shall fill our forfeit throne.

  PHILOCLES.   My gracious liege!

With justice do you in derision hold
The vain designs of your proud enemy;
Which more as matter for your laughter hear,
Than for your wrath.
    PHILIP.   Proceed.
    PHILOCLES.   The common talk
At Rome is of new warlike preparation
You have in hand, to subjugate the states,
Late in rebellion 'gainst your royal right !
And which, by treaties ratified at Rome,
You had acknowledged free.
    PHILIP.   What follows then?
    PHILOCLES. Forgive me that their insolent boasts I speak.
A force already have they set on foot ;—
The field already, in their thoughts, is won ;—
Then, to their victory to put the seal,
And surety for the future. . . .
    PHILIP.   Ha! so prompt?
    PHILOCLES. Yourself, my gracious liege,—
    PHILIP.   Proceed, proceed—
    PHILOCLES. Shall be deposed . . .
    PHILIP.   As modest as 'tis sure.
    PHILOCLES. Prince Perseus,—hated as his brother's loved,—
To exile doomed, or safe imprisonment;
So may Demetrius, on his quiet throne,
Assure to Rome a vassal and a friend,
Where now they see their most fell enemy.
    PHILIP. In sooth, right well devised !—a marvellous plan !
Simple, and easy, and straight on to the end !
Thus talk the people,—say you : but the Senate,—
What say *they* of us?
    PHILOCLES.   With more cautious voice
They laud your son ;——but for yourself, my liege,—
Forgive my speech,—with vilest epithets . . .
    PERSEUS. Oh my dear father! hear no more of this :
Or let such blasphemy to your private ear
Be whispered,—not i' th' face of men spoke out.

PHILOCLES. This letter, gracious king, from Titus Quintius.

PHILIP. Ha! 'tis his hand. What matter have we now?
(*He reads in silence.*)

1ST LORD (*to* DYMAS). His majesty looks not in wonted health.

DYMAS. This journey hath much dashed him.

1ST LORD. He's more pale,
And careworn.

DYMAS. Something's there that likes him not.
See how he grinds his teeth.

PHILIP (*folding the letter hastily*). Enough! enough!
I ask no more than this. The parricide!
Give me thy hand, my son. I doubted thee;
And fear'd 'twas malice, or intriguing strife
That moved thee 'gainst thy brother;—now I see
Thou hadst the sharper wisdom. But, fear not;
On every step that leads up to a throne,
There stand a myriad sharp, invisible swords,
To hew down lawless climbers.—For this traitor,
He shall not put one foot upon the stair;
Far less reach up to th' diadem. Thee, Perseus,
In the eye of all men do I now proclaim
My son, and sole successor. For Demetrius
I here abjure him,—cast him utterly off;—
And, as a cankered branch is hewn away,
And thrown into the flames,—so from my heart
Is he cut off,—and to such vengeance given
As the just Gods to crimes like his decree! (*A pause.*)
What say you, lords—am I o'erharsh in this?

SEVERAL LORDS. Your majesty is ever merciful.

PHILIP. Why—madman! did I send this egg to Rome
To have it hatched a crocodile?—Oh fathers!
If in your sons you would affection hold,
Still keep them in your eye;—for filial love,
Even like a fire untended, quickly dies
If love paternal feed it not. He's lost!

A traitor to his country, and his king !
The bosom friend of Rome !—Must Philip die—
Or see upon his throne a rebel son,—
Himself deposed,—imprison'd—and his kingdom,
That was erewhile earth's brightest, bowed to wear
The manacles of Rome ?—Or must *he* die ? (*A pause.*)
Had Saturn crushed the Thunderer at his birth,
He had not lost his heaven !—

  DYMAS (*aside to the* AMBASSADORS). How sorrow works
Upon his royal mind !

  APELLES.   He sees us not.

  PHILOCLES. Yet he looks on us.

  DYMAS.   With the balls of sight,
But not with that which should inform their sense.
Most royal Philip—vex not thus your soul
For one unduteous son, when still there lives
Another, to whose heart you are more dear
Than sunshine to the eye, or breath to life,
Or food to him who famishes. Noble prince,
Go to thy father, and assure his soul
How thou dost love him.

  PERSEUS (*kneeling*). Father, on my knee
I swear to thee—and may th' all-ruling Gods
So help me as in simple truth I swear !—
I have no wish but what to thee is true ;—
To thee who art my father, and my king :
I seek no power or honour but from thee :
From thee I had my life,—from thee must have
All that can make life glorious. When to thee
I prove disloyal,—let th' omnipotent Gods
Withdraw from me their favouring countenance !
And give me o'er to fate !

  PHILIP.   Rise—rise—enough !
As thou to me—thy children unto thee !—
Lords, for awhile farewell. We will retire,
To drink in solitude the bitter draught
Of filial ingratitude. Just heaven !   [*Exit.*

LORDS. Our duties to your majesty.
PERSEUS (*aside to* DYMAS).   He has it!   [*Exeunt.*

END OF THE THIRD ACT.

ACT IV.
SCENE I.—*A room in* PHILIP'S *Palace.*
(PHILIP *discovered.*)

PHILIP. There is no way but this. His guilt is plain
To dullest eyes—bold—monstrous—seen far off
As huge Olympus.—When a limb's diseased
Beyond the leech's art to make it sound,
He cuts it off;—thus saving the whole man,
Who else had perished with it.—Macedon
Is now that man,—Demetrius that limb ;—
And I, alas!—his father—am the leech
That must the sharp and cruel knife direct
To its stern purpose.

(*Enter a* SERVANT.)
What's thy business here?

SERVANT. The lord Antigonus, so please your majesty,
most urgently requests admission to your royal presence.

PHILIP. What would he now? I have forbid his coming:
But let him enter.   [*Exit* SERVANT.

(*Enter* ANTIGONUS.)
Well, old lord,—thy business?

ANTIG. Philip, thy happiness,—thy son's—the State's.
Forgive me, for I love Demetrius,
And know him innocent. He is your son,
And therefore should find mercy ;—he's a prince,
And should have amplest justice. That at Rome
He is beloved may be in him no crime :
Is he not young, and beautiful, and brave,—
Open—and generous—liberal in expense—

Gifted with qualities that make men love
And women worship? Are not these enough—
Being a prince beside,—to draw the hearts
Of Romans as of Macedonians?
Is it a treason then to be beloved?
If so the hated vicious are most loyal:—
Is it——

PHILIP. Stay—stay—old man,—thou'rt ignorant here:
He has found mercy,—and, be sure, sha find
The amplest justice.—I will hear no more.

ANTIG. Philip, farewell. Remember he's your son. [*Exit.*

PHILIP. I would I could forget it (*a pause*). He must die;
And presently;—or the mad people's love
Will fortress him against the siege of justice—
Demetrius, or Philip, must go out;—
Rome must be stabbed, or Macedon.—Who waits?

(*Enter a* SERVANT.)

Bid the lord Dymas enter. (*Exit* SERVANT.) It must be!
I cannot—may not—dare not shrink. Come hither.

(*Enter* DYMAS.)

Hast thou a heart to feel thy country's wrongs?

DYMAS. I have, my liege:—to bleed,—to die for her.

PHILIP. Hast thou unto thy king such loyal love,
That, well to aid him in a need extreme,
Thou'dst on thy gentle nature violence put,—
Drive pity and remorse from thy soft breast;—
And be,—even like the axe, that strikes the head off,—
Feeling no sympathy?—

DYMAS. What Philip bids,—
That will his servant act. I have no heart
But what is Philip's;—have nor hands, nor tongue,
Nor any power of sense—but what are his,
To use as likes him best.

PHILIP. Enough—enough—
He sups with you to-night.—

DYMAS. He does, my liege.
PHILIP. His life is dangerous to the State and us.
He must not live—
　　DYMAS. Then bring you him to trial?
　　PHILIP. That were but shallow wisdom. Of the mob
He is beloved,—the soldiers too :—his youth
And comeliness would be loud orators
In ears whereto his treasons could not speak.
Yet must he die ;—or, in his room, a host,
Whom his rebellion, to a bloody death,
Will bring untimely.—Something must be done ;
Instantly,—secretly,—yet, done, avowed ;
And his black guilt to all the world proclaimed
The cause of this great justice.—What is done,
Is borne with patience oft, as past recall ;—
Though, were it yet to do, a thousand swords,
And fifty thousand tongues, would interpose
To stay its execution—(*a pause*).
　　　　　　Dost thou think
He might be spared, and yet the State . . . but no !—
Advise me not to mercy,—for his guilt
Is broader than heaven's concave. Die he must—
Or Philip fall,—and Rome. . . . It shall not be ! (*A pause.*)
To-morrow let me hear thee say . . . dost mark me?
　　DYMAS. Most earnestly !—
　　PHILIP. To-morrow let me hear
That . . . Macedon is safe—that treason's flame
Hath been put out—that . . . dost thou understand ?
　　DYMAS. I see a fearful spectre in your words ;
But 'tis in darkness yet.
　　PHILIP. Dost dread to meet it ?
　　DYMAS. I would 'twere more substantial. But, that thing
Which Philip hath no fear to wish enacted,
I may not fear to act.
　　PHILIP. Thou sayst enough.
He sups with thee to-night.—Fill thou his cup.
What ! dost thou start ?—Thy words were bold enough.

DYMAS. So shall my deeds be. 'Twas a passing sting
Of foolish pity;—but the last. 'Tis gone!

PHILIP. I'd have him laid asleep;—but—tenderly.
Seek thou some drug that shall extinguish life;—
Not tear't to pieces.—I would have him dead;
Yet would not wish him feel what 'tis to die.
For oh! he's still my son,—my youngest boy!
Have ye no mercy, Gods?—Might he not live?—
But no—no—no—I'll think upon't no more.—
Fate calls him—he must go— [*Exit.*

DYMAS. So he but go,
I care not at what door. But go he must;
Or the bright honors that I seek to wear
Will prove a drunken dream.—What matters it?
Peasant, or prince—all must at some time die:—
His turn is now;—mine when the Gods shall please.
But not, I trust, before yon haughty dame
Her lofty head as low as mine shall stoop;—
Ay—call me friend, and kind deliverer.
I'll to her, and the tyrant paint so black,—
Tell her of deaths contrived so terrible,—
Shew her her children in their agonies
Herself to brutal lust exposed, and death
Horrid and infamous,—then, for one poor boon,
Promise escape.—She must—she shall be mine. [*Exit.*

SCENE II.—*A room in a Prison.*

(THEOXANA *and* ARATUS *discovered.*)

THEOX. So potent sayst thou?

ARATUS. Scarce the lightning flash
Strikes with more sudden stroke. Upon the eye,
Within the lip, or ear, one drop let fall,
Doth, even like water on the lingering spark,
All life extinguish.

THEOX. Without pain?

ARATUS. Sleep falls not
Upon the infant's eyelids with a touch

More tender than this gently dropping death.
'Tis but the breath breathed forth, nor drawn again.

THEOX. Oh thou most excellent balm of the bruised heart,
For all the laughing nectar of the Gods
I would not barter thy few joyless drops!
I thank thee, true and gentle friend,—I thank thee.
Commend me to the generous prince, thy lord,
And say I blessed him ere I died. Make known
The manner of our end, and for what cause,
Lest cruel and unnatural he should deem
The mother who her children could destroy.
Tell him to 'scape the torture, and a death
Of ignominy, she their innocent souls,
In gentle sleep, without a pang, set free;
Then hasted after. Say—but now no more—
Time urges:—the abhorrëd monster comes
With hellish suit again to file my ears.—
Take thou this jewel:—'tis the sole one left
By the rapacious spoiler,—yet so rich,
That in contentment mayst thou pass thy days
Unpressed by labour. Take it. Where I go,
I may not carry it. This little phial
Is worth to me a mine of gems.

ARATUS.   Oh heavens!
For such reward what have I done!

THEOX.   The best,
The kindest service;—oped for us the gate
That leads from shame and pangs to liberty.
But to thyself look now: no hand but thine
Could bring this help. Fly quickly, or thou'rt lost.
Adieu, and be thou happy.—Haste,—away:—
I would be on our journey.

ARATUS.   Oh farewell!
Most hapless lady—and dear innocents,
Farewell—farewell.   [*Exit.*

THEOX.   How is it to be done?
What is't that I would do?—Be firm, my soul;
    (*She opens the door of an inner chamber.*)

And let no woman's weakness . . . How they sleep!
Beautiful children—on their beds of straw!
Their death-beds! Like pure rose-buds do they lie,
All health and fragrance. 'Tis the spirit of life—
The in-breathed mystery from Divinity,
All freshly glowing in them : and that fire,
That light, I must extinguish! Can I do it?
'Tis but a touch :—better than—Oh! ye Gods!
To see their little limbs upon the rack
Writhing in agony—and hear their cries
To me, their mother, who might thus have saved,—
But, with false kindness and a cruel love,
Selfishly pitiful, dared not—Oh! the curse
Of every mother would pursue my name,
And brand me weakest—most unnatural!
But what if to that villain's horrid suit
I should appear to listen,—Hateful thought!
Foolish as hateful! Victims we must be—
Nor *could* he—would he, save us. Die we must!
Or thus,—or by the torture! Now to pause,
A trembling coward, when, with but a touch,
One merciful touch, from the black despot's bonds
I might release them thus—It shall not be!
Ye awful Deities, within whose hands
Are life and death to all things,—look not down
With eye of anger on this mortal deed,
Fate's, and not mine,—but, as your minister,
In mercy sent, uphold me to the end!
Fast locked in sleep! Now,—now, my soul, be firm!
   (*She goes into the inner chamber, and closes the door.*)

SCENE III.

(*The foregoing scene draws up, and discovers the inner
 chamber, with the* CHILDREN *lying on their couches,
 and* THEOXANA *sunk upon the floor beside them.*)

(*Enter* PHILIP *with the* JAILER.)

PHILIP. Soft—they're sleeping—Shade thy lantern, fellow,
Or they may wake.—Whose order did he shew?

JAILER. So please your majesty, he bore the ring
Of the lord Dymas.

PHILIP.   Dymas?

JAILER.   Yes, my liege.

PHILIP. I cannot think why Dymas sent him here.
He urged me give the fellow his release,
That he might use him to advantage me,
Someway—I know not how.—But, was he not
The servant of Demetrius, ere this woman's?

JAILER. So I have heard, my liege.

PHILIP.   Didst hear them talk?

JAILER. No word, my liege.

PHILIP.   He has been twice, you say.

JAILER. Twice, my dread lord.

PHILIP.   And brought he nothing with him?

JAILER. Nought that I saw, my liege.

PHILIP.   No letter?—nothing?

JAILER. Nought, to my knowledge. Coming from lord
Dymas,
I'd no suspicion.

PHILIP.   Let him be detained:
His looks were wild; I'll question him myself.
For old Antigonus—say I will not see him,
Bid him away—his presence doth offend me.
Put down the light, and leave me.   [*Exit* JAILER.
                Dead asleep!
I do not hear a breath.—And in a prison!
And on the night, too, that she thinks her last!
Might I but sleep like these.—I'd be the captive;
And let her sit upon the golden throne,—
And count myself the gainer. Shall I wake her?
She will not answer me,—or say a word
To bring my son in question. Yet she must;—
For I would have his guilt more bright than day,
To clear my terrible justice.—Ho—awake!—

THEOX. (*starting up*). What art thou?—Ha! the tyrant!—
have I slept?
My children.—Merciful Gods!—they're safe—they're safe!

PHILIP. And thou too shalt be safe, so thou confess
Thy treasons, and my son's.

THEOX. I *will* be safe.
One precious drop remains. (*Raising the phial to her lips.*)
                         His treasons?—fiend!
He is a God to thee, and all thy race.

PHILIP. But he's a traitor. Dymas hath revealed
His black designs: he knew them all.

THEOX. False! false!
Thy son is true;—and Dymas false as hell!

PHILIP. What ails thee, woman?

THEOX. Dying, tyrant.—Look,
My babes are gone before.

PHILIP. Ho! help—help—ho!
What horror's this?

THEOX. *Thy* work! Oh Gods!—one word—
Demetrius is most true—Demetrius—
Dymas—is false—is false—thy son—Oh Gods! (*She dies.*)

PHILIP. Help—help.—She's dead.—Ha! poison?
                         (*Taking up the phial.*)
JAILER (*rushing in*).   Good my liege!

PHILIP. She's poisoned.—All of them are poisoned!—Fellow,
What dost thou know of this?—Speak, on thy life!
If thou dost palter with me . . . (*Drawing his sword.*)

JAILER (*sinking on his knees*). Gracious king!
Have mercy on me! I am innocent!

PHILIP. Ha! now I see it—'Tis that menial's work—
Aratus—hence—drag him before me!—fly! [*Exit* JAILER.
We're mocked.—Hath Dymas known of this? What?—how?
She called him false—He dared not—To what end?—
If he be false—Demetrius may be . . . Ha!
A letter?—'Tis the hand of Dymas— (*He reads.*)

12

'Most beautiful, and unhappy—The king is enraged to the utmost. If no shield come between you and his wrath, yourself and your children will on the morrow die miserably in torture.'—Why thou shameless liar! 'I will visit thee again to-night. Consent to my wishes, and I can, and will save you. Refuse me—and bid farewell to hope,—the tortures are prepared.—I shudder to think of them.'—
'Tis sure the hand of Dymas.

(*Enter* JAILER *with* ARATUS.)

(*To the* JAILER). Hasten back—
Call in Antigonus: something he may know.— [*Exit* JAILER.
Have I been played on?—Fellow! wouldst thou live,—
Answer me truly:—palter with me now—
And I will scatter thee abroad like dust.—
Who sent thee here?

  ARATUS. Lord Dymas.

  PHILIP.   What the errand?

  ARATUS. I bore from him that letter.

  PHILIP.   And the poison?

  ARATUS. At her most earnest prayer I brought her that.
Lord Dymas knew not of it.

  ANTIGONUS (*hastening in*). Philip! Philip!
Thou'st almost broke my heart. Thou art betrayed!
Apelles, as he left the court to-day,
Was struck with death.—His conscience tortured him;—
He sent for me, and, with his dying breath,
Made full confession of such treachery
As chokes belief.—That letter was a lie—
Quintius ne'er saw it—'twas the damned issue
Of Perseus and black Dymas—

  PHILIP.   Sayst thou?—

  ANTIG.   Yes—
They forged it,—bribed the ambassadors to bring it,—
To poison you with lies against your son . . .

PHILIP. Away—away—Demetrius may be lost!—
Oh! if the horrid cup be at his lips—
Dash it away, I do beseech you Gods!
My guard ho! and my chariot! [*Exeunt omnes.*

END OF THE FOURTH ACT.

ACT V.

SCENE I.—*A room in the House of* DYMAS.

(*Enter* PERSEUS, *with a* SERVANT.)

PERSEUS. Dymas sups late to-night. What friends within?

SERVANT. Your brother, and the princess, good my lord;
None else.

PERSEUS. Go thou behind thy master's couch,
And whisper in his ear that I am come,
And would speak with him instantly. Beware
That none o'er-hear thee. [*Exit* SERVANT.
                      It *must* be to-night.
For every instant that he lives doth seem
To sting me for my folly.—He removed—
This arm is not more servant to my wish
Than will the soldiers be. The poor old king
Is merely frantic—should himself be ruled;
Not rule. 'Twere mercy on his withered head
To ease him of the golden weight he bears,
And lift the heavy sceptre. . . . Ha! my friend

(*Enter* DYMAS)

Thou'st been with Philip since we spoke together.

DYMAS. I have.

PERSEUS.   What said he?

DYMAS.   Wait but patiently,
And thou shalt hear the deed before the word—
This evening hath the marriage knot been tied,
No witness save her women and myself.

At turn of midnight, with his virgin bride,
Myself the guide and partner of their way,
Towards Rome he plans escape.

PERSEUS. How!

DYMAS. Ask no more:
Come to my chamber :—there lie hid awhile—
Thy fortune's sun will speedily break forth,
And I shall look to bask in't. Come away.

PERSEUS. When Perseus is the sun to Macedon,
Then shalt thou be a moon in the same heaven ;
As loved and worshipped. [*Exeunt.*

SCENE II.—*Another room in the House of* DYMAS.

(DEMETRIUS *and* JANIRA *are seated on couches.*)

DEM. 'Tis yet two hours of midnight, my sweet love ;—
Go to thy bed,—and steep those tender limbs
In balmy sleep awhile.

JAN. I could not sleep.

DEM. Nay but, sweet girl,—the cold moist air of night,
On bodies unrefreshed by wholesome rest,
Oft strikes diseases like a pestilence ;
But, to the limbs that gentle sleep hath fed,
'Tis as a cooling, and a strengthening bath,
Pleasant and healthful.—Prithee my sweet—WIFE.

JAN. Nay then, sweet lord, by *that* name first conjured,
I cannot say thee nay. Good-night—good-night.

DEM. Good-night, Janira ; and kind dreams be thine.
An hour past midnight will our horses wait.
Give to your women charge of watchfulness ;
For now is time more precious than fine gold ;—
And we must not be spendthrifts. Sweet—good-night.

JAN. I wish to-morrow were but come and past.
Something lies heavy here. Good-night.

DEM. Good-night :
And, after this good-night, a long—long life
Of days and nights as good.—One kiss, sweet love.

[*Exit* JANIRA.

What is this dark foreboding that comes o'er me?
I do not think we ever shall meet more.—
And yet no cause I know.—I'll call her back—
Yet why?—What shall I say?—Oh! I'm the fool
Of sickly fantasy!

(*Enter* DYMAS.)

DYMAS. How now, my lord?
Why you look cloudy as December night,—
And 'tis with you May morning.—Nay—be glad—
Such sombre brow, upon your marriage night,
Suits ill as doleful snow in merry June.
Where is the princess?

DEM. Gone to her repose.

DYMAS. Why she is wise; and 'twere in us more wisdom
To snatch an hour or two of wholesome sleep;
The nights are chill.

DEM. But we have much to speak of.

DYMAS. You are not fit for it. The length of way
Will give us leisure more than we can fill.
Such talk will then our over-fulness ease;—
Now—rob us of our little. Come, sweet prince,
With one full measure let us drown black care;
Then seek for merry dreams. I'll fill your cup.
(*Pouring out the poisoned wine.*)
Nay—nay—no drooping on your wedding night.

DEM. (*taking the cup*). Dear Dymas, I am even as a child,
And thou my gentle nurse.—Are there, dost think,
Foretokenings given us of unformed events?—
Dark shadowings on the soul, of coming ills?

DYMAS. Pshaw! 'tis mere foolery. Drink—drink it off.

DEM. Dost think 'tis so?

DYMAS. Nought else.

DEM. But I have seen,—
Long ere the tempest came, when not a breath
Was in the silent air,—the deep sea waves
Rolling laboriously,—and ever then

I marked the storm did follow : and, ere rain,
Or snow comes down, doth not the wind make moan,
Foretelling dreariness?—bees leave the flowers,
Feeling the storm that yet is far away :—
And so perhaps . . . thou smilest—

DYMAS.   Drink—drink—drink—

DEM. (*sipping*). What wine is this?

DYMAS.   'Tis good—is't not?

DEM.   Most rich.
'Tis Chios—no?—

DYMAS.   You have a delicate taste.
But drain it off.

DEM.   Would I'd a prophet's eye!

DYMAS. Why? my good lord.—What is't you'd wish to see?

DEM. I know not.—Gentle friend—thy health (*he drinks*).—
    Good-night.
Go to thy bed.   I'll stretch me on this couch :
But not, I think, to sleep.   (*He lies down.*)

DYMAS.   Good-night, my lord.
(*Aside*) Yes—you'll sleep soundly.   With no prophet's eye,
I can see that.   [*Exit.*

DEM. (*half raising himself*). Ha! ha!—my heart! my heart!
How's this?—Janira—my sweet wife—Oh come—
Come to me—I am cold—   (*Falls back.*)
                    Ah! me—'tis—death!   (*He dies.*)
                    (*A noise heard without.*)

(*Enter a* SERVANT.)

SERVANT. My lord—my lord—lord Dymas—

DYMAS (*entering at another door*).   What's this noise?

SERVT. The king, my lord, in furious haste is here ;
And calls for you, and for the prince—

DYMAS.   Soft—soft—
The prince you see is sleeping.   Close the door.
                                (*Noise increases.*)
I'll hasten to his majesty.—Good heavens!

PHILIP (*without*). Where is the traitor? Where's my hapless son?

DYMAS. What means this fury?

(PHILIP *bursts in, followed by* ANTIGONUS, *and several of his* GUARDS.)

PHILIP.　　　　　　　　Traitor! Where's my son?

(*He rushes to the couch.*)

Demetrius!—my dear boy!—awake!—awake!—
He'll wake no more! The bloodhounds have their prey!

(*He starts up and seizes* DYMAS.)

Oh! thou most damnëd villain of the earth!
What hast thou done?

DYMAS.　　　　Dismiss your train, my liege,
Ere we speak farther.

PHILIP.　　　　Thou foul dog of hell!
I have no speech for thee. Get home! get home!

(*Stabbing him twice.*)

Earth cannot hold thee longer.

DYMAS.　　　　Help! help! Oh!
Murdered! Oh foully murdered!

PHILIP.　　　　　　　　Murderer!
Foul! hideous murderer!

ANTIGONUS.　　　My gracious liege!
Was this not rash?

PHILIP.　　　Away! away! away!
Rash?—rash?—what's rash?—See! look what they have done!
He's dead!—my boy is dead!—*They* made me do it!

ANTIG. You, Philip?—you?—

PHILIP.　　　　　　　　Aye! me!—me—Philip—

ANTIG.　　　　　　　　　　　　　No!
You are distraught to say so!

PHILIP.　　　　Oh! they lied
So cunningly;—dropped to my very heart
Such rancorous poison;—painted him all o'er
So like a hell-thing, that—— But there's one left:

I'll have revenge—I'll make the villain know
What 'tis to drive a doting father mad—
I'll have him seized—I'll have him—Oh! my boy!
     (*He falls on the body of* DEMETRIUS.)
  (JANIRA *enters hastily, her hair dishevelled.*)
JAN. What dreadful larum's this?—Ha! murder here?
Lord Dymas murdered?

  ANTIG.   Gentle lady—nay—
Look not around you—go away at once—
This is no business,—and no place for you—
  JAN. The king?—Unhand me, sir—
  ANTIG.   Beseech you, lady!
  JAN. Off—off—old man! They've killed my husband too—
Villain—let go! Help! murder! help! help! help!
Ha—ha—ha—ha—
  (*She laughs and falls senseless in the arms of* ANTIGONUS.)
  PHILIP.   What frantic voice is that?
I thought she had been dead—and all her children.
I'm glad it was a dream.—No more of deaths—
I'll have no deaths within my kingdom : no—
No man shall die—I'll have an edict for it.—
Who's this?—who's this?—ha! he is dead! dead! dead!
Open thine eyes, my boy.—Nay, but one word—
Speak but one word—speak—I command thee—speak—
Dost disobey me?—Ha! he's dead! he's dead!
I'll creep into his grave—and lie with him—
He may awake—such things have been ere now—
I do believe he will awake again.—
Here—bear him to his bed—and make no noise—
Come, fellows—stir—and one of you bring here
My camp-cloak, for I'll watch myself to-night.
I know he will awake;—he will—he will.
   [*Exeunt* PHILIP, *and* GUARDS *bearing the corpse.*

  ANTIG. Unhappy king! he never will wake more!
Would thou couldst sleep as sound!—(*looking on* JANIRA)
  poor blighted flower!
It were a merciful stroke to crush thee now :—

For thou wilt wither day by day,—the worm
Gnawing thy heart out.—Oh! the mockery
Foul death puts on us,—shewing a ripe cheek,
And eyes of crystal brightness, while, within,
Lurks black corruption!

(*Enter* ARCHO, *and another female, hastily.*)

ARCHO. Help! my lady's dead!

ANTIG. Silence, fond girl! she hath but swooned.

ARCHO. Oh no!
She's dead—she's dead! dear lady!

ANTIG. Cease this noise—
And bear her to her chamber. Watch by her;
And with some slumbrous drug compel her sleep,
For, waking, she will rave. Go—speak no more.

(*The females bear out* JANIRA.)

Thou wretched clod that, for thine own base ends,
Didst put the dagger in the father's hand
Against his innocent son—thou hast thy due;
A stern, and fearful payment. Fare thee well.
Now to the wretched, mad, and guilty king.
Oh! my poor country! hapless Macedon!
Of foreign wars, domestic feuds, the prey,—
Who shall protect thee now? [*Exit.*

(*An opposite door is gently opened, and* PERSEUS *partly enters, speaking softly.*)

PERSEUS. Hist! Dymas—hist!—He's gone.—What means all this?
I'm sure 'twas Philip's voice.—What horrid rage
Hath seized him now?

DYMAS. Oh me!

PERSEUS. Whose voice is that?

(*He enters with a light, treading softly.*)

Here's some-one wounded—Dymas! is it thou?
Bleeding to death!—Who did this horrid deed?
Let me bind up thy wound—speak, if thou canst—
What damnëd hand hath done this thing?

DYMAS.   Oh! me!
I die!—Thy father did it—
  PERSEUS.   Ha!—the tyrant?
  DYMAS. Haste—fly.—He seeks for thee—I cannot speak—
All is found out—Demetrius—is—dead!—
  PERSEUS. What! hast thou crushed him?—
  DYMAS.   Great Gods! forgive me!
Give me thy hand—Oh Gods!—Oh! Gods! (*He dies.*)
  PERSEUS.   He's gone!
All his ambition,—all his glittering hopes—
Sunk—lost—in ever-during darkness quenched—
Even like the rapid, and eye-dazzling lightning,
That, for a space, doth seem to fire the heavens,
Making earth tremble, and the stars go out—
Then from his sky-path shoots into a bog,
And sleeps with rottenness!—Well, Dymas, well;—
I little thought thou'dst teach me moralize.
Thou'rt dead,—but I will make thee still my friend:
I'll show thee to the soldiers, thus carved up
By gentle Philip;—and it shall go hard
But thy eclipse shall make my beams more bright.
But no delay: the purchase of one hour
May be a diadem;—each minute then
Rates as a precious gem, and cries, dispatch,
Perseus—*King* Perseus! ROME—and VICTORY!   [*Exit.*

SCENE III.—*A room in the Palace of* PHILIP.

(*Enter* LYSIMACHUS *and* ONOMASTES, *with* CALLIGENES, *a physician.*)

  LYSIM. No hope—say you?
  CALLI.   None—none! His hours are few.
  ONOMAS. Unhappy king!—How doth he bear himself?
  CALLI. Even like a lion in the pangs of death.
His tortured soul it is that burns the body,
Which else hath no disease.

LYSIM.   He ever had
A spirit most untamed.   Doth his mind wander?

CALLI.   Most fearfully!—'Tis as a midnight tempest;
Dark and outrageous, with deep calms between—
I must unto him.

ONOMAS.   We will go with you.
Alas! poor Philip! is thy burning sun
Thus sinking into night?—

CALLI.   Good friends, I pray you,
What things so-ever you may see, or hear,—
As strange and dangerous is his discourse,—
Upon your lips put seals.

LYSIM.   Our memories
Shall be as graves, wherein, like things deceased,
His words shall be interred.   [*Exeunt.*

SCENE IV.—*The chamber of* PHILIP.

(PHILIP *lies on a couch.* ANTIGONUS, *and attendants are in waiting.*)

SERVANT. I think, my lord, he sleeps.

ANTIG.   His eyes are open;
Do not disturb him. Take those lights away,
And keep the chamber dark.—He is worn out,
And may sink down to sleep.

SERVANT.   Heaven grant he may!
That was an awful struggle.

(*Enter* LYSIMACHUS, ONOMASTES, *and* CALLIGENES.)
ANTIG.   My good friends!
Would I had seen you at a gladder hour!
But welcome now. Sorrow craves sympathy,
As well as merriment.

ONOMAS.   How is the king?

ANTIG. Even like some goodly temple, which the flames
Have almost vanquished,—silence now, and smoke,—
Anon fierce light, and roarings terrible.

One fearful agony hath just gone by,
And left him strengthless.

CALLI.   He is sinking fast.
I do not think he hath an hour to live.

PHILIP. Then bring him to me :—bring him to my face—
I'll see him ere he dies——

LYSIM.   What is't he mutters?

ANTIG. Hush—hush!—Still raving of his hapless son!

PHILIP. 'Tis pity he should die !—so beautiful !
So young and kind !   Oh Gods ! 'tis pitiful !
Art sure on't, Dymas ?—Tell me—art thou sure ?
Ah ! so ?—Then he must die !   Oh Gods !   Oh Gods !

ONOMAS. What dreadful groans are these !

LYSIM.   What words !
ANTIG.   Hush—hush!—

PHILIP. But do it gently ;—for he is my son—
Although he be a traitor !

ONOMAS.   Horrible !

LYSIM. Most horrible !

CALLI.   Nay, my kind friends,—beware,—
One word may turn this calm into a tempest,
'Twould madden you to hear.

PHILIP (*half rising and gazing in terror upon vacancy*). Why,
    who art thou ?
Take off thy bloody, glaring eyes,—foul thing !
It was thyself that did it.—Get thee gone,
With thy two livid brats !—Ha !—touch me not !
Thou'rt black and swoln !—Take off thy poisoned hand—
Off ! off !—thou smellest of the grave !—Go back—
And let the worms begin their meal on thee !—
Ay ! beckon as thou may, I will not go—
Why dost thou smile ?—What !—is thy husband there ?
Ha ! now I see him.   Wert thou not a traitor ?
No ?—Oh—no—no—I warrant thee no traitor—
Smile an thou wilt.—Farewell.—Even so ?—Oh Gods !
                               (*He falls back.*)

Lysim. He's gone! he's dead!

Calli. Not so—my good old friend.
Pray you be calm.

Onomas. Look where the princess comes.
Will you admit her now?

Calli. It soothes the king
To look upon her, for it makes him weep;
And in those showers the fires come harmless down,
That else might turn to lightnings. 'Tis his will
That she have all times entrance.

(JANIRA *enters—pale and haggard.*)

Antig. Hapless lady!
How fares it with you?

Janira. Have you seen him, sirs?

Antig. Pray you sit down. Come, child, thou'rt cold and faint—
Here—sit you down.

Janira. I thank you, reverend sir,—
But I'll not sit. He will be here anon.
I have a song for him,—a sweet new song;—
I know 'twill please him.—Shall I sing it to you?

Antig. Thou hast not strength, dear lady.—

Janira. Hush—hush—hush!
I made it as I sat beside his grave,
Last night, in the soft moonlight; and I sang it
Till morning beamed;—but he was fast asleep,
And did not hear me! 'Tis a sad,—sad ditty.
Pray you sit down, and I will *tell* it you;—
Not sing it till *he* comes . . .

'Up—up, sweet prince; for the morning is bright,
   And the clouds are purple and gold:
Up,—up,—thou dear sluggard, and come to the light,
   From thy bed so darksome and cold.
      What dost thou there,
      With thy amber hair,—

     Thy rosy cheek,—
     Thy skin so sleek,
  Thy limbs like the roebuck light?—
  Come,—skim o'er the valleys, and bound up the hills;
  And plunge in deep forests, and drink at the rills;
    And eat of the berries so bright:—
  What dost thou there, in the murky grave,
   Wrapp'd up in that ugly shroud;—
  Thou that are beautiful, young, and brave,—
    When the winds are singing loud,
  And the trees are nodding their beautiful heads . . .'

But indeed I can talk no more—so I will e'en sit me down on the grass here, and go to sleep. Ah! well a day! the sweet spring flowers are all gone. I thank you, kind sir. (*She sits on the floor.*)

ONOMAS. Poor lady! what an overthrow is here!

ANTIG. Each day she wastes, and wastes, and pines away. Yet still she talks, and sings;—and sometimes smiles,
As if she felt no pain.

LYSIM. (*to* CALLIGENES). How is the king?

CALLI. In a deep stupor that bodes little good. I dread his waking.

JAN. Did you, my sweet lord?—I' faith I heard you not—I cannot sing again;—so, pray you, get up and come to me. Oh! oh!

ANTIG. She grows paler and paler.

JAN. What! go to you?—Nay, you would hold me fast.—Pray you get up—I'm very faint and cold.—Well love,—I will but take one little sleep, and then I'll sing to you again.—Dark—dark—Oh me!

        (*She lies down, and dies.*)

ANTIG. She's fainted.—Help her, good Calligenes.

LYSIM. How deadly pale she is!

CALLI.   She'll never redden. She's dead.

ALL.   Dead?—
PHILIP (*raising himself*). Dead! Who's dead? who dares to die?
Where am I?—Bring me lights—'Tis not too late—
My chariot ho!—lights—lights! Ha! do not drink!
'Tis poison! dash it down!—Demetrius—
Drink not, I say—ha! fool!—he will not hear—
He drinks—he drinks—he drinks—Look in his face—
It has him! ha! it has him! see! see! see!
He dies!—he dies!—Oh, Gods! he dies! he dies!
(PHILIP *sinks back*.)
ONOMAS. Most dreadful sight!—Hast thou, Calligenes,
No drug that might a kind oblivion bring
Upon his tortured spirit?
CALLI.   Petty sorrows,
Physic may soothe,—but, to such giant ills,
There's no oblivion, but the great one—death.
(*Trumpets are heard without, and loud shouts.*)
PHILIP (*starting up*). Hark! hark!—the Roman trumpets!
Bring my arms!
Call up the soldiers——
ANTIG. (*to the* ATTENDANTS). Haste—and hush that din.
(*Two* ATTENDANTS *go out.*) (*Trumpets again.*)
PHILIP. Are we betrayed?—Where are the sentinels?—
Lights! lights! we cannot strike them in the dark!—
Ha! Quintius!—let me meet thee once again!—
My horse!—my horse!—Look! look!—They scale the walls!
Dash them down headlong! Grapple with them close!
Leap off! leap off!—Now let the Phalanx move!
They fly!—they fly! Come on—I'll lead you on—
Victory! victory!—death, or victory!
(*He staggers from the couch, waving his arm; and soon falls down senseless.*)
CALLI. Death—then!—unhappy Philip!
ALL.   Is he gone?
CALLI. No.—There is yet a flutter at his heart:

'Tis but the last weak tremble, while the soul
Bids farewell to its clayey tenement.

ANTIG. He opes his eyes :—his frenzy is past oft.
Let's lift him to the couch.

CALLI. Nay—move him not.
There's now so small a spark,—the lightest breath
May put it out.
(*Re-enter the two* ATTENDANTS.)

ANTIG. What is it you would say—
Yet fear to utter ?—

1ST ATTENDANT. Is the king no more ?

ANTIG. He is as one that's dead,—tho' yet he breathes :
All sense hath left him.

ATTENDANT. Happy then I am
That what I speak his ear can never know.

ANTIG. What is't you mean?

ATTENDANT. Prince Perseus is named king.

ALL. How ?—

ANTIG. Ere his father have paid Nature's debt ?

ATTENDANT. The army, with loud clamours, made him king ;
Crowned, and proclaimed him :—in return for which
He thanked and flattered them ;—and, on the spot,
Flung out defiance against Rome ; and War,
Even to the uttermost.——

CALLI. The king would speak.

PHILIP. Kind friends ! I have but little breath for speech—
Forgive me if I've wronged you—I've been mad—
There's somewhat I would say—I know not what—
Let me be buried by Demetrius—
And lay his hapless wife within his arms—
She's dead—so some-one whispered—yes—she's dead !—
I have been mad—and fierce.—Forgive me, heaven !
Where are you ?—It grows dark—I have no breath——

(*A pause.*)

Ha! Perseus! ha!—I see thee,—fratricide!—
I see thee, king—and captive.—Look!—he walks,
Barefooted, and with dust upon his head,
Before the conqueror's chariot—see!—his wife—
His children—Spare *them*, Gods!—they walk, and weep,
Shame-stricken, with their faces bowed to earth.—
I hear the Roman Triumph—hark! they shout!
They point the finger at him!—see!—see!—see!
Oh Gods!——(*He sinks and dies.*)
 CALLI. He's gone!
 ANTIG.   And, dying, hath he prophesied.
   (*Trumpets, and shoutings again without.*)
Ay! Perseus—now rejoice! The fruit is ripe—
Watered by father's—and by brother's blood!—
Eat of it while thou mayst—and gorge thy fill:
But there's a bitterness far worse than death
To follow on thy surfeit.—Thou art king,—
But there's a king above thee—King of kings!
Who sees, and will reward thee.—To His hands
We trust for justice!

    The Curtain Falls.

LOVE, POETRY, PHILOSOPHY, AND GOUT.

A Farci-Comedy
IN FIVE ACTS.

Persons Represented.

LAODAMUS—*A Noble and Wealthy Man.*
MELAS—*A Half-crazy Philosopher.*
PHORBAS—*A Mad Poet.*
PANTHUS—*A Gouty Old Man.*
ADRASTUS—*His Son, and Lover of Janassa.*
ANTILOCHUS—*A Young Gentleman of Thebes, and Lover of Janassa.*
ASIUS—*An Apothecary.*
OTUS—*A Slave.*
OTHER SLAVES AND SERVANTS.
HELEN—*Wife to Laodamus.*
JANASSA—*Their Daughter.*

The Scene lies in, and near, the house and garden of Laodamus.

The time comprehends the space of two days.

ACT I.

SCENE I.—*A field. A beech-tree with a seat under it.*

(*Enter* ANTILOCHUS *and* MELAS, *meeting* PANTHUS.)

MELAS. Good-morrow, Panthus. I am glad to see you on your legs again, even with two others to help them.

PANTHUS. I thank you, Melas. Give me your help a moment to seat myself under this beech, for I am somewhat wearied. Gently! gently! Take care of that left leg: the gout has swell'd the bone. Oh! oh!—don't touch my knees; and don't gripe my hand. Stay—stay—you must not touch that elbow!—Oh! my loins! Hah! murder!—hah! that shoulder! Merciful heavens! my back will break open!—A—h!—a—h! Thank you—thank you.—A—h!

MELAS. Well, you are down at last. Now tell me, Panthus, what several diseases are these that have, with such anatomical skill, seized upon every joint and member of your body. First for your leg;—but that you say is gout;—let us ascend to the knees; what ailment have you lodged there?

PANTHUS. Gonagra—Gonagra—curs'd Gonagra! I have not been on my knees to the Gods for these twenty years.

MELAS. And pray, how long hath Gonagra tenanted that part of your building, good Panthus?

PANTHUS. Oh! Jupiter!—for these five years have I been tortured with it.

MELAS. Ho! ho! Then there were fifteen in which you might have bent your knees to the Gods, and did not. But go on.—To the hands,—what joke-crackers have you there?

PANTHUS. Chiragra! cursed Chiragra!—My fingers are

nothing but chalk-sticks.—Oh Apollo! Apollo!—how have I sacrificed to thee,—and thou hast not helped me! But Fate is stronger than the Gods! Ah!—

MELAS. I dare say you think yourself very unfortunate. But go on. . . . What with the elbow?

PANTHUS. Onagra—horrid Onagra! I used to touch the harp a little, but that's all gone now. In my shoulder for ever sits damn'd Omagra, gnawing me to the bone:—and in my back, hellish Lumbago!—Oh! Gods! why have ye made man to be thus miserable?

MELAS. And dost thou really think such trifles as these ought to make a man miserable?—Are they not besides of thy own seeking?—Hast thou not, in thy youth, and in thy vigorous middle age, been a sitter at feasts?—a roarer among the mirthful over the wine-cups?—and a companion to midnight debauchees?—What couldst look for?

PANTHUS. Indeed 'tis o'er-true! Oh!—Ah!—But yet, methinks, for having smack'd a little of the honey, one should not be stung so damnably.

MELAS. Panthus, thou art in a mist,—a cloud of ignorance. Neither was thy past pleasure honey, nor are thy present distempers stings, wouldst thou but consider them aright.—Antilochus, do thou attend to this:—for though thou mayst be an excellent musician and poet, as I dare say thou art,—yet art thou, I fear me, but little of a philosopher, or thou wouldst not suffer that silly passion, love, to weave his web in thy brain, and catch thy senses like flies.

ANTILOCHUS. Indeed, I fear, sir, your censure is too justly merited. Yet shall I be glad to have my youthful ignorance made wiser by your experienced knowledge.

PANTHUS. And I should be glad if he could cure the gout. That would be worth all his philosophy, and grammar,—and your music and poetry to boot, young gentleman. What are the ten Predicaments to one such predicament as mine?—Or who would listen to the divinest music and poetry, when the gout makes him roar like twenty furies?

MELAS. Panthus,—Panthus! the gout hath crippled thy brain, as well as thy limbs. Study godlike philosophy; and then shalt thou learn to despise both pain and pleasure. In the midst of anguish, shalt thou be merry; in the tumult of joy, shalt thou be calm. Gout, colic, gonagra, chiragra,—omagra—onagra—all the tortures of disease,—and all gnawing, and burning thee at once, shall be merely things for thee to jest upon. Roasting before a slow fire, shalt thou almost burst thy sides with laughter, at the impotence of anguish on thy philosophic mind. Thou shalt rend off thy flesh, and pound thy bones in a mortar, for simple recreation.

PANTHUS. Hold thy cursed nonsense, Melas, or I shall go mad.—Hadst ever the gout?—or a right twist of lumbago in thy philosophic loins?

MELAS. No, Panthus;—for I never gorged my stomach with meats, nor inflamed my blood with wine. Divine philosophy hath been the pabulum of my soul and body. Yet, methinks, I could almost desire a good touch of colic, or gout, for a day or two, just to show thee how a true philosopher would smile at such pastime.

PANTHUS. Curse thy divine philosophy! and thy pabulum, and thy soul—and thy body, together! Oh!—Ah! my back! —my knee! Oh Gods!—If thou hast not gorged thy stomach, it is that thou hast had no meat:—and thou hast not been drunken, simply because thou hast had no drink.—Get out of my sight with thy damned philosophy:—or let my slaves pound thy skull with my crutches; and I will afterward listen to thy discourse. Oh!—Ah! I would attend thy lectures, hadst thou the gout: or if, teaching us to disregard torture, thou wouldst take thy seat on a well-heated gridiron the while. That would be philosophy to some tune. O—h!

MELAS. I tell thee, Panthus, it requires more philosophy to bear with the ignorance, and the impertinence, and the bad passions of our fellows, than to endure bodily anguish. Listen to me, and I will show thee how little this carcase of thine is worthy of thy care. What is it?—Nothing but a little blood and bones, interwoven with certain veins, arteries, and nerves.—

For your breath, 'tis but a little air drawn into your lungs, and let out again.

ANTILOCHUS (*aside*). Oh, Janassa!—thy breath is like the zephyr of heaven that sighs over fields of ambrosia!

MELAS. What dost thou say of Janassa? Dost thou know the daughter of Laodamus?—I trust thou art honest, young man.

ANTIL. I hope so too. Is the daughter of Laodamus named Janassa?

MELAS. She is. Dost thou know her?

ANTIL. I know her by report. She whom I love is named Janassa;—and when I thought upon her, I breathed forth her name.

MELAS. I shall teach thee to laugh at these follies; or thy reason shall prove untillable ground. But again I say, I trust thou art honest. I have promised to bring thee to my kind lord Laodamus, as one well fitted to instil into the tender mind of his child, the beautiful Janassa, a love for sweet music, and divine poesy; and I trust thou wilt not discredit my, perhaps, too hasty approval of thy qualities. But, as we return, I will farther question thee of thy birth and bringing up. Of Thebes, thou sayst?

ANTIL. Yes, sir; and my father's name is Paterculus. He is well known to Laodamus, yet would I wish not to be named as his son, lest the ancient enmity between them might disparage me in your lord's good grace.

MELAS. How! Were they foes,—sayst thou?

ANTIL. They were of opposite factions: no farther foes.

MELAS. Well, well. I'll question thee more anon. For the present let us proceed with Panthus. For thy body, Panthus, what—I say—is it but a little blood, bones, flesh, arteries, and other fragile earthy matter?—Thy breath, what but a little air that thou spoilest in the using? But next cometh thy mind, which was made to have the rule over thy body,—but thou hast made it thy body's slave.

PANTHUS. The furies fetch you! and your bodies,—and

your minds,—and your plaguy philosophy. Oh!—Ah! What matters it what your body is made of,—or whether you have a thousand noble minds to be kings over it, when the accursed gout will let you think of nothing but your toe, or your knee, hand, shoulder, or back?—Throw your philosophy to the first beggar; and see if he will take it instead of an obolus. Once for all, Melas, I tell thee, get rid of this cursed philosophy, which could not cure a cut finger,—much less assuage the burnings and rendings of cursëd gout. Oh!—Oh!

MELAS. Panthus, I can but laugh at thee.

PANTHUS. Oh!—Oh!—my back!—my shoulder!—Oh! Oh!

MELAS. Call'st thou that pain an evil?—Weak, silly man! Distort not thy agëd face with such unearthly grinnings. Smooth thy brow,—and compose thy horrid features to a benignant smile.

PANTHUS. Oh!—O—h!—Merciful Heavens!

MELAS. Nay—nay.—*They* heed thee not. They know well enough thy fond mistake.—Doth thy mind feel gout? No! 'tis thy poor and earth-formed carcase. Regard it not. Why— thou wilt burst thy eyes out! Take it as thou wouldst take a comfit, or a grape.

PANTHUS. Oh!—Oh!—O—h!

MELAS. Think but these tortures to be some pleasant titillation; and thou mayst smile, and bid them do their worst.

PANTHUS. Oh! O—h! mercy! mercy!

MELAS. Kind Jupiter! I never saw mortal less dignified in his sufferings!—And all for a little touch of the gout! Oh, Panthus! Panthus! had I thy pains, then shouldst thou behold the majesty of the man who laughs at agony.

PANTHUS (*hurling his crutch against the legs of* MELAS). Hell clutch thee!—thou scoffing dog!

MELAS. Oh! Oh! Oh! He has broken my leg. Oh! Oh! Help me away, good Antilochus. Help me away.—Oh! Oh!
[*Exit with* ANTILOCHUS.

PANTHUS. Oh! Oh! my arm!—my shoulder! Ha-ha-

ha-ha.—There's philosophy for you!—Ha-ha-ha-ha—(*laughing*). Here, slaves;—bring up my litter;—I will walk no farther. Ha-ha-ha-ha—(SERVANTS *enter, and begin to help him away*). Gently—gently! Reach my crutch. Ha-ha-ha —I did not know I had so good an argument to lean on. Ha-ha-ha.—How the majestic philosopher roared,—and rubbed his grammatical shins! ha-ha-ha.—Gently! gently! Oh! Ah!
[*Exeunt.*

SCENE II.—*A room in the House of* LAODAMUS.

(*Enter* LAODAMUS *and* JANASSA.)

LAODAMUS. Well—well, my child;—we'll talk more on't anon.
I am not one to bind the marriage knot
Where it would strangle love.

JANASSA.   My dear, dear father!
You ever are too kind.—If 'tis your will,
Your *earnest* will that I should lend my ear
When young Adrastus woos, I can submit;
And find a pleasure, even in that pain,
For that I act *your* pleasure. But my heart
Is not at my control. My hand, my fate,
I may resign,—and would,—at your command :—
But love will not be bid to *him*,—or *him*—
Put on, or off, as we our garments choose
For sunshine, or for rain ;—but, where he wills,
There fixes,—and there grows ;—or withers quite.

LAOD. Indeed Janassa! You are wondrous deep
In love's soft mysteries.—Nay,—blush not, girl,—
I do not chide thee. Doubtless thou hast learned
Of such things to discourse as of a *Mode—*
A *Substance—Being*, or *Not Being*,— *Words—*
*Cases—*and *Tenses—*mere indifferent things
Taught with thy grammar, logic, rhetoric ;—
And, when thou spak'st of love, it was but so
As thou hadst spoken of *a house, a lake,*
The horse of Cyrus, Alexander's wife,
A good boy,—a bad book,—Now was't not so ?

The learn'd grammarian, Melas, taught it thee,—
I know he did;—where else couldst thou have learn'd it?

JANASSA. My dearest father!—I have been too bold,
And you would shame me.—Tell me but your will,—
I ask no more.

LAOD. Janassa, thou art young,
And well mayst bid th' impatient wooer wait.
Adrastus for a year may seek thy hand:—
If then, or ere that time, thy heart shall say,
' I love Adrastus '—thou shalt be his wife;—
If not, I set thee free.

JAN. Upon my knees
I thank you, my dear father!

LAOD. Prithee up—
Thou art more grateful for a lover lost,
Than others for one gain'd. Well could I wish
For thee such husband;—for myself such son:—
Rich,—vigorous,—young—comely—and valiant—
Open, and generous, and well affined,—
And son of my old friend:—it is a match
Few maids would scoff at:—but I urge it not.
Consult with thy own heart:—and, if thou canst,
Let young Adrastus call thy father his:—
If not——but 'tis enough. Go to thy books;—
There thou mayst conjugate, nor break thy heart.
Well—well—I will not vex thee;—go thy ways—
Melas will call thee idler.

JAN. My dear sir!
Poor Melas is but just return'd,—much bruis'd,
His shin-bone batter'd to a very jelly.
He has it swath'd up with a score of cloths
Like a young infant:—but 'tis swell'd, he says,
Oh! monstrous! bigger than my waist.

LAOD. Good heavens!
How was this?—when—and where?

JAN. 'Twas done, he says,
By ruffians in the woods this very morn.

The wretches stole upon him, wrapp'd in thought,
Wandering alone in the dim forest's gloom,
Unarm'd, and unresisting. Can you not,
My dearest father, send abroad to search
The monsters out?

  LAOD.   I will, my love. Poor man!
Hath Asius seen the wound?

  JAN.   No; he is gone
To Tanagra. But Melas hath himself
Bandaged the sore. If any hidden power
Of medicine he trusts, I cannot say;—
But other hands, he vows, shall touch him not,
Nor other bandage take the place of that :—
Nor would he suffer any eye to look
On what he did,—or what he had endured.
His agony, I fear, is terrible.

  LAOD. What—did he groan, or shriek, or——
  JAN.   Oh! no--no.
Of late he much hath studied to despise
Pleasure, or pain, as things unworthy far
Of the immortal mind's regard :—talks much
Of man's true dignity,—and how the soul
Should hold the body merely as a cloak
To give it covering.

  LAOD.   A genuine Stoic!
I knew not, as it seems, but half his worth.'
I thought him a good, sound grammarian,
That had a smattering too of rhetoric,
But, otherwise, no deep philosopher.
I'm glad to find that, with so little glitter,
He yet is gold.—Hath he instructed you
In his new science?

  JAN.   I am far too weak
For such sublimities. But yesterday
I crush'd my finger till the blood flew out
In twenty different threads : I would not scream,
Yet, for the pain was dreadful, writhed, and groan'd,

And purs'd my brow, and closed my eyes,—indeed
It was a cutting pain ;—'tis easier now—
But all the while sat Melas, with a smile
Giving out maxims of philosophy.
' Conceive yourself not hurt,—and you are well.
'Tis but the body,—pay it no regard ;—
The noble mind is whole, and knows no pain.'—
And then his little finger held he up,
' *I* feel it not '—he said,—' *I* feel it not ;
Nor more shalt thou, wouldst thou forget thy hurt.'
And so on for a quarter of an hour
He lectur'd me.

  LAOD. A pleasant wag enough !
But there are many, bold as desert lions
To face their neighbours' torments,—yet turn lambs
If their own tooth but ache. Is Melas such ?
How bears he his own sufferings ?

  JAN.   Oh ! 'tis grand
To see the soul's omnipotence o'er pain !
Think but, my father, think,—his shin-bone bruised
To a mere jelly,—swell'd with agony
Big as my waist,—yet in his chair sits he
Smiling and cheerful as a pleasëd child ;—
Points to his tortur'd leg, and bids it rage ;—
And all the while breathes out philosophy,
Like sweet tones from some gentle instrument.
Oh ! it is grand, my father,—very grand !

  LAOD. I'll speak with him anon. 'Tis somewhat strange :
Hath he in aught, of late, appear'd unsound
Of mind ?—but I will see him soon.—What now ?

      (*Enter a* SERVANT.)

  SERVANT. A very strange-looking person asks to speak with you, sir.

  LAOD. Who is he ?—A gentleman ?—

  SERV. Oh no, sir ; or, if he is, he is a very odd-looking

one. His cloak is patched, and has not seen a brush for this
month past—and his———
  LAOD. Go — go — and send him in. (*Exit* SERVANT.)
   Janassa, see
What half the world esteems *the gentleman*.
They ask not, 'Is he learn'd?—accomplish'd well
In elegant arts?—of rare capacity?
Gentle—humane—generous—and true?'—
But if his cloak be of the finest cloth?—
Cut to the changeful fashion's newest freak?
Whether his sandal-clasps be brass, or gold?
Or, better still, of some rare, costly gem?—
And with this ready measure of his worth
They take his altitude. The face of Jove,
Wrapp'd in a beggar's cloak, to half mankind
Were but a beggar's:—and the foulest slave,
Wearing a diadem, would be a Jove.

     (*Enter* PHORBAS.)
Good-morrow, sir.
  PHORBAS. The just Gods smile on you!
  LAOD. Why, thine's the better greeting. Please you go
At once to that which brings you here.
  PHORBAS.   Fame speaks
Right nobly of you, sir. You have a child
For whom you seek out teachers in two arts
Of priceless value.—Sir, I am a poet,
And would be her instructor.
  JANASSA.   Dear father,
Melas already hath, in part, engaged—
Waiting but your approval—one well skill'd
In music, as in poesy. Each hour
He looks to see him here. Were it not well
This gentleman should wait a day or so
Till you have proof of that sufficiency
Which Melas warrants you?
  LAOD.   It shall be so.

For some few days, sir, please you make my house
Your dwelling-place.
  PHORBAS.   You are right noble, sir.
  LAOD. Who waits? In which time, sir, I shall well learn

    (*Enter a* SERVANT.)
Your rival's qualities, and your deserts,
Which shall be fairly balanc'd. In short time
I'll speak more fully with you ;—for the present
My books perhaps may keep you company.
Conduct this gentleman into my study ;
And see he wants for nothing.
  PHORBAS.   Sir,—the Gods
For *this* have chiefly their true worship paid,—
That they do give us all things ;—taking nought
But our poor thanks,—which I do render you.
Yet have I somewhat :—but I will not boast.
No eye hath seen it yet,—and shall not see
Save only yours,—but at a fitter time.
Right noble sir, adieu.—'Twill fire you, sir.

  LAOD. Good-morrow to you. I shall look for much
To answer my expectance. [*Exeunt* PHORBAS *and* SERVANT.
  JANASSA.   This poor man
Stands not in your approval, sir, I'm sure.
  LAOD. I have not rung him yet,—but much I fear
He hath more lead than silver. If his brain
Be lean as are his ribs, his verse shall be
All lines,—lines,—nought but lines. There are such poets,—
And much bepraised too of a class of men,—
Whose verses are like cobwebs in the grass ;—
Spun only in fine weather,—very pure,—
Most delicately fine,—most truly wrought,—
But substanceless, and flimsy as a dream.—
They glitter in the sunshine ;—in the shade
Become invisible ;—from end to end
Are shaken if a breath but blow on them.
And, for these cobwebs, are there critic-flies,

Who deem them produce of ethereal looms ;
And thereupon do make a mighty buzz
Among the lines, and cry—' How beautiful !
How fine !—how pure !—we cannot break away—
How fascinating !—and how *very* strong !
Look to our legs and wings !—if they bind *us*,
Let none presume to touch them, and go free !'
And so on will they buzz and bounce about,—
Till comes a shower that drowns the critic-fly,
And breaks the web forever.

  Jan.   And then comes
Another spider, and another fly—
I know 'twas in your mouth.—

  Laod.   It was so, girl ;
For here's the spider hopes you'll be his fly.

  Jan. And so I will,—and fly away from him. (*Going.*)

     (*Enter* Adrastus.)

  Adras. Stay, stay, Janassa ;—for one moment stay.
I crave your pardon, sir,—pray bid her stay.

  Laod. Janassa, stay, or go—as is your will.

  Jan. I thank you, dearest father ;—so adieu.
Adieu, Adrastus,—I can ne'er be yours.

  Laod. Tell Melas I'll be with him presently ;
And let a slave go summon Asius here.
Philosophy is madness, push'd to this ;—
And must so be dealt with.

  Jan.   I'll send this instant. [*Exit.*

  Adras. What crime is mine, sir, that you 'bate me thus
In your esteem ?

  Laod.   No crime, Adrastus, none.
Listen a moment, and I'll tell you all.

  Adras. You might command, sir,—force her, by the law,
To be my wife, if so far went your will
To serve me.

LAOD.   By the law, we might do much
That, by our conscience, we're forbid to do.
And I must say, young man, it argues ill
In one impatient thus of all restraint,
That he would seek to use the father's arm
To place the child in bonds.

    ADRAS.   Sir, 'tis my love
That goads me on to madness.

    LAOD.   Love seeks not
Its pleasure in the loved one's misery.
Say rather 'tis your rage, revenge, or pride,
For that she smiled not, when you deign'd to smile
And honour her with love.   Had she then stoop'd
To your first offer, you'd have thought her cheap ;
And turn'd away to look for costlier goods ;
But, since she prized herself above your price,
You think her priceless.—I have been your friend
And help'd you in your suit :—make me not fear
That I have help'd th' unworthy.—In few words,—
Janassa's heart returns not yet your love ;—
Her hand shall not be forced.—If, in one year,
You thrive not better, she shall be releas'd
From farther importunity.   Till then,
Lay gentle siege, and win her if you can.

    ADRAS. Her mother, sir, is earnest in my suit ;
And you *were* friendly.

    LAOD.   And remain so still,
While you remain deserving.   That's our bond.
I'm friendly while you're honest.—Alter that,
And you shall cancel all that binds our hearts,
And break all covenant loose.—I wish you well ;
And will well aid you in love's soft blockade,—
But not in fury's storm.—And now adieu.
You seem but little pleas'd ;—yet, think upon't,
And you shall say 'tis right.

    ADRAS.   I must submit.

    LAOD. Then do it with a grace.   The slave submits,

When the whip threatens;—the free man submits,
When reason bows him to't;—yet so submits
That it seems not submission, but free will.
Be yours such. So adieu. [*Exit.*

    ADRAS.   Must I submit?—
I'll have a reason for't. The bull submits
His strong neck, and falls helpless as a lamb:—
But 'tis the axe compels him. Till he's down,
Beware his horns.—I am not struck as yet,
And will not bow.—By fair play, or by foul,
I'll have her; spite of him,—and her,—and all.
By Jupiter I'll have her!—I submit? [*Exit.*

END OF THE FIRST ACT.

ACT II.

SCENE I.—*The apartment of* MELAS.

(MELAS *on a couch, with his right leg bound up to a prodigious bulk.* JANASSA *sits near him, with a book in her hand.*)

    JANASSA (*laying down the book*). Indeed, sir, 'tis in vain.
My mind knows not
That which my eyes do read. How can I think
Of Nouns, and Cases, Verbs, and Adjectives,
When still I look upon that tortur'd limb;
And feel by sympathy, the pangs you feel,
But will not own?

    MELAS.   Now, prithee child, go on.
These pangs are our derision. 'Tis the soul—
But here's your father.

(*Enter* LAODAMUS.)

                    Sir, I cannot rise
To do you courtesy,—so pray you sit.
This worthless leg doth chain me to my seat,
Spite of th' immortal mind.

LAOD. I grieve to see it.
But, gracious Heaven!
JAN. Oh! Is't not terrible?
LAOD. It is most fearful.
JAN. Asius is returned
And hastens hither. Oh! he comes. Good sir!
(*Enter* ASIUS.)
Such a most dreadful case!—Well may you look!

ASIUS. Oh! Great Apollo! what do I behold!
Good-morrow to you, sir;—lady, good-morrow.
(*Aside to* LAOD.) It is a mortal case.

LAOD. I fear'd it, sir.

ASIUS. How do you, Melas? Have you made your will?
I am not one to joke where death is by.
Your hours are few: bethink you of your end.

MELAS. What think'st thou, Asius, of th' immortal mind?

ASIUS. That what's immortal shall for ever live.

MELAS. Dost think the mind exists within this clay?

ASIUS. Yes, certainly.

MELAS. Then what is death to me?
I live,—and shall live. What great matter is't
If here, or elsewhere?

ASIUS. That's the priest's affair,
Or yours:—the body is my care. Come, sir;—
Compose yourself while I shall search the wound.

MELAS. Hold, sir—hold off.—No hand shall touch that limb
If 'tis my fate to live,—I live:—if not, I die.
Dost think that Providence can need thy aid
To cure me if it wills it?—Or, if Death
Be summon'd hither, will he slink away
At thy head-shaking?—Surely men are mad,
To think a dose of rhubarb can annul
What Fate hath said shall be!—Think well of this:
And quit thy impious trade;—and get thee home;
And cultivate thy garden honestly:—

Pray to the Gods ;—and after wisdom seek ;—
And make divine philosophy thy guide,
And live to virtue.

Asius (*to* Laod.). Sir, a word with you. Your preceptor's mad, sir :—essentially mad. You perceive he laughs equally at pain, death, and the doctor. An undoubted madness, sir! I make it a fixed rule in my practice, that he who sets up for philosophy must be mad. Look at him, sir. He has taken again to his book with as much indifference to pain, as if his leg were the leg of the table ; and those monstrous contusions merely knots in the wood. The disease of the mind fights with the body's disease, and overcomes it.— The case is mortal, sir.

Laod. I fear it is. Have you no remedy to minister to hope,—if not to pain?

Asius. It shall be tried, if 'tis your pleasure, sir. We will bind him down,—forcibly uncover his leg and examine the wound. If he resists us, a few stripes will quickly make him yield. A sound flogging is an excellent thing for a mind unsound.—Provide us ropes, and scourges, and I'll answer for the event. His death, you know, sir, is unavoidable ; and why may he not, therefore, as well die in our fashion as his own? 'Tis common, sir.

Laod. I cannot consent to this. We will try him again. You shall learn from him the manner of the accident, and the extent of the injury : from this judge what course it were best to take regarding diet, physic, sleep, and so on :—and meantime, for a day or two, we will wait and see the event.

Melas. Th' immortal spirit spurns the earthly shell!

Asius. You hear, sir. Most indubitably mad!

Laod. Come now and hear his story. (*They return to* Melas.) My good Melas! It lives yet in our hope that, if not for your own sake, yet for ours, who suffer in your sufferings, you will somewhat soften down the austerity of your Stoicism ; and permit your wound to be searched, and, if there be in drugs or herbs such balm, its agonies to be mitigated. But, for the present, all that we ask of you is only to relate to us how this dreadful calamity befel you, and to detail to us the full nature and extent of the injury; and this we know you will not refuse to our loves.

MELAS. Immortal Gods! What is a leg,—an arm,— Nay the whole body, that the noble mind Should therewith vex itself!—But, for your loves,— If truly in my memory it yet live, And be not with like trifles mix'd and lost, I will this foolish thing unfold to you.

ASIUS. Methinks, Melas, that had my leg, on any occasion, been crushed to a mummy, I should have retained a very clear recollection of it, though I had lived a thousand years after. But make haste, or you may not live to finish the story. I would gladly help you to longer life; but he that will fall on his sword, must expect to be pricked. I am sorry for you. Go on. I will place my finger on your pulse, that I may give you warning when the last stroke is at hand.

MELAS. Ay! place thy finger there,—and feel how true, How firm, the dying Stoic's pulse.—How is't? Is consternation there?—or grief—or pain?—

ASIUS. One—two—three—four—five—six—seven—eight. By the son of Latona! 'tis the oddest death-pulse I ever felt. (*To* LAOD.) Sir, it comes as strong and regular as the strokes of a smith's hammer;—and his hand is as cool as a vestal's! This will be a very extraordinary and curious decease,—I am happy to have an opportunity to witness it.—A very odd pulse! Now go on, sir.

MELAS. You know the forest northward of the town. There 'tis my wont to take my morning's walk, Breathe the pure air, and with my soul converse On happiness, and misery,—pleasure—pain— Good—evil—virtue—and the general state Of man,—his twofold life,—his birth, and death.—

ASIUS. And very pleasant speculations are they; especially the two last.—One—two—three—four—a most odd pulse! Some singular appearances after death, no doubt. Sir, I shall examine your diaphragm with particular attention. Pray go on.

MELAS. There, as this morn I walk'd, four ruffians came;
Seiz'd;—in a moment hurl'd me to the ground;—
Tied to four separate trees my separate limbs,
And bade me answer them.

    JANASSA.   Is it not horrid?

    LAOD. It is indeed, my love.

    MELAS.   'Is pain,' quoth one,
'An evil? Thou'rt a Stoic;—answer us.'—
To him I answer'd,—' Try it on yourselves,
And you shall judge.'—But then again he spake,
'Is pain an evil?—Answer for thyself—
Or on *thee* will we prove it!'—To him then
These words I said: 'The pure immortal mind
Knoweth no pain;—'tis the dull body's lot,
And, so, unworthy of the mind's regard.
Imagine 'tis not pain,—and you're not pain'd:—
What is to all men common, good and bad,—
Can never be an evil.'—At that word,
A hideous blow upon my leg he dealt,
And question'd me again. I, all unmoved,
Again replied the same;—and he again,
With his huge, knotted club, upon my leg
Rain'd down a long-continued shower of blows
Till his arm fail'd him,—and for ever ask'd
'Is pain an evil?' But I answer'd him
With cool words, and with smiles. Thereat incens'd,
He swore to end me; and against my head
Prepar'd a savage stroke: but still I smiled,
And bade him strike. At this, asham'd, he stopp'd;
And begg'd forgiveness on his bended knees;
And bandaged up my crush'd and shatter'd limb,
And homeward bore me;—shook me by the hand,
And said he would himself become a Stoic.
This is the whole.—Now do not ask me more;
But let me to the garden be borne forth,
That I may feel the sun and pleasant air,
And meditate at peace.

LAOD. Were not your bed
The better place, good Melas?

MELAS. For the sick,
Or weak in mind, or body. I am strong;
My soul is vigorous, and would be abroad,
Discoursing with all nature. Pray you, sir.

LAOD. Who waits?—
(*Enter a* SERVANT.)
Come four of you, and bear this gentleman with all care into the garden. [*Exit* SERVANT.

ASIUS. Now, Melas, once again do I most solemnly warn you——

MELAS. Asius, forbear.—Why threaten me with death,
Who hate him not,—but rather this vile breath,
Which holds th' immortal spirit in dull clay,
That else would mount, and soar thro' space away.

(*Enter four* SERVANTS.)
Now bear me off. (*They carry him out.*)

LAOD. Be gentle, my good fellows.
I'll follow you erelong. Go thou with them,
And still admonish them to gentleness.
Then come to me again. [*Exit* JANASSA.

ASIUS. I never saw a more determined madness;—and he hath taken to rhyming too. How long hath that frenzy been on him? 'Tis one of the very worst symptoms.

LAOD. I never heard it till this moment. We have a poor poet come to our house this morning, and Melas hath, I am told, held some discourse with him. Perchance he merely quoted somewhat that he had read.

ASIUS. Depend on't, sir, the breath of that poor poet hath infected him. The Plague is not more contagious than this disorder. One lucky rhymer will give the disease to a hundred, who shall straight come out with their hearts, and their darts, —their dreams—their streams—their dark eyes—their groans and sighs—till you would think Parnassus merely a place for sickly youths to go a caterwauling in. This very morning have

I been chastising a knave of a boy who hath this cursed itch, and must for ever be scratching. I caught the scoundrel in the very act of scribbling, when I had entrusted to him the compounding of a most invaluable medicine, the preparation of which would have found him ample employment for a summer's day. Sir, in that most unheard-of remedy are there no less than two hundred and fifty-three drugs, and simples of sovereign efficacy. Yet the knave had got to his old trick. There stood he, with the pestle in one hand, and the pen in the other, arranging an imagined discourse in verse,—a sort of lecture, sir, on disease. I flogg'd the puppy soundly, and took his trash from him. You never saw such stuff. I have it in my pocket, if you would like to look at it.

LAOD. Poor boy! I fear you dealt somewhat harshly with him. The whip, if used at all, might perhaps have better been reserved for worse crimes than bad rhyming. But let us see his verses.

ASIUS. Sir, I flogg'd him for the love I bore him. A broken limb may be cured, and the man may grow rich after it:—a child may fall into the deepest well, and yet live to an old age; —but an unhappy youth once thoroughly infected by the madness of rhyming, must live poor, and despised,—and die raving. 'Tis a horrid thing, sir: and the only chance of cure is a sort of perpetual blister, kept open by the rod, till the venom is evacuated. A horrid thing, sir! Here are the verses.

LAOD. Pray read them, sir.

ASIUS (*reading*). 'Disease in all its branches will I search;' Do but mark the rascal, how confident he is.

    'Disease *in all its branches* will I search,
    And challenge death to leave me in the lurch.'

You understand, sir, this is a sort of lecture that he supposes himself about to begin.

LAOD. I perceive the drift. Pray you go on.

ASIUS (*reading*).
    'But, as the time allow'd us craves despatch,
    I'll simply touch upon the heads of each ;—
    That is,—just shew the most important features
    Of all diseases, that assail all creatures.'

LAOD. He allows himself scope enough.
ASIUS. Oh! 'tis an arrant knave, sir. Hark now.
'But to be brief. You will soon, I flatter me,
Learn from my mouth the science of anatomy.'
LAOD. A neat rhyme that—flatter me,—'natomy.
ASIUS. 'The various uses of each various member,
Which I'll explain as fast as I remember.
On fevers,—brain-disease,—I'll next discourse;
Colic, and jaundice follow them in course;
Phlebotomy and measles next I'll mention'—
You see, sir, the ignorant varlet classes phlebotomy among diseases! I wonder he did not include the doctor also.—The puppy!
LAOD. 'Tis wonderful indeed.
ASIUS. 'Phlebotomy and measles next I'll mention—
Coughs—colds—catarrhs—lumbago, and consumption.
On scald-head—scurvy—and St. Vitus' dance,
Some observations next I shall advance:
Then, erysipelas and tooth-ache spoke on,
Investigate the cause why bones are broken.'
This last line, sir, he had just written down; and, with his head uplifted, and his right arm expanded and waving with inexpressible dignity, he stood spouting forth to the drug-bottles, when, coming suddenly behind him, I took him a cuff on the cheek that shook pen and pestle from his hands, and sent him rolling on the floor, confounded and chop-fallen.

LAOD. Believe me, sir, that was rough handling. I fear you hurt him.

ASIUS. Not in the least: he is used to such things, sir. But, sir, 'twas the choicest fooling. I have laughed twenty times at it since. There he stood in all his pomp,—and with a most swaggering accent,—Oh! 'twas admirable!
'Next, erysipelas and toothache spoke on
Investigate the cause why bones are broken'——
Here is one cause, said I, and knock'd him down. Oh Apollo! 'twas the choicest fooling! ha—ha—ha!

LAOD. A witty stroke, sir, no doubt; tho', like some others, somewhat rough. Take heed that he do not some day favour you with a repartee. Boys, you know, sir, have a trick of becoming men; and these witty jokes are debts that most people like to scratch out of their books. But now, sir, for my poor friend Melas :—what course shall be pursued with him?

ASIUS. Sir, 'tis quite indifferent as to what measures be followed. Could I inspect the wound—perhaps—but I know not. —— 'Tis a case of horrid fracture,—laceration,—and mental hallucination. Physic cannot touch it, sir. Die he must.

(*Enter a* SERVANT.)

SERV. A young gentleman, sir, waits, whom Melas bade me name to you as the instructor for your daughter.

LAOD. Oh, very well—the young poet and musician. Pray bring him in. Hath Melas seen him even now, said you?

SERV. He has this moment parted from him.

LAOD. Let him come in. (*Exit* SERVANT.) I grieve, Asius, that you have so little hope. (*Enter* ANTILOCHUS.) Good-morning to you, sir. Your name is, I think, Antilochus?

ANTIL. The same, sir :—and much devoted to your service.

LAOD. Somewhat of the youthfullest, sir, to be already master of the double lyre.

ANTIL. My pretensions, sir, stand at a far humbler station. Something I know, which I can teach; but more have still to learn. What is poor in my knowledge shall, I hope, be enriched by my diligence.

LAOD. I'll speak with you anon. Amuse yourself, the while, with this group. 'Tis from the chisel of Phidias.

ANTIL. I thank you, sir. Pray use no ceremony.

LAOD. (*aside*). Where have I seen that face? (*To* ASIUS) You were about to speak, sir.

ASIUS. I say, die he must, unless, by sacrifice and prayers, some one of the heavenly powers be moved in his behalf. I will go offer a cock to Esculapius. To-morrow I'll call again: and meantime let him even do as he lists. If, however, death seems at hand, command, I pray you, that I be instantly summoned,—for his decease must be singular and interesting. I should like much to open him. A very singular case!

LAOD. Pray offer a dozen cocks to Esculapius if you think that of any use. Cure him, and I care not by what means. You shall be prodigally rewarded.

ASIUS. Sir, you are truly noble. What art can do shall assuredly be done:—and that rather for the love I bear to you, sir, than from the hope of any reward. Yet I know your generosity will not be denied. Sir, your most humble servant.

LAOD. Asius, adieu,—and think of us, I pray you.

ASIUS. Most earnestly. Singular case! [*Exit.*

LAOD. How like you that, sir?

ANTIL. Truly, sir, it pleases my eye much: but, having no skill in the art, I profess not to have much judgment.

LAOD. A most unusual modesty, young man: for I have ever observed that, of the works of the painter, the sculptor, the musician, and the poet, almost every man thinks himself an infallible judge; and will allow of no appeal from his sentence. I dare say you have found it so.

ANTIL. Indeed, sir, 'tis but true: and, with the smallest capacity to judge, is commonly found the greatest pretension.

LAOD. I hear from Melas, sir, much commendation of your parts: and my own brief observation consents to his report.— You will find in my daughter much quickness of apprehension, together with a gentleness that sinks speedily under reproof;— which, as I think she will not often deserve, so I incline to hope you will be sparing to bestow. I will send her to you.

[*Exit.*

ANTIL. What will she say?—This poor disguise not long
Can hide me from her. She will read my eyes
If I look on her:—if I turn away

She'll read me in my fearfulness :—if speak,
My voice will be informer 'gainst myself;—
And, if speak not, why then my silence speaks,
And says, 'This is a cheat.' It cannot last.
Yet I shall see her :—I shall hear her voice :—
Breathe the same air she breathes :—touch the same book ;—
Perhaps her hand :—shall speak to her ;—shall say—

(JANASSA *enters unperceived by him, and goes to the table*)

Oh! heavens! what shall I say?—What dare I say?

JAN. (*aside*). The gentleman seems deeply wrapped in thought. Perhaps brooding over some vast poetical conception. — I almost fear to disturb him: and yet I must. (*Aloud*) Sir, I attend your leisure.

(ANTILOCHUS *turns hastily, and gazes on her in silence. She stands turning over the leaves of a book.*)

JANASSA. Shall my first lesson be in music, sir,
Or poetry?

ANTIL. Oh! both—both—both.—

JAN. Which first?
Shall I go fetch my lyre?

ANTIL. Oh! no—no—no ;
I want no other music than your voice.

JAN. He is distracted! I dare not remain.
(*She goes to the door.*)

ANTIL. Janassa! (*A pause.*) Oh! Janassa! pardon me.

JAN. Antilochus!

ANTIL. Oh, stay. Hear but one word.

JAN. I've heard too much. If you would farther speak,—
Be't to my father; for no act of mine
Shall wear a cloak to hide it from his eye.
I'll hear no more. [*Exit.*

ANTIL. You must, or I am mad. [*Exit, after her.*

SCENE II.—*The garden of* LAODAMUS: *with an arbour.*
(PHORBAS *is discovered, seated in the arbour, with his cheeks propped up on both palms, in profound study.*)

PHORBAS. 'Why let the thunders crack the ebon sky!'
That's good—that's very good—that 'ebon sky'—
But stay——
  'Why let th' immortal thunders split the rocks!'
Ah!—A—h—that's *very* grand! let us try them again.—
  'Why let the thunders crack the ebon sky!'
That certainly is fine—
  'Why let th' immortal thunders split the rocks!'
Stop—stop—I have it.
  'Why let th' immortal thunders of the Gods split,—crack
    the ebon rocks!'
Oh, Jove! Jove! Jove! that's it!—What a sound there is in that line! There is thunder in its very rolling:—and the rocks are heard to burst asunder.—Let me not lose it.—
                                                          (*He writes.*)
  'Why let th' immortal thunders of the Gods split, crack
    the ebon rocks!'
I never heard a line of such majesty! Jove—Jove! I thank thee. This one line must, *must* immortalize the poem!—Could I but make that line's fellow, the world were my own. —— Stay — stay — stay — stay — stay — stay — Jupiter! Apollo! Minerva! I see it—I see it—stay—stay—'The seas dash out the stars'—Oh! oh! what a thought is that!
  'The seas dash out the stars;—against high heaven
    earth knocks!'
It is impossible to outlive this! Great Jove! I thought not words could reach such unutterable sublimity!—Would I could die this moment!—For what is dull existence now?—Here's for the thousandth,—ay—the ten thousandth generation. What myriads of spirits will fire at this, and think of thee, O Phorbas. (*He writes.*)
  'The seas dash out the stars,—against high heaven
    earth knocks!'

Methinks I see the bright lamps washed away; I hear the jarring of a hundred continents!—How will they read together?
—I almost tremble to pronounce them:—

 'Why let th' immortal thunders of the Gods split, crack
  the ebon rocks;—
 The seas dash out the stars ——'

Stay—stay—I don't think the sense is quite clear there. It won't do to say '*let* earth *knocks*'—and yet I must have *knocks*, because of *rocks*.—Pshaw! 'tis the simplest thing in the world. I have only to scratch out *let*, and write *if*, and all is clear.

 'Why *if* th' immortal thunders of the Gods split, crack
  the ebon rocks;
 The seas dash out the stars; against high heaven earth
  knocks!'

Here, do I prophesy, shall be the touchstone on which, to the end of time, will be proved the poet's imagination. The man that feels not this, feels nothing! Its grandeur is terrible! I am interrupted.—I must go—I cannot now mingle with common men.

   (*Enter* LAODAMUS.)

LAOD. Once more, good-morning to you, sir. I trust my servants have attended to you in all things.

PHORBAS. The seas dash out the stars—against high heaven earth knocks!   [*Exit* PHORBAS.

LAOD. Then I wish heaven would open the door, and take earth in. Poor man! his wits are crazed.

   (*Enter* JANASSA.)

JAN. My dearest father, I've been seeking you.

LAOD. And you have found me. What is't you would say? Why—what's amiss, my child? You're pale as death. Hath aught alarm'd you? Are you ill?—Come, come, Speak out at once. Is our poor friend no more?

JAN. My dearest father, pray forgive me this.
I've somewhat much at heart, which I must tell you.
And yet I know not how.—For our poor friend
Be not alarm'd: I heard him even now
As I pass'd by, with some-one in debate

Within the temple's porch. What I would say,
Concerns myself, and . . . one beside.

LAOD.   What one?
Adrastus?—hath he——

JAN.   No, sir, 'tis not he.

LAOD. I must await the kindling of your lamp
To guide me in this darkness.—Come—take heart.
Now.—Let the lion forth ;—I'm on my guard.
There is a youth——

JAN.   Oh heavens, sir! do you know it?

LAOD. What! Is't so wonderful for me to know
There is a youth?—

JAN.   But, sir,—the youth I mean
Is he the same?

LAOD.   Now, prithee, child, go on,
And tell thy secret. I know nothing on't.
But, by thy pale face, and thy gleaming eye,—
Thy palpitating heart,—and quick-drawn breath,—
Thy trembling fingers,—and thy restless foot,—
I guessed that, somewhere in this lower world—
In Greece perhaps—there *might* a youth exist.
But farther I know not. Now get thee on.

JAN. Were you like common fathers, my dear sir,—
I had not dared do this.—— There is a youth—

LAOD. I thought so, girl!

JAN.   Who loves me——

LAOD.   Or says so—
Do you believe him?—But I'm sure you do.
'Tis th' only creed that, to the end of time,
Weak woman shall confide in ; tho', each day,
A thousand dupes give warning of the cheat.
But to thy story. This most loving youth—
Why art thou silent, child?

JAN.   You shame me, sir :
And may, I fear, be angry.

LAOD. Am I prone
To causeless anger?

JAN. Oh! no—no.—At Thebes
I saw him first. Oft in my morning walks
We met, but spake not. Yet at last he spake;
And then we grew acquainted; for he loved
The books I loved,—and liked the walks I liked;—
Was fond of music too, and poetry.
So morning after morning passed away;—
At last he said,—he loved me.

LAOD. Very odd!

JAN. Was it not, sir? *I* thought it *very* odd.

LAOD. Most marvellous!

JAN. Nay, now you laugh at me.
Indeed to me it seem'd——I know not how.
I had heard Adrastus say it many times,
And it displeas'd me.

LAOD. But 'twas different now.

JAN. Oh! very different!

LAOD. Well—what said you then?

JAN. I, sir?

LAOD. Yes, you. What answer did you make?

JAN. Oh! I said nothing.

LAOD. What said he to that?

JAN. He told me so again.

LAOD. Persisting dog!
What answer made you then?

JAN. I told him, sir,
To speak with you. He said he dare not do it,—
You were his father's enemy.

LAOD. Indeed!
A bitter one!—for I forget our feud,—
And knew not I'd a foe. But what's his name?

JAN. Paterculus.

LAOD. Of Athens?

JAN.   Yes. Oh heavens!
see he spake too true.

LAOD.   Is he,—you love—
Calista's son?

JAN.   His mother's name is so.
Oh! my dear father! why that heavy sigh?
Tell me but what to do, and I will do it—
Whatever be the cost.

LAOD.   Go on, my child.
What since hath pass'd between you?

JAN.   I broke off
Our conference; and bade him speak no more
What it might grieve my father to know spoken.
That morning I left Thebes—and, till to-day,
Have not beheld him.

LAOD.   That is six days back,
According to the calendar:—to love,
As many months.—And you have seen him now?

JAN. I have, sir.

LAOD.   Bid him come and speak with me.
I never was his father's foe. The world
Thought I *must* hate him :—yet in truth I loved him,
Tho' we've been strangers since——but that's all past.
How looks Calista? She was once—Pshaw! Pshaw!
Hath he his mother's face?

JAN.   I saw her once.
Somewhat he's like her,—but more handsome far.

LAOD. Well—well—well.—Where is he? let me see him.

JAN. I'll send him to you instantly.—Dear father!
My dear, dear father!

LAOD.   Go—go: get thee gone.
                              [*Exit* JANASSA.
Calista! Oh, Calista!—And thy child
May still be mine;—and mine be thine!——Hence thoughts!
I will not entertain you.——Twenty years

To vanquish you,—and *then* submit, were shame!
What have we here? (*Takes up a paper.*)
'Why if th' immortal thunders of the Gods split, crack
   the ebon rocks,
The seas dash out the stars,—against high heaven earth
   knocks.'
Why, then 'tis fair play 'twixt the heaven and the earth,—
hard knock for knock.—Poor Phorbas! this is thine.—'The
seas dash out the stars.' Then for dark nights. But what
becomes of the moon, I wonder, in all this hurly-burly?—Oh!
these happy poets!—Here comes another: but truly of a
different sort. This now, I should think, would sing of dying
swains, and cold-hearted nymphs. What brings him here?

(*Enter* ANTILOCHUS.)

A pleasant morn, sir,—is it not? How sweet
The wanton air comes thro' that woodbine bush!
Methinks, were I a poet, such a day,
And such a scene,—these flowers, and plants, and trees,
That brook,—and yon majestic deep-blue arch
That folds the globe and firmament about
As 'twere the drapery of Father Jove
Wrapping his children, and their cradle earth,—
Methinks, sir, things like these would warm my soul
To an unwonted ardour. Is't not so?
How say you, sir? Speak boldly.—Why is this?
Is aught amiss?—What would you have with me?—

ANTIL. You sent, sir, for me.

LAOD.   No—'tis some mistake.
Stay—*you* are not—and yet.——   Who bade you come?

ANTIL. Your daughter, sir.

LAOD.   Are *you* Calista's son?

ANTIL. I am, sir.

LAOD.   Let me look on you.——Oh! God!
                                                    (*A pause.*)
You love Janassa?

   ANTILOCHUS.   Oh! most fervently!

LAOD. But this disguise!—And yet I know it all.
How are your parents?

ANTIL. Well, sir.

LAOD. Once again
Let me behold you.—'Tis enough.—Go now:
In a few hours I'll speak again with you.
Go to Janassa:—tell her you have seen me.
Heaven bless thee, boy! (*embracing him*).

ANTIL. Oh! sir,—I have no words,—
But a full,—bursting heart. Heav'n guard you, sir! [*Exit.*

LAOD. Her very picture!—And the father's form,—
Some twenty years back.—Do they know of this?
But here comes other business.—Well, sweet wife?—

(*Enter* HELEN *and* ADRASTUS.)

HELEN. Laodamus, why will you vex me thus?

LAOD. How do I vex you, Helen?

HELEN. Do not ask,—
For you know well the cause.—Why is this youth,
The son of our old friend, thus, day by day,
Put off in his most honorable suit
By girlish fickleness?—Why will you, sir,
Not only not command her to this match,
But to her whimsies lend your countenance,
Upholding her in all her waywardness?
It vexes me;—I tell it you aloud,—
It vexes me.

LAOD. So do not you vex me.—
Adrastus,—not two hours back we have spoken;
And I did give you then my well-weigh'd thoughts,—
Not likely to be changed so soon.—Once more
I tell it you:—and do not hope to sway,
By importunities, or lowering looks,
My firm resolve.—Janassa's hand is free,—
To give, or to withhold.—You have a year
For gentle wooing. If she then consent,
You win her for a wife:—if she refuse,—

You never ask her more.—This is our bond;—
From which I'll 'bate no jot.—I pray you, sir,
Break not my peace with these distemper'd heats;
Nor, failing of yourself, with others league
To push me from my purpose. 'Tis in vain,—
And may be worse than vain.

  ADRASTUS.   I take my leave.
(*Aside*) But I'll have vengeance yet!   [*Exit.*

  HELEN.   'Tis mighty well!
A noble match!—and will be thrown away.—
But, nowadays, good matches are like crabs,
That everyone may gather when he likes.
'Tis mighty well!—All for a puling girl,
That knows not what she sneers at. Mighty well!
This comes of music,—logic—poetry—
Grammar—and painting,—and what not beside.
How can you hope such bright accomplishments
Can stoop to humble duty?—What know *I*
Of all these baubles?—Yet I hope I live
To as good purpose as the wisest she,
That never saw a pudding of her own.—
But 'tis in vain to speak. You are more deaf,
When 'tis your will, than adders, or stone walls;
For one *will* give an echo,—th' other bite;
But you'll do neither.—Sir, I'm vex'd with you,—
And so good-day.   [*Exit.*

  LAOD. Dear Helen, a good-day.
Janassa cannot love him;—and this bond
Will be but useless;—worse than that;—to both:
To her a clog,—a treacherous hope to him.—
But *'tis* a bond,—and shall be truly kept;—
So he keep true. No longer.—What, again?
And with a brow more lowering than before?
Then, my dear Helen, for thy sake, and mine,
I'll shun thee till thy frenzy shall grow cool.
The gardener hath left his shed unlocked;—
I'll use it.—There's a fitness too in that,—

For 'tis a tool-house,—and they'd make me one,
Could they but soften, twist, and hammer me.

(*He takes out the key; goes in, and locks the door.*)

(*Enter* HELEN, *hastily.*)

HELEN. Where is he gone?—I cannot bear it more,
And will not. I must speak my mind, or burst.
Laodamus—where are you?—

(*Enter* ADRASTUS.)

ADRASTUS. Stay—stay— stay—
Don't call again. I've glorious news to tell.

HELEN. Then tell it quickly.

ADRAS. There's a lover here.

HELEN. A what?

ADRAS. A lover :—a pernicious wretch-
A minion of Janassa's—

HELEN. Not so loud.
Come hither in the arbour.—Quickly now.—
A lover of Janassa's?—

ADRAS. Yes.—The wretch
Brought here by that old fool-philosopher
To teach your daughter music, poetry,
And other liberal arts, no doubt.—Oh Gods!
He shall not live!—he shall not live!

HELEN. Hush! hush!
You will be heard. Keep cool. How learn'd you this?

ADRAS. From your slave Otus. He o'er-heard their talk;
Heard him protest;—and her refuse his love,
Save with her father's sanction; which to gain,
She left him suddenly.

HELEN. But where was this?

ADRAS. Within the grotto, where the slave had crept,—
Seeing Janassa hastening down the walk,—
In hope to hide himself. But there came she;
And after her, in full pursuit, the wretch;

Before the tempest of whose cursëd vows
She seem'd driven in for shelter.—When she went,
There stood he in an agony of sighs,—
Tears—groans—accursed villain !—there he stood,
Awaiting her return.

  HELEN.   But where went she?

  ADRAS. Oh ! to her father,—to declare her love,
And ask his leave, no doubt ;—for, in short space,
She came again,—and placed her hand in his,—
And bade him go,—and fear not a rebuke,
For all was well. And then he kiss'd her hand,—
I'll tear his heart out,—villain ! Then he raised
His eyes and arms to heaven,—and sighed,—and went
As to his death.—And then out-pourëd she
A flood of tears,—and press'd her heart,—and cried
' Oh ! prosper him, kind Heaven !'—Needs more than this
To prove her false to me, and fool to him ?—
He shall not see yon sun set !

  HELEN.   When was this ?

  ADRAS. This very moment ;—since I left you here.
I saw the slave, with a most timorous tread,
Steal from his hiding place,—and questioned him.
He knew his secret's price, and kept it back ;
Yet shew'd enough to make me bid for it ;
And I have bought it :—and I'll use it so,
That others pay the cost.—His blood I'll have,
Tho' mine be spilt to get it !

  HELEN.   Nay—not so.

  ADRAS. By Jupiter I will !

  HELEN.   Come, come :—you're mad.
Did I believe you guilty,—but in thought,—
Of such a wickedness, I'd cast you off
For ever from my heart.—Say nought of this.
Keep cool, and quiet. Be as you have been ;—
Come, as you came ;—and go, as you have gone.—
I have a plan shall give you all you wish,
And keep your hand unsoil'd.—I'll see the slave

He can assist us much.—In half an hour,
Come to my room,—and I will tell you more.
But, once again,—keep cool.
    ADRAS.   To keep me so
Give me, tho' but a crumb, of your design,
That I may feed upon it the fierce thoughts
That prey upon my heart.
    HELEN.   The scope is this :—
The manner, yet, as shapeless as a dream.
You shall bear off Janassa :—if by stealth,
So much the better,—she'll forget it soon :—
If not,—by gentle violence; your love
Shall well excuse it to her. For her father,
He's wise in most things, but a fool in this;
And must be guided. In a little while
He'll say 'twas best so.—Let us now away.
Run all things truly, and to-morrow night,
You'll call Janassa wife. But—cool—cool—cool!
When she would catch the mouse, the cat lies still.
    ADRAS. To-morrow night!—to-morrow night! Oh heaven!
Then for immortal vengeance.—Come away.—   [*Exeunt.*
        (LAODAMUS *comes out from the shed.*)
    LAOD. Indeed!—indeed!—'Tis a right duteous wife!
A noble, and true-hearted son-in-law!
I 'must be guided'—I'm 'in most things wise,
But a mere fool in this thing.'—'If by stealth,
So much the better :—she'll forget it soon'—
Indeed! forget it!—a forgiving soul!
'If not,—by gentle violence :'—Ho! ho!—
By *gentle* violence.—How very kind!
Good shed, I thank thee.—And to-morrow night!—
No doubting, half-work this. They strike at once.
And 'cool—cool—cool!—when she would catch the mouse,
The cat lies still.'—Why, thou'rt a duteous wife!
And thou'rt a generous son!—Our bond is broke.
Thou art no son of mine!—But I must haste :
The cat's upon the watch.—I'll place a mouse
Shall this time, if I err not, catch their cat!   [*Exit.*
        (END OF THE SECOND ACT.)

ACT III.

SCENE I.—*A library in the House of* LAODAMUS.
(ANTILOCHUS *stands looking at certain books.*)

ANTIL. I know not what I look at :—yet I look ;
Toiling to cheat the time.—'Tis all in vain !
I force my eye to pore upon the words,
But cannot read them ;—for they melt away ;
And, in their room, I see Janassa's face
Smiling—how beautiful !—as then she smiled,
And blush'd—and trembled, when she spake that word
Which, while I live, will dwell within my ear
Like an undying echo.—Now he comes—
What is my fate ?—Orsilochus is true,
And would not slander me.—Oh ! patience, heaven !

(PHORBAS *enters hastily: snatches up a pen and begins to write.*
ANTILOCHUS *turns again to the books.*)

PHORBAS. Exquisite !—exquisite ! I never had a more sprightly thought.
'The big and burly elephants
 Shall dance about—shall dance about,—
 The big and burly elephants
 Shall dance about—about.'—
'Fore heaven ! 'tis absolutely the neatest thing I know ! What gaiety in the music of the numbers ! 'The big and burly elephants'—Hark ! hark !—the very words sing of themselves.
(*Singing.*)
'The big—and bur—ly el—ephants
 Shall dance a—bout ;—shall dance a—bout.'
Why, the lines dance !—they dance—they dance.—I see them—I hear them—They would make the side of a house dance with them. Ha !—ha !
(*Singing and dancing.*)
'The big and bur—ly el—ephants
 Shall dance a—bout—shall dance about—
 The big—and bur—ly—el—ephants
 Shall dance a—bout—about.'
(*In dancing backwards he falls against* ANTILOCHUS.)

Antil. I am glad to see you so merry, sir;—but you have crushed my toe!

Phorbas. Heed not your toe.—Here—here are ten of mine. Jump on them,—crush them—dance upon them.—What is a toe, or a foot, compared to the feet in this verse? Hark, sir— hark!
> 'The big and burly elephants
> Shall dance about—shall dance about—
> The big and burly elephants
> Shall dance about—about.'

Ha! sir—what think you of that?

Antil. Really, sir, 'tis very surprising.

Phorbas. And the music of the metre,—did you mark that?

Antil. Sir, 'tis so plain that a child might sing to it;—and with twenty different tunes one after the other.

Phorbas. Ha! my dear and excellent friend! you have said it;—and you have an undoubted, and most perfect judgment.— And did you note how the bulky loftiness, and buoyancy of the sentiment is, as it were, borne in upon the ear by the sprightly and jocund vastness of the verse?—that resemblance, sir, between the expression, and the thing expressed, which makes them seem mere counterparts of each other.—I am sure you apprehend me, sir.

Antil. Most perfectly.

Phorbas. My dear sir!—Do but note it, and you shall see in the dancing of the numbers, the bulky frolickings of these sublime and stupendous animals.— Hark, sir—
(*Singing.*)
> 'The big and bur—ly el—ephants
> Shall dance a—bout—shall dance a—bout.'

Antil. Sir, I see them as clear as the sunshine. The conception of the subject is most certainly novel and surprising.

Phorbas. Excellent young man! I am enraptured with your genius. Let us be for ever friends! And you are a poet too.—You shall show me your verses some time: but just at the present it might interrupt us; and I am just going to give you a glimpse of my design in this work; which I intend to be no slap-dash, off-hand matter, sir,—but a thing for posterity, sir,—for posterity.

ANTIL. Sir, your condescension is most flattering.

PHORBAS. Why, truly, it is not to everyone that I should shew this favor. The world, sir, is filled with common, vulgar souls; and with such, we spirits of the higher order cannot mix. But in your countenance, sweet youth, I behold the poet's raptur'd eye;—and my soul leaps, as it were, and clasps yours in its arms.—We will live together.—You shall daily see my verses, and I yours.—I have extraordinary things to shew, sir. Oh! Heavens!—but I'll say no more. You shall judge:—you shall judge.—This very day, sir, have I composed two lines that will outlast eternity. They'll shake you, sir—they'll shake you horribly. But not now. And yet—but no—it might be too much for you;—and we must speak now of the singular piece before us.—Now mark me, sir.

ANTIL. It is impossible that I should not.

PHORBAS. Ah! sir—the force of genius! The world little knows what it loses by neglecting genius. But it will not always neglect it.—No, sir.—In this little work have I shadowed forth the time when all men shall be poets:—when trades—professions—arts of government—wars—contracts—*all* shall be no more: but man shall live in the fertile plains, and on the majestic mountains; feeding upon the fruits of the earth, and drinking of the limpid rills;—when to the rising sun they shall chant their exulting hymns;—and with hymns shall sing him to his bed of repose:—when all men shall be gifted with immortal poesy; and all women shall be beauteous, —and chaster than snow.—Ah! sir, I see it moves you.

ANTIL. That were indeed a most blessed time!

PHORBAS. 'Twill come, sir—it will come.

ANTIL. And at that time it is, I presume, that the elephants——

PHORBAS. Oh! gifted youth! thou see'st it—thou see'st it. —To be sure!—

'Then shall the elephant dance—the sea-horse sing——'
But stop, sir;—I will give you a morsel.—After a brief, but lofty induction, setting forth the new and beautiful state of things to be,—I go on thus :

> 'The big and burly elephant
> Shall dance about—shall dance about
> The big and burly elephant
> Shall dance about, about.'

Now, sir, mark the change of the numbers. Mark!
' Then shall the elephant dance,—the sea-horse sing.—
Then shall great whales leap up—and make sweet jargoning.
Then shall the mammoth shake his sides; the huge mastodon smile,—
The sleek rhinoceros laugh outright, his sorrows to beguile—
Sea snakes, and happy toads'—now mark this well.

(*Enter* LAODAMUS.)

ANTIL. Oh! my dear sir!

LAOD. Stay—stay awhile.

PHORBAS. Oh! ye good heavens!—Sweet youth, I'll come again :—
You shall not lose it. Tarry but awhile—
I'll not forget you. [*Exit.*

ANTIL. What is my fate?

LAOD. I'm satisfied in all.
Orsilochus reports you to my wish ;—
Somewhat beyond my hope,—though that was much.
You say your parents know of this your love?

ANTIL. They know I love her: but, of more than that,
I dared not speak. But, Ah! to call her theirs,
Would be a joy almost as great as mine.

LAOD. How know you that?

ANTIL. 'Twas ever in their mouths
How beautiful she was ;—how good,—how pure—
How bright a jewel for some happy man—
How blest to call her child!

Laod.   Well—well.—Take this— (*Giving a letter*)
Post with all haste to Thebes. Bring their consent ;
I think you have Janassa's,—and then mine
Shall give her to you.—For all other things,
As dowry, and so forth,—take no account,—
She's heiress to my wealth. Of this great haste
Ask nothing now :—suffice it that I say,
If all prove happy, by to-morrow night
Thou'lt call Janassa wife.—Now hence—nay—nay—
                               (Antilochus *kneels.*)
    Antil. I can say nought but, thank you—thank you, sir.
    Laod. Then say't another time.—Go—get you gone.
                                    [*Exit* Antilochus.
Now for the slave. Who waits ?
    Servant (*entering*).   Your pleasure, sir ?
    Laod. Send the slave Otus here.   [*Exit* Servant.
                                     What moles are we,
Even when we see,—or *think* we see, the farthest !
Philosophers will tell you how this earth
Was form'd !—how long 't has lived,—and when 'twill die ;—
They tell the cause of earthquakes, and of tides ;—
And how the worn-out moon grows young again ;—
And whence the winds arise ;—and why the stars
For ever wheel, and wheel, yet never fall :—
Of everything they pierce the hidden cause
With wisdom like to Gods ;—yet a dull knave
Hiding his foulness with a holy veil,
Shall cheat them to the beard.—Come hither, sir,

                (*Enter* Otus.)
And to my questions give direct reply.
Whence come you now ?—No pausing.—Answer straight.
    Otus. From my kind mistress, and your lady, sir.
    Laod. What was't you spake of ?—Make reply at once.
One lie will gender soon a hundred more,
To fight together, till they fall on you
And make you rue it.—What was your discourse ?

OTUS. I don't know what to say, sir. If I am false to my lady, she will punish me ;—and if I am true to her, you will punish me.

LAOD. Be true then to the truth and honesty ;—
'Tis the best master.—For a moment stop :—
Your next step brings you to a smooth, plain road,
Or throws you down a precipice.—Look well !

OTUS. I know not what to think, or say—or do. I would gladly do what is best, if I knew how.

LAOD. To do what's best, do ever what is just ;—
Not what will profit most. In every heart
There is a guide that points the path to right,—
A fair broad road ;—but in the head there sits
A puzzled, calculating fiend, that still
Directs to some by-lane,—some shorter cut—
Not easy to re-tread—yet hard to keep—
And ending in a quagmire. In your head
That fiend is whispering,—in your heart that guide
Is calling you aloud.

OTUS.   Most honor'd sir !
I pray you pardon me.

LAOD.   Then speak at once.
No harm shall come to you : nor, from your words,
Disgrace or punishment on those you serve,
But must no longer serve,—or serve for me,
To help me thwart their treachery. Come, come—
Speak out.—Adrastus with my wife is leagued
Against my child and me,—and you're their tool.
Can you deny this?

OTUS. It is all too true.

LAOD. Which party is the guilty?—which the wronged,
In this foul plot?

OTUS. Oh! I am very guilty, sir. Forgive me, and I will serve you faithfully while I live.

LAOD. Wilt thou be true to me ?

OTUS. To death, most honor'd sir.

Laod. Then mark me. You are master of their plot,
And I must be so :—not to punish them ;—
But that I'd catch them in their own sly snare
To laugh at them, and let them go again.
Be true to me,—and the third morning hence
You shall be free ;—and whatsoever bribe
They offer you, that sum shall doubled be,
So you to me prove faithful. To be false,
I think you dare not. Now—speak out at once.

Otus. Why, my honor'd lord, for the matter of out-speaking there is but mighty little for me to say. All what my honor'd lady, your wife, and the young gentleman, Master Adrastus, wish for to go about for to contrive is that my young lady, your daughter, should be married to the young gentleman, Master Adrastus, who is certainly a very comely and generous young gentleman, and loves my honor'd young lady, your daughter, mightily :—and my honor'd lady, your wife——

Laod. Go on—go on—and how's this to be done?

Otus. Why, my honor'd master, they say it will be the simplest, and most harmless, and virtuousest thing in the world. My honor'd lady, your wife, is to procure of a certain wise woman a certain sort of a kind of a drug, which she will put into my young lady, your daughter's wine when she goes up to bed; and that, of a surety, will put her into a sweet sleep in the twinkling of an eye.

Laod. And what then?

Otus. Why, what is then to be done, sir, but that the young gentleman, Master Adrastus, is to carry my young lady, your daughter, away in a coach, which I am to have at hand, and he is to take her to a priest, and so be married to her before she is quite awake.

Laod. Ay truly ! that would hardly be legal.

Otus. They say it would, sir ;—for that many people are married that way when, if they had had their eyes open, they would have kept single.

Laod. And in one sense that may be true. Yet, having

married with their eyes shut, it would perhaps be better never to open them. But is this all? Are you not bribed to listen again to what may pass between my daughter and the young gentleman you saw with her?

OTUS. Truly, my honor'd master, I am. The young gentleman, Master Adrastus, hath promised me twenty drachms if I can overhear aught of concernment:—but I will not listen nevertheless.

LAOD. For which, according to our bond, I must owe you forty drachms. I suppose.—Now Otus;—*I* have also a plot which you must communicate to your employers; and which will, I think, tempt them to alter theirs. What it is, I am not yet quite perfect : but before night I will speak again with you —and the plot that I shall then draw you out, you must pretend to have overheard in a discourse between the young lady and gentleman. You understand me?

OTUS. Oh ! yes, sir—-very well.—Cheat upon cheat.

LAOD. But theirs for knavery, and mine for right.

OTUS. Ha ! sir.—That's just what my honor'd lady, your wife, said to me, to persuade me to help them away with my honor'd young lady, your daughter.

LAOD. Ay, indeed ! And who was going about to cozen her?

OTUS. Why, who but yourself, most honor'd lord ;—so she said :—for that the young gentleman, Master Adrastus, had particularly the best right in the world to my honor'd young lady, your daughter ; and you only wanted to cheat and cozen him shamefully and 'bominable out of it, and throw my honor'd young lady, your daughter, away upon a poor 'poster of a poet not worth an obolus : and so thereupon my honor'd lady affirmed that they were only going to set about for to cheat you, for to hinder you from cheating them ; which, she said, would certainly be doing a very virtuous and upright and dutiful action ; and that if I helped them in such a righteous matter, why, certainly my virtue should be well rewarded ; which I thought good reason enough.

LAOD. Go now : and within half an hour after sunset come

to me again. Meantime, whatsoever you may hear or know farther of their intentions, that treasure up in your thoughts, and truly and fully impart to me. You know the consequence of faith, and of falsehood. Heed well. But I fear you not.

OTUS. My humblest duty to you, my honor'd lord. [*Exit.*

LAOD. What sophists are we!—even to ourselves!
Let's rail no more at guile in other men,
When each one gulls himself,—and knows it too,
Yet cheats himself to think it is no cheat.—
Let but the right eye wish its fellow blind,
And straight a hundred reasons are at hand,
Urging to quench it.—Where's that monstrous crime,—
That glaring error,—finds no argument
To prove it truth and virtue?—Then what ties
Of blood or contract shall defend from guile
Each passes on himself?—Well, Helen!—well!
Thou'dst cheat thy husband foully of his child,—
And call thy baseness 'virtue.'—Thee he'll cheat—
Give it what name thou wilt.

(*Enter* PHORBAS *hastily.*)

PHORBAS. Now you shall have it—now you shall have it.
'Sea-snakes and happy toads at length on golden wings shall soar——'

LAOD. Happy toads and sea-snakes truly! How do they manage that?

PHORBAS. Oh! merciful heavens! you are not the poet. Where is that most sweet and gifted youth? I *must* see him. Sir, good-day—good-day. 'Sea-snakes and happy toads——'

(*As he goes out he runs against* ASIUS, *who enters.*)

ASIUS. Curse the fellow!

PHORBAS. You have broken my nose, sir. Are you not fond of poetry?

ASIUS. No—I hate it worse than horse-aloes. Your cursed nose has almost fractur'd my cheek-bone.

PHORBAS. 'Sea-snakes and happy toads——' [*Exit.*

ASIUS. Sir, it came against me like a battering-ram.

LAOD. The common course seems reversed here; for, when the doctor and the madman encounter, the poor lunatic is, I fear, more frequently the sufferer.

ASIUS. That infernal cartilage of his must be totally ossified. I should like to examine it. But now, my dear sir; how is our poor patient? I have had him continually in my thoughts since I saw you, and have offer'd up three cocks. Hath any amendment ensued?

LAOD. I have seen him but once since you left us, for I have had business of some urgency on my hands. I hear, however, that his situation is just as it was:—his spirits good, —his voice strong, and his mind excursive. He is still in the garden, whither, if you please, we will attend him. I am most anxious about him, for I begin to doubt if he be perfectly in possession of his senses.

ASIUS. Sir, the pain of such contusions would be enough to drive a whole senate of philosophers to distraction. Let us see him immediately.

LAOD. With all my heart. [*Exeunt.*

SCENE II.—*The Garden.*

(MELAS *on a couch, with a book in his hand,* JANASSA *stands beside him.*)

MELAS. Thou'rt no philosopher to think on't thus.
Pain is a pleasure to the Stoic's mind:—
For, in defeating that, more joy he feels
Than if he felt no pain.

JANASSA. But, my dear sir,—such excessive agony as you must now undergo is surely enough to overcome the strongest philosophy. I wish, my dear good Melas, you would give way a little. The oak, you know, is sometimes torn up because it will not bend to the tempest;—and I am really afraid that the energy and resistance of your mind may at length burst your heroic heart. I wish, my dear sir, you would bow a little. I am sure a few tears and groans would ease you. I have often found it so.

MELAS. *I* bend?—*I* groan?—*I* shed unmanly tears?—

And for a worthless limb?—There—there—vile clay!
(*Striking his leg with a stick*)
Take that—and that—

    JAN. Oh! my dear sir, forbear! for my sake hold!

    MELAS. *I* cry and weep? Here, slaves:—bring fire and steel;—
Burn me, and hack me—an immortal soul. . . .

    JAN. Gracious heaven! hush—hush—

    MELAS. Shed tears and groan, for a vile limb of earth!
Where are these slaves?—Bring here your strongest rack!

    JAN. Be still—be still,—good sir!

    MELAS. Lay me upon it:—tear me limb from limb—
And I will smile, and thank you.—*I* shed tears?

    JAN. I crave your pardon, sir. I meant it well. Pray you be cool. I never saw you so much shaken from the gravity of your philosophy.

    MELAS. You are mistaken. Never sat my soul
With a more perfect steadfastness than now
On her firm throne.—But come,—no more of this.
Go read Chrysippus—his seven hundred tracts,—
And godlike Zeno,—they will ope your eyes—
That you shall long for some great agony
To make your sport with.

(*Enter* LAODAMUS *and* ASIUS *behind.*)

    JAN. Heaven forbid, sir! I am sure a very little agony would make sport with me.—Adieu, sir. I heartily wish you amendment.

    MELAS. I thank thee, child. Adieu. And don't forget that I would speak with Antilochus when he returns. I must a little farther catechise him; tho' truly he seems a youth of noble parts, and of rare acquisitions. Yet he is young.

    JAN. I will not fail to let him know your wish. [*Exit.*

    MELAS. Now, godlike Zeno—let our souls discourse.
(*He begins to read.*)

LAOD. Do you mark in him, sir, any change for the worse? —Any token of dissolution at hand?

ASIUS. Dissolution, sir? He looks as hale and sound as a young ash-tree. It will be one of the most extraordinary dissections in my practice. I cannot understand it.

LAOD. Must not his pain be great?

ASIUS. Unutterable, sir!—unutterable! Unless indeed—but I don't know—I should hardly think—and yet 'tis just possible that the whole limb may be mortified, and dead;—in which case it would be insensible to pain:—but then there would surely be symptoms of such a fatality.—A man half mortified could never keep up such a rubicundity of countenance as this;—but pain, sir, pain may and does ensanguine the cheeks, and brighten the eye;—and, you see, sir, his cheek is as red as a huntsman's. Oh! sir—his pain must be mortal. How in Pluto's name he bears it I cannot think.

LAOD. 'Tis his philosophy upholds him. The mind, he insists, has absolute control over the body, and can do with it as it wills.—

ASIUS. And, seeing this, I do believe it all. If philosophy can do this, I shall not marvel to see a man die, and lay out his own body;—get into his coffin, and carry himself to the grave:—ay—and cover himself up with his own tombstone.

LAOD. That would indeed be a singular spectacle.

ASIUS. Not a whit more so than this! Great Apollo! A man, whose body, or one quarter of it at least, is actually reduced to a jelly, a mere pulp,—to sit there before me with a steady hand—a cool eye—and a cheek like the south side of an apple!—'Tis a riddle that would puzzle the Oracle!—But he must die—Jove be thank'd!—and then we'll satisfy ourselves.

MELAS. The mind is of th' Eternal Nature part—
Ethereal, and immortal. Flesh is dust:—
Misfortune, poverty, and pain, mere jokes
To him can laugh at them.

ASIUS. Ay! ay! master.—There's the point of the pimple:

—to him can laugh at them.—I feel more and more sure, sir, that his wits must be unsettled ;—and this may partly account for his florid face. Your red-checked people are commonly fools. I could never do anything with them ;—and they have as commonly a sort of antipathy to the doctor ; which is a bad sign.

LAOD. For the doctor, or the patient?

ASIUS. For both indubitably. But I see, sir, you are waggish upon us.

MELAS. For poverty, what is't ?—for pain, what is't ? For hunger? nakedness?—Can't I live on, And, spite of them, grow wise ?

ASIUS. No—no—my good friend ;—if you are not wise already, you have not much time to learn it in, I promise you.

LAOD. Can you not suggest some course of diet, sleep, and so forth, that might be useful,—or, at least, harmless?

ASIUS. No doubt, no doubt! Where there is pain, there must be fever.—Fever, sir, must be combated by strong wines, and long-continued watchings.—Let him be made drunk with wine :—let him have no sleep, day or night ;—spice up his food till his palate take fire ;—place watchers in his room to drive away slumber ;—let his ears be distracted by the shrieking of trumpets, and his eyes be dazzled by the flashing of torches ;—wear him out till nature is just sinking——

LAOD. But, my good sir ;—this seems a somewhat harsh method of cure. Is it so unquestionably the best as to warrant us in disregarding its immediate evil, in consideration of the succeeding good ?

ASIUS. Your scruples, sir, are very amiable ;—but we never regard such in practice.—The object, sir, is to cure : and, that accomplished, what matters it for the method taken ?—If a man gets safe to the end of his journey, he does not heed whether the horse he rode on was brown or black.

LAOD. Yet even then it is of some consequence to him whether his paces were rough, or easy. But, surely, before he *begins* his journey he likes to examine if his horse's knees are whole, and his wind sound :—and so, before trying this uninviting course of cure, I should like to enquire if there be no gentler mode in esteem by others of your learned faculty.

MELAS. I tell thee, a ragged philosopher, whose habitation is with the swine, and whose food is acorns and wild berries, is a far nobler creature than the barbarian monarch of the boundless East, who sits on his diamond-pillar'd throne of gold.

ASIUS. Do you hear that, sir? A throne of gold placed on diamond pillars.—I fear there is little doubt of his lunacy; and that will be an additional reason for his taking down large draughts of wine. Sleep, sir, is most particularly desirable in all cases of disordered brain ; and every one knows that wine inviteth to sleep :—therefore, in cases of madness,—brain fevers, and so forth, we invariably begin by making the patient dead-drunk ; and that seldom fails to throw him into a deep sleep.

LAOD. From which he sometimes forgets to awake. Is it not so?

ASIUS. I deny not, sir, that in our travels we occasionally meet with such falls ;—and I admit that there are physicians who insist upon a course directly the reverse of that which I have laid down. But, sir ;—of two methods diametrically opposite, if one be right, the other must be wrong :—and I presume, sir, that my long course of practice may sustain me in thinking my method is *not* the wrong one.—But, if you please, sir, let us make a closer examination, and try the indications of his pulse.

LAOD. Certainly, sir.—Well, my good friend—(*they go up to* MELAS) how are you now?

MELAS. Excellent well, sir!—Do you not see that I have with me the divine Zeno?

ASIUS. One—two—three—four—five—six—seven—eight. —A pulse for a hundred years to come! Monstrous odd! But how is your leg, sir?

MELAS. Why, what is that to me?—Do I carry my legs with me when I pass thro' the universe? When I discourse on moral good and evil, do I take counsel of my knee-joint?

(*Enter* PANTHUS—*helped in by two* SERVANTS. *They place him in a chair.*)

ASIUS. Well, here is one whose knee-joints have given him counsel for many years. My excellent friend—how do you do? How is Podagra?

PANTHUS. Oh!—ah! gently—gently.—Asius, I am glad to see you.—Oh! Ah!—take care of that elbow.—Oh!—thank you—thank you.—O—h! you may go, and come again for me at sunset. Oh!—Ah! [*Exeunt* SERVANTS.

LAOD. Well, Panthus—I am glad to see you. But why are you so late? Dinner is almost ready, and we began to fear you would not come.

PANTHUS. And truly, my good friend, it was my intention to excuse myself, for I had a little flustration this morning that somewhat shook me—Oh! Oh!—But the sad accident that has befallen poor Melas came to my ear—Ah!—a—h!—and so I resolved to come and condole with him. (*Whispering*) It seems a bad business, I fear. What says Asius?

LAOD. He has no hope;—none at all:—and yet methinks he does not look so much amiss. What think you? It confounds Asius.

PANTHUS. 'Fore heaven! I wish I looked half so much amiss!—Why, his cheek is as round as a pumpkin, and as rosy as a morning cloud.

LAOD. *That* Asius imputes to the excess of his agony.

PANTHUS. Ay, marry! Then methinks my face should outflame the blood-red sun. I never knew till now that pain was so good a painter.—By Jupiter! I ought to be the most rubious, and handsome old youth existing.—It gravels me—Oh! Oh!—my back!—It perfectly gravels me, Laodamus.

LAOD. 'Tis truly a most surprising effort of heroism to endure pain thus. But what will not an enthusiastic mind accomplish?

PANTHUS. May I be hanged if he does not look as quiet and easy as an elbow-chair! Has he much pain, think you?

LAOD. Asius affirms that his pain must be unutterable. He is stagger'd, I assure you.

PANTHUS (*aside*). And so am I.—I am sure he did not always bear pain so comfortably; my crutch can witness that.

ASIUS (*aside to* LAOD.). Perhaps it might.—I have, also, somewhat else in contemplation that may be serviceable. Shall we go?

LAOD. If you please.—For a short time, my good friends, we leave you.   [*Exeunt* LAODAMUS *and* ASIUS.

PANTHUS (*aside*). I wonder if that be the same leg. Poor fellow! My blow was only a sort of rap at the door just before the others came in to pull down the house. And yet he certainly rubbed his shin.—It gravels me;—it *does* gravel me.— But Asius of course has dressed the wound, and ought to know best. It never *can* be a hoax. (*Aloud*) Well, my good Melas,—how do you? I am sorry to hear of your misfortune; —very sorry.

MELAS. Misfortune? Who told you I had met with any misfortune? But I am glad to see you again, Panthus. Have you well digested what I threw out this morning touching the pleasure the noble mind feels in conquering pain? Have you learned to laugh at your gout and lumbago?

PANTHUS. For love of the Gods, Melas, don't put me in a passion with your cursed philosophy.—No—I tell you,—I cannot laugh at gout and lumbago,—and I never shall, unless I should ever see *you* in their clutches.—But excuse me, my dear Melas :—you have enough to bear now:—I am a testy old fellow,—and apt to misbehave when I get into a rage. Oh! curse this infernal gonagra!

MELAS. You are, of a surety, somewhat hasty, my good friend:—but age and pain are not foes that every arm can subdue. I freely excuse you.

PANTHUS. Thank you—thank you. I was, in my youth, of as sweet a disposition as need be:—but this gout,—this lumbago,—gonagra—omagra—Oh! curse 'em all!—have held me in an everlasting fermentation till I am become little better than vinegar.—But how are you, my old friend? how are you? Oh! blessed Apollo!—*there's* a leg!—My dear, good old friend,—how I pity your misfortune!

MELAS. Misfortune? Why, my dear Panthus, will you talk of misfortune?—I have had none.

PANTHUS. No?—Why what's *that?*—Is not your leg converted into jelly?—into a sort of stiff broth?

MELAS. And what is that to me?—Call you that a misfortune?

PANTHUS. Now, don't put me in a passion, Melas:—don't put me in a passion:—I tell you don't put me in a passion.

MELAS. Doth it prevent me from worshipping the Gods?— Doth it make me dishonest?—Doth it wash out from my mind the precepts of divine philosophy?

PANTHUS. Oh! curse divine philosophy!—I tell you you will put me in a horrid passion. Oh!

MELAS. Doth it prevent me from being brave and truthful?

PANTHUS. Oh! curse him! he has got the bit between his teeth.—

MELAS. Bold and judicious?—quiet and temperate? Is my leg *me?* Is it immortal? Doth it think,—reason?—Or is it not clay merely? worthless clay?

PANTHUS (*throwing down his crutches*). Hold your cursed noise, I tell you,—or I shall be forced to break your bones.— But, thank heaven! I flung my crutches at the ground this time, and not at you.—

MELAS. Is this leg——

PANTHUS. Melas, you'll distract me.—Don't speak any more— (*shouting*) I'll not hear you. By Jove, you'll throw the gout into my stomach. You will, by Jove!

MELAS. And what then?—My excellent friend: what then? Pray you keep cool.—The immortal mind should not be puff'd about by every change of the blast, like a boy's kite. Answer me gently, my friend. Suppose the gout *should* be thrown into your stomach,—what then? I ask you :—what misfortune would there be in that?—What harm?—What harm?

PANTHUS (*almost choking with rage*). Harm?—harm? you old villain!—Do you want to murder me? Help—help—

murder—murder—I wish I could reach you—you cursed old villain! Murder! Murder!

(*Enter two* SERVANTS *in haste.*)

SERVANTS. What is the matter, sir? Lord's sake, what's amiss?

PANTHUS. Pound him to dust! Mash his old bones! give me my crutches—kill him, I say—The horrid old villain!—kill him—kill him.—

1ST SERV. For heaven's sake, sir, what is it you mean?

PANTHUS. Oh! O—h! my back!—my legs! Oh!—O—h! my stomach! Oh—Oh—Oh—Oh—It's all over—I am going—call my son—*he* has done it (*pointing to* MELAS), but I forgive him—Oh—Oh!—Melas—I am going—Oh! Oh!

MELAS. Rejoice then, my good Panthus—rejoice. Thou art going on a pleasant journey;—and I would fain go with thee. But we must wait our time. Rejoice, my dear and valued friend;—thou wilt now shake off the vile clay that holds down the ethereal spirit :—thou wilt leave that dirty old carcase to the hungry worms.—Never hadst thou a better, or a kinder friend than that agony which is now carrying thee off. Adieu! adieu! I wish I could reach thee, that I might take thy hand, and bid thee good speed.

PANTHUS. Pr—pr—pray you,—ca—ca—carry me to him.

(*They bear him to* MELAS.)

MELAS. Ay, my good friend,—thy hand burns. Thou hast lived a bad life :—thy bones are nought but chalk and rottenness;—and now kind gout comes to bear thee away.—How pleasant is it to behold the Spirit parting from its earthly fetters! What!—dost grin yet?—not even now able to smile at agony?—Be calm—be calm—Subdue these last, foolish pangs,—and die like a philosopher.—

PANTHUS (*striking* MELAS *with his fist on the cheek*). Curse thee—and philosophy too! Take that—and that—and that.—

MELAS. Panthus, hold off—hold off.—

PANTHUS. Curse thee! there's more for thee,—there—there—there.—

MELAS. And there—there—(*striking* PANTHUS) there's for thee—thou abominable old chalk-stone!

SERVANTS. Pray gentlemen forbear!—pray sir—now pray sir—Nay then, I must move you away, sir,—or you'll be the worse off. (*They draw* PANTHUS *back.*)

PANTHUS. Why do you draw me away? Let me kill him.—Give me my crutch.—The old villain!

1ST SERV. Pray sir be quiet:—here comes my mistress.

MELAS. You do well, Panthus;—you do well.

PANTHUS. Oh! Gods! my arm! my shoulder! my back! my loins! Oh! my knees!—Is your mistress coming?

1ST SERV. No, sir;—I think not. She has just met your son, Master Adrastus, by the orange walk,—and they are now going towards the house.

PANTHUS. I hope she did not hear anything of this infernal squabble—Oh!—O—h!—

MELAS. Bear me away from this ungoverned person:—bear me away, I say. Panthus, I forgive you.

PANTHUS. Return for me. I cannot be moved just at present. Oh—Oh—

(SERVANTS *bear* MELAS *away.*)

For a man half beaten to a rotten jelly, I must say his fist is a cursed heavy one.—My head rings as if every nerve were a bell-rope, and twenty furies sweating at them:—and my bones shake about like walking-sticks strung up in a windy day.—Oh! Jupiter! he's a strange fellow!—But, for a man just dying, he has simply the hardest gripe in the world!—Hang me if he has not pinched my arms till the bones are become almost invisible! Oh!—Oh!—And that cursed elephant-leg too of his, that would have kept another man down as firm as a wedge,—may I be broiled if he did not shake it about like a lamb's tail! Oh! Oh!——Why, who is this?—who's this?—Great Gods!—a madman!—

(*Enter* PHORBAS, *in a frenzy.*)

PHORBAS. Rend mountains up,—and fling them at the moon:

Empty th' Atlantic—drink it at one gulp—
Then squirt it to the stars!—Leap into space—
Take worlds for marbles—be the sun thy top—
Thy whip, the comets' tails.—Lash systems round—
See—see—the heavens are spinning!—hark! hark! hark!
Dost thou not hear them hum? Hark!—bang!—bang!—
  bang!—

PANTHUS. Oh blessed Apollo! who shall save me now?—

PHORBAS. Worlds are exploding!—terrible!—hark! hark! Bang!—bang!—Hiss—hiss—there go a hundred comets— Ha!—ha!—I'll ride on one.—Whew—flash!—flish! flash! Away we go——hark how they roar and hiss; Soho!—soho!—good-bye to you, earth—good-bye——

PANTHUS. Jupiter grant he may be going! If he looks at me, I must die.

PHORBAS. Mind, helmsman—mind—there's Saturn in the way——bear off—or we shall clash——bear off—bear off.— Holla—holla—you with the ring and the seven moons—stand clear, stand clear!

PANTHUS. Oh! all ye deities!—if ever I have sent up to you well pleasing sacrifice——.

PHORBAS. Hold hard—hold hard—we shall knock together ——hold—hold.—Now for it——Bang!—shatter—and clatter blunder—and thunder.—We have burst through the ring, and knocked out the planet!——Look where she tumbles—look— look—down—down—down—down—down—down—(*he sees* PANTHUS). How do you do, sir?

PANTHUS (*aside*). Now for it!—Oh blessed Jove! Now for it!—'Tis a hard death!—I think I had better shut my eyes, and be resigned.—

PHORBAS. How do you do, sir?

PANTHUS (*aside*). Now he's going to begin on me.—Oh! Jupiter!——Where will he bite first?

PHORBAS. I think, sir, you are a poet. I perceive in your distracted look, sir, the signs of intense rumination. Give me your hand, sir. You are in a cold shiver. Oh, sir! deny it not,—you *are* a poet,—and that which you have just overheard,—tho' I will be free to say, sir, that I was not conscious of having so distinguished an auditor—hath o'ermaster'd your too sensitive soul. Tell me, sir, I beseech you,—are you not smitten with the charms of sacred song? Are you not enraptured with divine poesy?—Pray you, speak.

PANTHUS. Oh! dreadful fond of it, sir.

PHORBAS. Ha! I knew it. Let me embrace thee, thou godlike old man.

PANTHUS. Oh! curse it, sir,—you kill me! Oh! my shoulders! arms!—back! loins! legs! Oh! oh!

PHORBAS. Good heavens, sir! what ails you?

PANTHUS. Oh!—you have killed me!—Gout—gout—gout—from the crown to the toe, all gout—cursed gout, sir.

PHORBAS. I pity thee.—That must, in a slight degree, abate the heat of thy poetic fire.—Brought on by hard study, I suppose, sir——

PANTHUS. Oh! yes, sir—yes—horrid hard study. Pray, sir, will you oblige me by shouting for the servants—I would not be so bold to ask you to trouble yourself to step for them, or——

PHORBAS. My excellent friend! you don't intrude at all upon me :—nay, I shall be most glad if you will spend the whole day with me. And pray show me some of your verses. But indeed I must not, and cannot suffer you to go yet. What is your forte, sir? Do you most wanton in the grand—the terrible—the beautiful—the sublime—or the pathetic?—

PANTHUS. Oh! sir—the terrible and pathetic : for when this terrible gout comes I do nothing but roar and groan.

PHORBAS. Give me a touch of your verses ;—one little touch of your *terrible :*—I must have it.

PANTHUS. Not just now, sir :—my memory is poor—another time, sir—another time, sir, with pleasure.

PHORBAS. Come, then,—I will give you an atom of my *Terrible.*—What you have partly overheard, sir, is a morsel from an unfinished drama ; the *Scene* of which is *Unlimited*

Space, and the *Time* is *Eternity*:—so that you will immediately apprehend, sir, with what a perfect nicety I have preserved the Unities.—Ah! sir—when that work is finished!—But no—no —I'll say no more o' that at present. Yet I think I may modestly affirm it to be at once the most novel and sublime of human labours. But what I shall give you now, sir, is the more common kind of the Terrible. You apprehend me, sir?

PANTHUS. Oh! yes—certainly, sir. (*Aside*) I wish to heaven somebody else would apprehend him, and carry him to the bottom of the sea. Now for it—now for it—Oh! Jupiter! he's beginning again!

PHORBAS. The dead man came at the hour of noon,
  And he sat at the board, with a bone for his spoon.
  The fire went out as he sat him down;—
  And the beef grew cold at his deadly frown;
  And the wines were all frozen,—the puddings were ice;—
  And the chairs and the tables went *crack!* in a trice;
  Shrunk up by that dreadful frost.—
  And the host, and his wife, and their guests all died;—
  Shoulder to shoulder, and side to side,
   They sank—and gave up the ghost.—
   The corpse spake no word,—
   But stuck to the board;—
   The meat he munch'd,
   And the bones he crunch'd,
  And the puddings he threw down his maw.
  The wines he swallow'd—bottles and all;—
  The mustard-pot short, and the cruets tall,
  And the knives and the forks to atoms small,
   Did he grind with his terrible jaw.
  The cheese, and the raisins, and nuts eftsoons;—
  The table-cloth next,—the dishes and spoons,
  Down his horrible throat thrust he.

  And when all was done,
  He swore 'twas good fun,
   But he hadn't had half enough——
So he took up the host,
Like a piece of toast,
  And munch'd him merrily.
His coat was blue—and his breeches were brown,
  But body, and breeches, and coat went down,
And the corpse did neither choke nor frown,
  He gulp'd him so easily.
  And then, on my life!
  Down went the wife——
And the guests, one after another.
He dipped *their* heads in the salt-pot first,—
For now he was full, and ready to burst,
  And ate but saucily.
The last guest stuck in his throat, I ween!—
'Twas a horrible sight as ever was seen;—
  For the body was in, and the legs hung out;—
  And the corpse began to fidget about,
   And swallow, and strain
   With might and main,—
And push in the legs, and swallow again,—
  But he could not get him down.
  So he swore, in a huff,
  He had had enough,—
And that he'd pull him out.
  But little knew he
  What a job that would be :—
He pull'd him, and shook him, and toused him about,—
But he stuck in his throat like a roach in a trout.
  Oh! his case was truly pathetic!
  He pull'd,—and push'd—and pull'd again,—
And urged, and retched,—but 'twas all in vain,—
  And he wish'd he could take an emetic.
But there was not room to swallow a drop—
  For he stuck in as tight
  As a thick wax light

Jamm'd hard in a narrow socket.
At last he came up—with a smack and a plop,
Like a cork from a bottle of ginger-pop,
 Up with a smack came he :—
  The corpse was pleased
  To find himself eased,
 And laugh'd most solemnly :—
With many a laugh—and many a roar,
Away went he to the chamber door,
 But there he made a stop,
For he saw the last guest on the table :——
  'That very guest,
  Did I like best,
Yet to eat him I am not able ;—
 And ah !—he's a delicate sop !
Of all the guests I liked him chief ;—
To leave him were deadly sorrow—
Gadzooks ! I'll eat him to-morrow !'
So he folded him up in his handkerchief,
 And carried him off in his pocket.

Now, my dear sir, what do you think of that ? That's a specimen of my Terrible. How do you relish it ?

PANTHUS. Oh ! wonderful ! I never heard anything like it. Holla !—come hither, you knaves.

PHORBAS. What !—interrupted again?—My dear sir, I'll see you soon, and hear some of your verses. I am sure your Terrible must be very fine ; you seemed so much affected by this. Ha ! sir—I long for that happy moment. Adieu—adieu. —Let me embrace you.

PANTHUS. For heaven's sake, my excellent sir, don't touch me.—Holla—here—carry me in.—

(*Enter the two* SERVANTS.)

PHORBAS. Adieu—dear friend,—adieu—I'll see you soon again. [*Exit.*

PANTHUS. Jupiter forbid !—Oh ! you idle knaves ! To leave me exposed thus to a raging madman, or a Fury for aught I know.—I am near dead.—Carry me in.—But stop.—I cannot move just now. Oh me!—Did you see his eyes?

1ST. SERV. Sir, 'tis only a poor poet that our master has in his house for a day or two. He's quite harmless, sir, only a little odd in his way.

PANTHUS. A little odd—do you call it? 'Fore heaven! it passes all I ever saw or dreamed of.—I don't think I shall outlive this day.—But how is the Stoic? I was too choleric. I hope he is not hurt:—curse him! he has hurt me, though! But how's his leg? Oh!—Ah!

1ST SERV. Oh, just the same, sir:—he says it's nothing to him.

PANTHUS. Then I am sure 'tis nothing to me. Which of you assisted when his leg was drest?

2ND SERV. Nay, sir,—it has not been drest at all, for he refuses to let Asius see it.

PANTHUS. Not drest?—

2ND SERV. No, sir. I don't think, sir, it can give him very great pain, for I perceived when he was shaking you, sir, that he wagged it about without flinching a bit.

PANTHUS. Not drest?—not let Asius see it? What think you of this, my masters?

1ST SERV. I am sure *I* don't know, sir.

2ND SERV. Nor I, sir. Other folks commonly show their bruises to the doctor.

PANTHUS. Wh——ew!——Will you do me a little service, my lads? It shall do harm to nobody;—and good to yourselves, for I'll fill your pockets for you, if you be faithful.

1ST SERV. I am sure, sir, we will both do anything to pleasure you.

2ND SERV. Yes, sir,—I am sure we will.

PANTHUS. Then I'll tell you what, my lads. We will see this leg of his whether he likes it or not. I'll give you a dose, that one of you shall put into his wine after supper. In five minutes it will send him asleep as sound as the foundation of the house. Let me then be called; and we will untruss this mammoth limb of his, and satisfy ourselves. What say you, my lads?

1st Serv. Oh, sir, I am sure we will do it with all our hearts.

2nd Serv. It cannot hurt him, you know, sir.

Panthus. Hurt him?— No.— It may be the curing of him. But carry me in now. Gently—gently—Oh!—mind—mind.—That's it.—Wag it about? To be sure he did.—Curse him! we'll untruss him.—But for your lives don't speak a word of this. —Curse him! we'll untruss him. [*Exeunt.*

End of the Third Act.

ACT IV.

Scene I.—*A room in the House of* Laodamus.

(Laodamus *and* Janassa *discovered.*)

Laod. I told you for one year that he might sue
To gain your love; but, failing then, should cease.
This was the bond 'twixt him and me;—yet still
With this reserve,—that no unworthiness
Should prove his seeming gold but counterfeit.—

Jan. I cannot love him, my dear father,—no—
Though earth had but one youth, and this were he,
I could not love him. Why then for a year—
A month—or even a day?—

Laod.   Wouldst thou but wait,
And listen, ere thou answer'st.—

Jan.   Pardon me—
I do forget myself.

Laod.   Then hear me now.
Not for a year,—a month—a day—an hour,
I bid thee listen to him. Every bond
Is broke between us; and I cast him off.

Jan. And am I free, then?

Laod.   Yes—from *him* thou'rt free.
And yet the chains are on the anvil, now,
Shall fetter thee again.

Jan.   But still I hope
No desperate crime of his hath sever'd you;—
I love him not, yet wish him nought but good.

Laod. He is not honest;—that is crime enough,—
And so no more of him. But, tell me now,
And truly:—should Antilochus thus sue,—
As he indeed doth sue,—what wilt thou say?
Wilt bid him wait a year?—or but six months?
Or three?—or two months?—or, at least, a week?
Or surely till to-morrow?—What wilt say?
Hast thou no answer?—

Jan.   'Twere not modesty
In me to answer that. My mother, sir,
And you, my dearest father, know the best;
And I resign me to you.

Laod.   Well, my child—
I'll put thee to the proof. I'd have thee wed,—
And at short warning:—but thy mother's voice
Hath nought to say in this;—our purposes
Do clash together;—and, if hers hold on,
Mine must fall down. Speak thou no word with her.

Jan. Does she refuse consent?

Laod.   Ask nothing on't.
Here is a letter from Paterculus.

Jan. Then is Antilochus return'd?

Laod.   Stay—stay—
'Tis somewhat short, and rough, for he that bore it
Could tarry for no flourishes of speech.
I'll read thee but one sentence.

Jan.   Is he come?

Laod. (*reading*). 'To-morrow, my much-loved and long-lost friend, I will write more to thee. That our son Antilochus

should espouse thy daughter Janassa is the dearest wish of both
our hearts : and I would say that his merits deserve as dear a
treasure, if I did not know that her virtues are above———'
But what comes next you shall read for yourself:
And, as I see your patience burns down quick,
I'll only say——Antilochus *is* come,
And waits you by the temple.—

  JAN.   Oh ! good heavens !
My dearest father ! thank you. (*Going.*)

  LAOD.   Stay—stay—stay.
If such a speed as a stout man of forty
Can travel at, be not too slow a rate
To pace with your impatience, I'll go with you.
I would not have you seen in any way
To wake suspicion. But I'll tell you more
As we go on.—Wilt bid him wait a year ?

  JAN. My dearest father !   [*Exeunt.*

  SCENE II.—*The Garden—with a Grecian Temple.*
  (ANTILOCHUS *discovered walking to and fro.*)

  ANTIL. *That* was a footstep sure—No—no—Oh ! heavens !
What a mere cheat is this which we call Time !
Whose minutes unto some appear long hours ;
Whose hours, to some, seem minutes. 'Tis a day,
Told by my restlessness, since I stood here ;
While, to some happy tippler, 't has not been
The space 'twixt cup and cup :—and, by the stars,
Some fourth part of an hour perchance. Hark !—hark !
That *is* a footstep—Ha ! 'tis she—'tis she—
But not alone—who is't with her ? He's gone ;
And she comes on again. Oh ! Gods ! Oh ! Gods !
And she is mine !

      (*Enter* JANASSA.)

  JAN. Antilochus !

  ANTIL.   Janassa ! (*A pause.*)
I wish this minute were eternity,—
That we might ever be embracing so.

I could be happy, for unending years,
To press thee thus,—and feel thy gentle breath ;—
And hear thy heart's loud throb :—and nothing more,
Not even thy voice I'd ask :—but just to lie
On some soft couch beneath the moonlight sky,
With those bright stars for ever wheeling round,—
And a scarce-whispering breeze, perfum'd like this
From yonder orange walk,—and not a sound
To tell of aught in the wide world beside :—
And so, methinks, for ever I could lie,
Nor wish to move, or think, save the one thought,
That thou wert in my arms.—Why dost thou sigh?

JAN. I cannot tell ;—unless that I'm too happy.

ANTIL. The melancholy sigh ;—so do not thou.

JAN. There's melancholy in too sweet a bliss.
I cannot tell thee why ;—but so it is.

ANTIL. Who was it came with you, and turn'd again?

JAN. My father.

ANTIL. Say *our* father.

JAN. Say it thou.

ANTIL. When wilt thou let me truly call him so?

JAN. Ask that of him.

ANTIL. To-morrow shall it be?

JAN. Oh! no, no, no, no, no. A month or two,—
I pray you grant me that. But, ask my father.
I yield in all to him.

ANTIL. And will you swear
T' abide by his decree?

JAN. Oh! gentle love,—
Talk not of swearing between thee and me,
If I do promise,—wouldst thou ask an oath
To make it sure?—Give me thy lightest word,
Nay, even a nod, a smile ;—'tis bond enough
Tho' thou hadst promised kingdoms.

ANTIL.   *Say* but then
His word shall be thy law.—

JAN.   'T has ever been
My law, and my best good; for, to obey,
Was ever to be happy. 'Tis too late
To turn a rebel now.

ANTIL.   I ask no more.
What think'st thou of to-morrow?

JAN.   As the day
Shall follow this sweet night.

ANTIL.   And is that all?

JAN. Is't not enough? Methinks, to stand before,
Or after it, or but in the same week;
Were note enough for the best day i' th' year.

ANTIL. But tell me truly:—shall it be to-morrow?

JAN. To-morrow never shall be:—for when *'tis*,
'Tis not to-morrow. Look at yon bright sky.

ANTIL. But shall it be to-morrow?

JAN.   Ay! for ever!
Silent, and bright, and beautiful!—Methinks
Those stars are happy lovers, whispering
Their holy vows in absence of the sun.

ANTIL. But shall it be to-morrow?

JAN.   That it shall.
The eastern sky shall rear his standard first,
Ruby, and golden hued;—and thro' heaven's gate
The Sun shall ride in on his flaming car;
And bowl away o'er heaven's triumphal arch;
And, as he passes, all created things
Shall hail him monarch of the boundless sky,
And father of all life.—

ANTIL.   But, dear Janassa!
Say—shall it be to-morrow?

JAN.   Prithee, love,
Now do not tease me more. Have I not said

Most eloquent things to quiet thy *to-morrow* ?
In truth I know no more :—so now be still.
I am not counsellor to agëd Fate,
And cannot tell thee what shall be to-morrow—
Yet what shall *not* be, I could tell, methinks.—

 ANTIL. Oh ! speak.

 JAN.   If that I would :—but I will not.

 ANTIL. *What* shall not be to-morrow ?

 JAN.   *Thou* shalt not
Be——I'll not tell thee what. Now ask no more.
My father's will is mine.

 ANTIL.   Belov'd Janassa !
Then will I tell thee what *shall be* to-morrow :
And yet I will not :—is not that the way ?
To shew the sparkle of some brilliant thing
Then snatch it from the sight ?

 JAN.   Yes ;—that's the way
Yon little cloud is dealing with the stars.
But soon it passes on and lets them shine ;
And so thy secret will, erelong, peep out
Without my breath to speed it.—Some-one comes.

 ANTIL. Hush !—hush !—no, love ;—'tis but the whispering wind.
I thought I heard a score of coming feet,
Ere thine did come indeed. Each glancing leaf
Seem'd thy white garment waving ;—every sound
Was thy light footstep. But I'll tell thee, love,
What 'tis shall be to-morrow.

 JAN.   Ha ! so soon ?
But now I will not hear it.

 ANTIL.   But thou shalt.

 JAN. But if I stop my ears.—

 ANTIL.   Why then I'll tell it
Without a word, and thou shalt know't as well.
I will but point to where the sun shall rise,—
And then to his bright chamber in the west :—

Then to yon temple's altar ;—then to thee ;—
And then to me ;—and then I'll clasp thee thus—
And kiss thee thus ;—and that shall tell thee plain,
That on to-morrow night thou'lt be my bride.

JAN. Why then, methinks, I'd better shut my eyes.
How wilt thou tell it then?

ANTIL. Why, then I'll count
How many minutes till to-morrow night ;—
And for each minute will I give a kiss ;—
And that shall tell it thee.

JAN. But, if it fail?

ANTIL. Why, then I'll call to mind that every minute
Hath threescore seconds ;—and, for every second,
I'll give three kisses.

JAN. Well—I have not heard it ;
No—nor yet seen it ;—nor shall kisses tell me ;
But only my dear father. Come away,
And tell thy wish to him.

ANTIL. I may not go
Within the house ; he hath some reason for it ;—
Not till to-morrow evening :—I had, else,
Not linger'd here so long. Hast read the letter?

JAN. 'Tis here, Antilochus.

ANTIL. But hast thou read it?

JAN. But hast *thou* read it?

ANTIL. Yes—even while 'twas written.

JAN. Art not asham'd, then, to be flatter'd thus?

ANTIL. My cheek burn'd as I read. If *that* were shame
I was indeed ashamëd. Didst *thou* blush?
For all my praise was not a tithe of thine ;—
And yet thou wert not flatter'd.

JAN. I blush *now*.
But let us walk.

ANTIL. I hear a nightingale
Somewhere this way.

JAN.   'Tis in the jasmine bower.
I listen'd to't last night.

ANTIL.   How sweet this breeze!   [*Exeunt.*

SCENE III.—*A room in the House of* LAODAMUS.

(*Enter* LAODAMUS *and* OTUS.)

LAOD. I think you perfectly understand me now.

OTUS. Oh! yes, my honor'd master;—very well.

LAOD. Then see my wife and Adrastus as soon as you can, and bring me word what their intentions are. This plot of mine will make them change theirs, I have no doubt.

OTUS. I will, most honor'd sir. I think I see master Adrastus at the end of the gallery. Yes—it is—and he is coming this way.

LAOD. Now remember your tale. Keep a clear head, Otus;—and think on your reward.   [*Exit.*

OTUS. Oh yes, sir; don't fear that. When a slave has been promised his freedom in the morning, he's not likely to forget it before supper. I hope *you* won't forget it, my good master. But now for laying the birdlime that is to catch these two magpies that want to come for to steal my good master's fruit; or, in other words, his daughter, my honor'd young lady; which truly may be called a sort of a kind of fruit, tho' not a fruit to be eaten;—and yet I don't know—— But here he comes:—and now will I tell him some horrible lie, and he will pay me for it.

(*Enter* ADRASTUS.)

Oh! Master Adrastus—I have such a thing to tell you.

ADRAS. Quick then—out with it. What is it?

OTUS. Oh! Master Adrastus! such a thing! You won't forget what you promised me.

ADRAS. Speak quick, or I'll give thee more than I promised thee. Here—here are thy twenty drachms.

OTUS. Thank you, Master Adrastus—thank you. Oh! if you did but know what a sort of a kind of a business this has been to come at this here 'telligence, I am sure you would hardly mind how much you gave me. Oh, sir!

ADRAS. What! did they catch thee listening?

OTUS. Nay, sir, or I should not have lived to tell you. But sir, first of all, I was forced to stand for half an hour among the rushes at the side of the fish-pond, almost overhead in water.

ADRAS. But how so?

OTUS. Why, my honor'd sir, I'll tell you how it fell out. Being on the look-out, as your honor bade me, and seeing what a fine moonlight was abroad, I said to myself as I stood peeping out of the window,—'Bless me!' said I—'here's a fine moonlight night'—and so it is, honor'd sir;—has your honor been out?

ADRAS. No—no.—Be quick with your story.

OTUS. So said I to myself, 'Here's a beautiful moonlight, to be sure; and, they say, lovers like moonlight. Why, Otus,' said I— 'it's drachms to oboli but they are now in the garden.'—And with that off I went; and, to be sure, there they were, walking backwards and forwards beside the fish-pond. But how to come at them to listen seem'd clear impossible, for there's neither tree nor bush, you know, sir, near that path.

ADRAS. Well—well—go on.—

OTUS. However, my honor'd sir, I saw that they sat 'em down every now and then on a seat pretty close to the pond,— and, said I to myself,—'The young, and handsome, and honorable gentleman Master Adrastus——'

ADRAS. Come, come,—no more of this nonsense.

OTUS. Nay, sir, I must tell my tale my own way, or I shall be so puzzled I shan't know the saddle from the horse's tail.

ADRAS. Get on, then.

OTUS. 'The young, and honorable, and handsome Master Adrastus'—said I—'hath promised to reward thee nobly,—do thou do what thou canst to serve him, ay, tho' thy life may answer it; for I'm sure he'll not grudge thee thy due.'

ADRAS. I understand you. Go on.

Otus. So, with that, I stood ready; and, as soon as they turned their backs, off set I to hide among the reeds just before the seat. But, sir, when I came to creep in among them, the first step soused me up to the middle in water,—and I should certainly have roared out if it had not been that I so desired to serve you.

Adras. Well—well.—Here are five drachms more for thee. But, be quick.

Otus. Your honor'd mastership is very kind; and I humbly thank you. But this was not all. For, if I had stayed so close to the side, they would certainly, I thought, see me, and that would spoil all; so I was e'en forced to go out three steps farther; and that, for certain, brought me up to the chin, and a little above. However, my eyes and ears were above water, and that was all I wanted. So there I stood to wait; and to be sure, at the very next turn they came to the seat, and down they sat, and he began to tell her of a plan he had in his head for getting her off. This made me prick up my ears; and I fancy I must have ruffled the water a bit; for my honor'd young lady, Miss Janassa, stops him, and says, ' My dear Antilochus——'

Adras. Did she say, my dear Antilochus?

Otus. Oh yes, sir—and a deal more.

Adras. Curses on him! but, go on.

Otus. 'My dear Antilochus,' says she,—' what strange thing is that in the water among the rushes? it looks, for all the world, like a man's head.' Oh, sir! how I began to sweat at that!

Adras. What! in the water?

Otus. Oh! yes, my honor'd sir; but I knew it was all for you, and so I didn't mind what might come to me. But certainly it put me into a horrible sweat :—yet I durst not stir. —'Ay'—says he,—'it does indeed,' says he,—'very much like a man's head:'—and, with that, up he jumps, and comes close to the brink of the pond to look at me.

Adras. That must have frighten'd you.

Otus. Oh! sir,—I knew you would pity me.—So there he

stood and looked at me. 'It's the oddest looking thing I ever saw,' says he—'just for all the world like a monstrous ugly man's head.'—That's what he said, sir. And then he kneel'd down for a better view of me, and stared me full in the face.— Oh! sir;—it was a dreadful thing!—And so he stared—and stared,—and went hither, and thither, and looked up and down;—at last he says—' Prithee, my dear Janassa——'

ADRAS. Curses on him!

OTUS. 'Prithee come'—says he,—'and look. It is the od-dest—ug-liest thing.'—So then she came, and they both stared, and stared at me; and I durst hardly breathe, or wink. 'It *is* the que-er-est thing'—said she;—'why, it certainly is a man's head.' And, with that, she took up two or three little stones and pelted me over the nose and eyes:—but, you know, sir, I durst not move. ' How odd it sounds!' says she,—'pray, my dear Antilochus, do get a stick and hook it out.'

ADRAS. Thou art certainly a cool and resolv'd fellow, Otus, —and I'll not forget thee.

OTUS. I was cool enough in the water, sir.

ADRAS. Except when you were in that horrible sweat.

OTUS. Oh! sir—that was a cold sweat.—But, of a truth, I feared I should be forced to give up at last; for what should master Antilochus do but begin to whistle for his great dog, that he might send him in after me. Oh! sir, that was a dreadful moment, for that monstrous brute would have toused me like a rat. But, as good luck would have it, the dog was not within hearing;—and so then he fetches a pretty long, thick stick, hooked at the end, and begins to grope for me.—I was almost done, sir:—for he pokes his hook round my neck, and pulls me on.—At that down dips I my head, and lets the hook slip; and then comes up again:—and then again comes he with his hook, and tries me again, and again; and it was all I could do to keep from sneezing or choking.

ADRAS. It must indeed have been awkward for you.

OTUS. Oh! sir—you can't tell, or think what it was. At last says he—' It must be fast to the bottom,' says he :—' I fancy it must be only a pumpkin?'—and, with that, he gives me a pretty hard rap on the skull. ' I'm pretty sure it's a pumpkin '—says he :—'hark! how hollow it sounds.' — And then again he whacks me on top o' th' head,—and then on this side,—and then on t'other side,—and then on the top again ;—and, all the while—' do but hear,' says he,—' how odd it sounds :—and it feels odd too. Try it, my dear Janassa.'

ADRAS. Poor fellow! Here are ten drachms more for thee.

OTUS. Oh! sir—you are a truly generous gentleman. But, as I was saying, then he gives her the stick, and then she begins to push, and pull, and knock my head about on all sides; and, at every bump—' La !'—says she—' how *very* odd and hollow it sounds.'—At last they left me, and went back to the seat, and he finished telling her of their plot. And, when I have told it you, sir, you will stare. I was glad enough when it was done, and they went away, and let me get out of the water.

ADRAS. I dare say you were. But now for their plot. Tell it in as few words as possible.

OTUS. Then, my honor'd sir,—it's just this. My young lady has got leave of her father, my honor'd master, to go to-morrow on a visit to her cousin about five miles in the country.

ADRAS. 'Tis six miles. I know the place perfectly. What of that?

OTUS. There's somebody coming, sir :—we may be listen'd to,

ADRAS. Oh, 'tis your mistress. Let her hear it too.—My dear madam—you are just in time.

(*Enter* HELEN.)

'Tis as I said it would be. She's going to be off with the poet : —all settled.

HELEN. But when is this to be? Perhaps your turn may come first.

ADRAS. Ay, Otus—when is it to be?

OTUS. To-morrow night, my honor'd sir.

ADRAS. Yes—but she goes to the country in the morning, I suppose.

OTUS. No, sir, not till the evening.

HELEN. But how is all this? Let me know the whole.

ADRAS. Begin again, Otus. You must understand, madam, that Otus has over-heard the poet and your duteous daughter plotting this in the garden. She has asked leave of her father to go to-morrow to visit her cousin.—Now for the rest, Otus.

OTUS. Well, my honor'd mistress, and sir;—and so my young lady is to go;—and Master Antilochus is to meet her there ;—and they are to be married ; and to come home ; and my honor'd master is to scold 'em a bit; but for all that, he's at the bottom of it;—and then it's to be all right. And so that's all.

HELEN. And enough too. Have they engaged a priest?

OTUS. Oh yes—my honor'd mistress ; I forgot that. And they are to be married in masks. The priest is old Diocles. Master Antilochus said to Miss Janassa that the old fellow would marry almost anybody for a good fee, but yet he thought it would be safer to go in masks, because the old priest would know her, and perhaps be afraid of her father.

HELEN. And you over-heard all this?

OTUS. Yes, my honor'd lady.

HELEN. I could hardly have thought this of Janassa: and yet what could be expected from a lady of such accomplishments? I always told her father he would ruin her by such follies as grammar, logic, and music, and poetry : and that to make a pudding was a much better thing than to make a poem. But he was for ever blind.—But I'll tell you what, Master Adrastus ;—I spy a way by which we will contrive to eat the dinner they are cooking, in spite of them.

ADRAS. Pray, my dear madam, give me your help. I must win Janassa, or Antilochus shall not live. By heaven he shall not !

HELEN. I don't like to hear you talk so. You shall have Janassa,—that be sure. Antilochus must, either by stratagem, or by force, be kept out of the way.—You must meet Janassa: the mask will conceal both voice and face;—and you shall marry her instead of Antilochus.—'Tis as plain and easy as to walk.

ADRAS. 'Fore heaven, madam! you rejoice me.

HELEN. And in truth, Adrastus, if to win my daughter be matter for rejoicing, you ought to rejoice; for this new blow of fortune shall thus be made to glance from us, and hit the striker. Had we pursued our first scheme, and carried off Janassa, there would have been much anger to encounter from her father, which now the shame to be caught in his own snare will make him hide. And his cunning shall be the fitting excuse for our own.——But truly I forgot to tell you, Adrastus, that your father is asking for you. He is about some joke upon our philosopher, and wishes you to help him. When you have been with him, come to my room, and we will talk farther.

ADRAS. My dearest madam, I give you a thousand thanks. I'll help his joke with all my heart; for it was that cursed old fellow that brought the poet here. I'll be with you again presently. [*Exit.*

HELEN. Otus, come you along with me. I must hear more fully in this matter. And remember to keep still on the watch. Something or other may cause them to change in their scheme; and you must dodge them like the air, that catches every word that is whispered, tho' the whisperer himself scarce hears it. Mind, Otus—catch—catch—catch.—

OTUS. Oh yes, my kind and honor'd lady; if there's any fish stirring, I'll catch it,—be sure o' that. (*Exit* HELEN.) Now is she going to try if she can catch any of my fish :—but they shan't bite, mistress, depend on't. And it shall go hard but I'll make you pay for the sport too. [*Exit.*

SCENE IV.—*The apartment of* MELAS.

(*Enter* LAODAMUS *and* ASIUS.)

LAOD. He is coming here immediately. The slaves are now bearing him away from the supper-room.

ASIUS. It was merely my wish to caution you that his death must now be very nigh. He will take no wine, I am told,— and what chance have we therefore to bridle the fever that must be running away with him?

LAOD. I have often remarked, my good Asius, that, upon certain minds, a recommendation to pursue any specified course begets an obstinacy that infallibly turns the unhappy being into a path directly opposite.

ASIUS. You are perfectly correct, sir ; as in lunatics and pigs. I have often thought it, sir, a very curious subject for philosophical disquisition, why those animals, on the least intimation that their road lies *here*, become immediately anxious to take it *there*:—and I have conceived, sir, that among the many analogies which Nature presents us in the most heterogeneous matters, we might perhaps trace one between the pig, and the obstinate madman. But go on, sir; I interrupt you.

LAOD. Sir, I am sure so profound a thought ought not to be called an interruption. I trust you will pursue it, and that mankind may profit from your ingenious researches. I was merely about to suggest than an injunction to refrain from wine might perhaps be a sufficient incentive to an indulgence in it. Here they come. Use the hint as you think best.

(*Enter* MELAS, *carried in by four* SLAVES.)

MELAS (*as they enter*). Who bids you bear me gently? *I* do not.
I rather wish your walk were rough and quick,
That so this worthless limb were shaken well,
And I might smile at it. Thanks, fellows—thanks.
'Tis for your labor, not your gentleness.   [*Exeunt* SLAVES.

LAOD. How now, good Melas?

MELAS. Sir, I saw you not.
Right well: I thank heaven for it.

LAOD. But your leg?—

MELAS. Pray think no more on't. Will the worlds stand
still
Because my bones are powder'd?—Doth this joint
Discuss philosophy?—or doth this calf
Discourse on good, and evil—chance—and fate?

ASIUS (*aside*). I know one calf that talks a good deal upon
all those matters.

MELAS. Oh, sir! these earthly limbs are but my mock—
Who cares to have his fetters bright and sound?
Or rather joys not, when the hungry rust
Is fixing his sharp teeth?—Such are these limbs;
Mere bolts and shackles to th' immortal mind.

(PANTHUS *enters behind—and sits down unseen.*)

PANTHUS (*aside*). Oh! curse his immortal mind! He's at it
again. But I'll keep cool.—I'll keep cool. Oh! A-h!

ASIUS (*feeling the pulse*). One—two—three—four—five—six
—seven—eight—(*Aside*) 'Tis truly the most obstinate pulse I
ever felt. The man must be in a raging fever, and yet his pulse
is as quiet as a ploughman's on a Saturday night.

MELAS. How do you find it, sir? Is death at hand?
Don't flinch, if that's your thought. Say it at once;
And I will call that word a blessed one.
Death is my dearest friend,—for then I mount
And leave this dunghill earth.

PANTHUS (*aside*). Oh! you cursed lying old rascal! You
ought to mount first, and die after, on a gallows. But we'll
tickle you.

ASIUS. One—two—three—four—five—six—seven—eight.
—Sir, there are symptoms here that baffle me. How for-
tunate that I came in at this time! Sir—had you, under the
present state, followed my prescription in the matter of wine, I
cannot say what might have been the dreadful result. Your

agonies would have been horrible. Avoid wine, sir, as you would avoid the adder's sting.

MELAS. I hear you; and am thirsty.—Bring me wine—
That I may taste new agonies to laugh at.
Now bring it me, I beg you.

LAOD.   My good friend!
I will not put the scourge in your own hand,
To tear your flesh with. Pray you now, be ruled,
And let the learned leech inspect the wound,
And use his deepest art upon it. Pray you.

MELAS. Were I, my good and honor'd sir, like men
Unread in our divine philosophy. . . .

PANTHUS (*aside*). Oh! Curse your divine philosophy!

MELAS. Who think mere pain an evil,—pleasure good,
It may be I had listen'd to you :—but,
No pain is pain to me that leaves the mind
Able to act ;—no pleasure pleases me,
That springs not from the soul. And, for this leg,
What is it?

PANTHUS (*aside*). Oh! you cursed old villain! I shall burst if I have to bear this long.

MELAS.   Might not such an accident
Have chanced to thousands,—whose unmanly souls
Had sunk beneath it?—Then should I rejoice,
That on *me*, rather, hath the burthen fallen,
Whose strength is equal to it.——To endure
With philosophic soul, is happiness
More than to feel no pain.

ASIUS. Well, my good friend, I must leave you now.—One —two—three—four—five—six—seven—eight.——Remember, sir, that wine is present death. One—two—three—four— Present death, sir.—Good-night to you, sir.—Present death, sir.

LAOD. Good-night to you, Melas ;—sound sleep, and a pleasant waking.

PANTHUS (*aside*). One of which, at least, I'll take care he shall have.

MELAS. My kind friends, a good-night to you both.

LAOD. (*aside to* ASIUS). What think you of him now?

ASIUS. You may as well ask me what I think of a man who died a thousand years ago. I would give half of what I possess to have the opening of him. He must infallibly, sir, be devoured by fever, and yet that infernal pulse of his goes as true as the sun. Pray you let him have wine. I will see what can be done by sacrifices; for physic can do nothing. Sir, I will offer up a sheep to Apollo. I have known wonderful cures performed that way.

LAOD. But may I be allowed to ask why wine should be forced upon him to check fever, when you confess that his pulse gives no indication of fever existing?

ASIUS. But, sir, he *ought* to be in a fever, and a dreadful one.—Great Gods, sir!—A man, pounded like blanched almonds, not to be in a fever? Sir, he *must* be in a fever, and his pulse deserves not to be trusted.

LAOD. Take what course you think best; and your services shall be amply considered.

ASIUS. Sir, your generosity is well known. Of all the cases in my practice it is surely the most puzzling!—A pulse like a water-wheel!

[*Exeunt* LAODAMUS *and* ASIUS.

PANTHUS. Well, my good Melas,—how is it with you, now?

MELAS. Ha! Panthus—are you there?—What says Podagra?—and what says gentle Colic?

PANTHUS. You and I were rather rough this morning, my good Melas.—

MELAS. *You*,—but not *I*.—Who waits?

PANTHUS. I don't know what you call rough, but by Jove!—

(*Enter a* SERVANT.)

MELAS. Bring wine.

PANTHUS. And here, my good fellow, help me a little nearer to my poor friend.—Thank you, thank you.

MELAS. I tell you, Panthus, the slim willow-twig that bends with every sigh of the air is not more pliant than was I before the storm of your fury.—(SERVANT *places wine before* MELAS.) I drink to your better mind : for your health, what matters it?

PANTHUS. And I drink to your better leg :—for your confounded philosophy, what matters that? Curse it, man!—can you walk upon a syllogism? Or, if a scoundrel affronts you, can you kick him with your immortal mind?—Tell me that, man.

MELAS. I drink to you again, Panthus :—and may you soon be set at liberty from that horrid old carcase that chains down the ethereal spirit !

PANTHUS. I won't go in a passion—and that's flat. I tell you, Melas, you *shall not* drive me into a passion. But I must tell you that you are the most infernal old scoundrel unhanged.

MELAS. Panthus, I love thee. That sweet tongue of thine
Doth lash me ;—but it teacheth to endure,
And therefore is it sweet to me.—Again
Unto thy health I drink—to thy mind's health :—
And may Gonagra, and most blessed gout,
Take thee off quick ! I love thee to my heart.

PANTHUS. And I love thee,—and thou shalt find I love thee.—
Why dost drink so often ? Is that philosophy?——

MELAS. Thou takest wine for pleasure ;—I, for pain.
The learned leech hath threaten'd agony
If I should drink,—and therefore I take wine.—
And truly 'tis a glorious torture comes.
Dear friend ! what are lumbago,—colic,—gout,—
To the sweet pangs *I* feel!—Seize—seize thy crutch—
And smite thy joints till they shall burst abroad :—
And take sharp drinks till thy old back shall rend
With thy fierce agonies ;—then, let us sit
And smile at one another, and be friends.—
Ha ! Panthus—to thy health.— (*Drinking.*)

PANTHUS. Earth never bore such a monster as thou art,—thou diabolical old plague ! Smite my joints !—oh ! merciful heaven !—and rend open my back with fierce agonies !—and then sit and smile ! Oh, curse thee !—But I'll keep cool. Curse thee ! I shall have the fit at my stomach again if I don't keep cool.—Thou cursed old villain !—But I'll keep cool—I'll keep cool.—Oh curse thee !

MELAS. Oh ! blest philosophy ! who'd bear to live
Unwarm'd by thy sweet sunshine ?—Panthus—friend—
Prithee indulge me. Let us take hot coals,
And press them in our palms :—and thrust sharp knives
Into our flesh ;—and drink boil'd pitch for wine,—
And so be merry.—Prithee, my kind friend—
Call for quick fire,—and place thy gouty foot
Within it, and rejoice.

PANTHUS. Oh ! curse thee ! I can't bear it. Here—give us more wine. Does thy leg sting thee now?

(SERVANT *fills the cups.*)

MELAS. With an immortal and delicious pang.
What think'st thou of divine philosophy ?
Ha ! lovely Panthus ! I will bruise thee soon,
And reason thee to take it with delight.—
Oh ! how I'll pound thy much-loved gouty limbs !
Thou'lt be in heaven. Once more I drink to thee.

PANTHUS. And I to thee. (*Aside*) Ay—swig it down, my friend ; and then *thou'lt* be in heaven.

MELAS. Oh ! Panthus !—Think but on th' immortal mind ! And these poor limbs.—Heigh-ho.— (*Yawning.*)

PANTHUS. I promise thee I am thinking even now of that poor limb of thine.—Thou growest sleepy, Melas.—'Tis the body that sleeps, I take it. The immortal mind keeps broad awake :—doth it not ?

MELAS.—Oh, certainly—cer-tainly.—To-morrow—
Or any other time.—Who are you, sir ?—
Divine philosophy.—For this vile leg—— (*He sleeps.*)

PANTHUS. Ay—for this vile leg, my old fellow ;—we will

soon see what ails that.—Call in your mistress, and my son.— Oh!—Ah!— (*Exit* SERVANT.) Now, thou infernal old scoundrel!—that callest on gout and lumbago to take me off quick ;—and promisest to pound my much-loved gouty limbs; —we'll untruss thee :—we'll behold how thy bones are powder'd :—we'll find out the cause of thy delicious and immortal pangs. Ha! thou abominable old rascal!

(HELEN *and* ADRASTUS *enter with the two* SERVANTS.)

ADRAS. Is he asleep?

PANTHUS. As sound as Caucasus.—Come, knaves—despatch. Get out your knives and scissors, and let us unpack this bale, and see what kind of merchandise we have therein.

HELEN. Stay :—let us first have the doors locked :—and pray you, go gently about it; for I cannot but think he hath some grievous hurt; tho', perchance, not of a measure equal to the report he hath given out. And, pray you now, keep all quiet : and, for your lives, let not a word of this escape : for Laodamus would be in a towering wrath.

ADRAS. What is that first covering?

1ST SERV. Can't tell, sir, till we've got to the end of it.

PANTHUS. End of it? Why, there is no end of it. Did you see him wag his leg when he cuff'd me to-day?—Curse him! I shall never forget it.

HELEN. Why, good heavens! what has he wrapp'd his limb in?

PANTHUS. Why the main-sail of a ship, I think. He might well thwack his leg as he did to terrify poor Janassa. I could stand it myself beneath such a fortress of canvas.

2ND SERV. We have got to the end now, sir.

PANTHUS. And how does the leg look?

1ST SERV. Oh sir—'tis terrible big now, sir.

PANTHUS. Perhaps there is another main-sail to be overhauled. But, my lads, get on with your work. There is a kernel to this shell, and we must come at it.—Zounds! boy— don't touch my elbow! Oh!—Ah!—confound you!

ADRAS. I beg your pardon, my dear sir.

HELEN. What's that?

2ND SERV. Why, madam, I think it be—I can't think what it be.—And here's another something.—

1ST SERV. Why 'tis master Melas' old cloak, that came back from the tailor last week irrecoverable.

PANTHUS. Well—he has made it coverable, at all events.—What! Anything else?

2ND SERV. Bless you, sir!—why there's no knowing when we shall ha' done. Here be two waistcoats, and two nether garments.

1ST SERV. Hold—hold.—There's blood here: we must go gently. Would you have us take this wrapper off, sir? It may make it gush out again, you know, sir, and perhaps——

2ND SERV. Blood?—Yes, 'tis pretty blood! A pair of blood-red garters.—Here we have it, sir.—Pray you, look sir.—

PANTHUS (*shaking his fist at* MELAS). Why, thou cursed old fox!

HELEN. Good heaven!—Why, his leg is as sound as mine!

ADRAS. What would Laodamus say to this?

PANTHUS. Or Asius?—that said his face was red with his unutterable torture. I shall never forget it.

MELAS. Oh! divine philosophy!

HELEN. What does he mutter?—He will surely not awake?

PANTHUS. Not he! He's only dreaming of his old work—his cursed philosophy—hush!—

MELAS. Here—rack these worthless joints.—Pound small this shatter'd leg——

PANTHUS. Oh! you cursed old rascal!—here's a shattered leg truly! Sound, and strong enough for half a dozen porters. I'd give half my estate for such a shatter'd leg. No wonder he wagged it about as he did, when he was shaking my bones out of their sockets this morning. Oh! you sly old villain!

ADRAS. Is he crazed, think you, madam?—or has he done this for some cheat?

HELEN. I cannot say :—but, in truth, I have considered him little better than a fool for some time past. 'Twas but th' other day he wished me not to cut a corn that pained me horribly, because, forsooth, it was virtuous to endure pain with fortitude. He had even the kindness to recommend a tight, hard shoe,—as an improvement.

ADRAS. Let us call in Asius, and Laodamus, and expose the old knave——

PANTHUS. No—no—no, no, no, no. Leave him to me. I have a plan, growing in my head, that shall bear good fruit for to-morrow night.—The old immortal-minded, divine-philosophy'd knave ! I'll teach thee to shake my bones like dice ; and to bang my head like a blacksmith's anvil.

PHORBAS (*without*). Open thy door, immortal Stoic !— Quick !—

PANTHUS. Heavens ! There's that infernal madman ! Roll up the bandages quick—that fellow will rouse the whole house if he cannot get in.

PHORBAS (*without*). Open thy door, I say ; I would speak with thee.

HELEN. Whisper him thro' the key-hole that the Stoic is dead.

PANTHUS. I thank thee for that.—Go, fellow.—

PHORBAS (*without*). Divine Melas ! My soul would commune with thee. Open thy door.

1ST SERV. (*at the key-hole*). Pray you, sir, depart. The divine Melas is no more. Disturb not his ashes, which we are preparing for their mother earth.

PHORBAS (*without*). Oh heavens ! Is that immortal spirit fled ? He was too great and glorious for this earth. I'll write his elegy :—and to-morrow will I pronounce it above his much-loved remains. Oh ! heavens ! Good-night, friends —good-night—I go to my solemn task. Good-night—good-night—Oh ! O—h !

SERV. Good-night, sir.—

PANTHUS. Good fellow ! I'll remember thee for this ; that

horrid madman would have almost killed me with the very aspect of his death's head, and his fire-ball eyes. Oh, Gods! I shall never forget him. But, come now. Carry the rest of the bandages away with him into his bed-chamber, and finish your packing up there. And mind you roll all up orderly, so that he may not discover the trick we have put on him. Adrastus, lend a hand to carry the old hunks off. Pray, you, madam, give me your help to rise up.—Gently—gently.—

ADRAS. Lift—fellows—lift. By Jove, he weighs like a rhinoceros!—Steady—steady!—

PANTHUS. There goes philosophy!—There goes an immortal mind. I thought what sort of marrow we should come to, when the bone was cracked. Softly—my dear madam.— Oh! my back! Oh! my knees! And he talked of pounding my much-loved gouty limbs!—Pray you, give me that crutch.

HELEN. Tread softly, fellows.—

(ADRASTUS *and the* SERVANTS *bear* MELAS *out.*)

PANTHUS. Oh! thou unutterable rascal!—But, to-morrow night!—to-morrow night——

HELEN. I, also, have a little sport for to-morrow night.

PANTHUS. Ay, marry? Let us hear it.

HELEN. Thou'lt know it in good time. [*Exit.*

PANTHUS. Well—well—I'll teach the old knave to make bell-ropes of my joints,—and cuff my head about like a tennis-ball. Curse him! Oh! A—h!—Curse him! And to beg, too, that lumbago and gout would carry me off quick! Oh! the infernal rascal! I shall never forget it—I shall never forget it!—Pound my joints, too!—Oh! curse him—O—h!—A—h!
[*Exit.*

END OF THE FOURTH ACT.

Act V.

Scene I.—*A room in the House of* Laodamus.

(Adrastus *discovered walking to and fro.*)

Adras. I wonder she does not come to me. It must be high time now to set off. (*Looking out*) Why, Zounds! the sun is just sinking. I shall be too late. (*Enter* Helen) My dearest madam, are you not late?

Helen. All in good time. Otus has just given me notice that Janassa is gone, and that Antilochus has received her pretended letter; and will not, therefore, depart for this hour to come: so that you have time enough. Remember to speak no unnecessary word; and, for the same reason, don't urge her to break silence; for, in the reply, you may betray yourself.

Adras. Oh! my dearest madam! I owe you much. Have you carefully instructed the slave? Will she not, think you, betray herself?

Helen. What matter if she do?—You will be first married to Janassa; and whether Antilochus afterwards wed the slave, or not, can signify but the value of a joke carried, or lost.

Adras. 'Tis very true. And yet I would be glad that he should be mocked, as well as deceived; for I hate him with a mortal hatred.

Helen. Poh! poh! You'll have revenge enough in carrying off his prize; let it rest there.—But now, away—away—your horse is at the postern gate. Ride coolly. You will easily be there before Janassa, for she takes the longer road.

Adras. Adieu, my dearest madam:—soon to be, I hope, my dearest mother. (*Aside*) Now for love, and revenge!

Helen. Hark you, Adrastus. [*Exeunt.*

(Laodamus *and* Janassa *enter on the opposite side, treading softly.*)

Laod. Hush—hush!—Did you hear that? In good faith we were near treading on the fox's tail.

Jan. Did they see us?

Laod. No—but did you hear? 'Farewell, dear Adrastus,—soon, I hope, to be my dear son!'—Oh! Helen! Helen!

Jan. My poor mother!

Laod. Come, come, my dearest child:—no more of this.
Leave her to me, and to her better self.
She'll wake from out this dream, and be right glad
To find 'twas but a dream.

Jan.   My poor, poor mother!
I never yet deceiv'd thee.—

Laod.   But must now.
And she shall thank thee for it. But come, come;
Antilochus awaits you; and the priest
Is putting on his vestments.—Go you first;—
He's in the temple porch. Nay, nay, my child;
Sighing and tears are not for such a night;
Why, that's a face to tend a funeral,—
Not to be married in.—Go—go along.

Jan. It is so *very* sudden.

Laod.   Sudden, girl?
Why, in six days, this earth, and the deep sea,
And all that lives,—and the star-lighted heavens,—
Were plann'd and form'd; and the enormous sun,
Ev'n at a thought, amid the dark, void sky
Stood blazing!—Surely four-and-twenty hours
May serve to patch a wedding up.—Come, come;—
I'll walk with you,—and bring the priest anon.
Lean on my arm.—Oh! 'tis a horrid business!
Hanging is curds and cream to't.

Jan.   My poor mother!
[*Exeunt.*

Scene II.—*The Garden—and the Temple.*

(Antilochus *stands in the porch.*)

Antil. Oh heavens! when will she come? My heart is sad.
What can it mean?—All is so solemn still:—

There's not a breath amid the leaves ; no stir
From out the city ;—not a cloud in heaven,
Whose smooth and silent course might look like life
Amid this death-like stillness.—Oh ! come—come—
My loved Janassa—come—and comfort me,
With thy mild looks, and thy celestial voice,—
Sweeter than breath of June.—Oh ! come, my love :—
My heart is lone and sad.—I've heard it said,
These darkenings of the soul are auguries
Of evil nigh at hand.—Ye gracious heavens !
Be merciful !—hark—hark ! There is a foot.— (*A pause.*)
'Tis she !—Oh ! my Janassa !

(*Enter* JANASSA, *leaning on* LAODAMUS.)

LAOD. (*giving her to* ANTILOCHUS). There—there—there.—
JAN. (*holding his hand*). Pray do not leave me !
LAOD. I'll be back anon :
Comfort her, youth ; for she is sore distrest
At thought of such a death.—My dear—dear child ! (*Embracing and kissing her.*) [*Exit* LAOD.

ANTIL. Janassa !—What ! in tears ?—Is aught amiss ?
Will you not speak to me ?—Do you repent
Your hard-wrung promise ?—Am I hateful to you ?

JAN. Oh ! no—no—no.—Pray do not question me.
This sudden marriage ;—and my mother's grief ;—
And this deceiving of her——

ANTIL. Prithee, love,
If this be all, lay by that sorrowing look.
I hoped those rebel thoughts were all subdued,
Never to rise again. Come—come ; look up.—
Is this an hour for melancholy, love ?
I ask thee that, and yet myself am sad ;—
But 'tis a pleasant sadness, now thou'rt here—
Dearer than all the boisterous joys of life.
Look up, my love.

(*Enter* LAODAMUS *and a* PRIEST.)

LAOD. This way, good father. We will come anon.
(*The* PRIEST *goes into the temple.*)

Come, my dear child:—life hath severer pangs
Than even this.—But no—I'll rail no more.
Lean on my arm.—Antilochus—go in.

ANTIL. Janassa!—look not so!
(ANTILOCHUS *goes into the temple.*)

LAOD. My dearest child!—even from thy cradle up,
Thou'st been a blessing to me. Thee Heaven bless!
(*They go into the temple.*)

(*Enter* PHORBAS.)

PHORBAS. Oh! mourn! mourn; mourn! ye solitary shores!
The great, the good is dead! His spirit soars
Far—far away,—(his bright immortal mind,—)
And leaves the vile, dull clay behind:—
Melas—the great—the good! Oh! earth, make moan,
Ye oceans,—mountains—rivers—groan! groan! groan!
[*Exit.*

SCENE III.—*The apartment of* MELAS.

(*Enter* PANTHUS, *with the two* SERVANTS.)

PANTHUS. Which is the place?

1ST SERVANT. Here, in this closet, sir.—This thin screen will hide you as well as a wall, and yet you can see, and hear everything through it.

PANTHUS. Come, then — help me in. Softly — softly!— Remember I am not a man of marble. Oh! Ah! gently—gently—that arm!—that knee! Oh! Ah!—Now, place the seat so that I may be quite easy:—and put me a stool for each foot. It won't do to cry out, you know. Help me to sit down easy. Oh! Ah! Thank you—thank you. Now, my lads, play your parts like stout fellows, and I'll fill your pockets with gold.

2ND SERV. Oh, sir, don't fear us. They are bringing him along now.

PANTHUS. Then off with you. And remember your parts. (*Exeunt* SERVANTS.) Curse him! we'll tickle him. Oh!— but Zounds! I must not cry out so. Curse him, but he shall though, and lustily. The villain! Smite my joints till they burst abroad! Oh! the remorseless fury! I shall never forget it—and rend open my back with fierce lumbago! Ha! thou hell-dog! And thrust my tortured foot into hot coals! Thou most unheard-of miscreant! And pound my much-loved gouty limbs! I shall never forget it. Curse him! but here he comes. Now for it.

(MELAS *is carried in by four* SERVANTS.)

MELAS. Fellows, I thank you. Know you what you are?

1ST SERV. We be men, sir, I hope—and good servants to our good master.

MELAS. Oh ignorance! Now listen what you are;
And bear't in mind. You all are living souls,
That drag about you earthly carcases.

2ND SERV. Oh, sir! I am sure we carries you about with a deal of pleasure. Pray say no more about it, sir.

MELAS. Poor, simple things! Stay, fellows: give me wine,
And that huge folio.—Then go your ways.

[*Exeunt* SERVANTS.

(*Enter* ASIUS.)

ASIUS. I cannot stay a moment; but must just ask how you are to-night, my good Melas.

MELAS. In admirable health, I thank you, Asius. The immortal mind——

PANTHUS. Oh!

ASIUS. What was that?

MELAS. 'Twas a strange noise.

ASIUS. What! have you wine? Said I not that wine would be present death to you? How is this?

MELAS. Even as you see. I drank, and yet I live.

ASIUS. One—two—three—four—five—six—seven—eight—Melas, thou'rt better: thank Apollo for it. I have sacrificed to him for thee, and am, even now, about to offer up new sacrifice. Erelong look for wonderful things. Adieu—adieu. The God listens to me; and thy natural fever is coming upon thee. May it increase! And so fare thee well. [*Exit.*

MELAS. Asius, adieu. Now for one cheering cup: then to my studies. (*Drinks.*) Was I drunk last night? I must sip more sparingly. Of a certainty I never before was so overtaken by total obliviousness.—How I got to bed,—or how, and when that pestering gouty old fool left me, is as strange to me as the history of the moon.—Let me think.—Who carried me to bed? —Why, nobody.—But did I walk, then? Yet how could I walk with such a shattered leg? And the bandages, beside, weigh half a hundred. I never could walk in my sleep with such a clog to my foot, and not be wakened by it:—to say nothing of my leg being beaten to a sort of paste; as it certainly is. And yet—(*a pause*)—and yet I sometimes doubt it, too.—Who did it? I cannot tell rightly. But there are the bandages :—let them speak for themselves.

PHORBAS (*without*). Now for my doleful task. Oh! Oh!

MELAS. There's that cursed mad poet coming. If I speak to him, he'll plague me all night. I'll feign myself asleep.

(*Lying down.*)

(*Enter* PHORBAS, *walking slowly; with his eyes bent on the ground.*)

PHORBAS. Oh! mourn! mourn! mourn!

PANTHUS (*peeping out*). Oh! blessed Jupiter! what shall I do now?

PHORBAS. Mourn, earth, thro' all thy caves;—
  Mourn, sea, with all thy waves;
Mourn, all ye forests, and ye mountains high!—
  For he is gone,—
  The great, the mighty one,—
And left dull earth behind,—and fled into the sky.
  Mourn, mourn, oh! mourn!
  For earth is now forlorn—
   Melas is dead!
  The immortal mind is fled;
And on this night shall never burst the morn,—
  For he's above—and we're below—
  O—h! O——h!

Let me now once more behold his much-loved remains.
                              (*He looks on* MELAS.)
Good heavens! how beautiful he looks in death!
Fresher, methinks, than even in his life.—
And he'd been drinking when the death-pang came!
And so they've left him!—Let me taste his wine. (*He drinks.*)
'Tis good! 'tis *very* good!—I'll try again.
I loved the man;—and now I love his wine.
                              (*He drinks again.*)
Oh! he's a lovely corpse! Yet 'twas not well
To leave his eyes half clos'd,—his mouth agape:—
I'll do him this sad office,—close his jaw;
And seal his eyes up.—Oh! Oh! Oh! Oh! Oh!
     (MELAS *bites his finger, and rises up, still keeping hold.*)
Oh! mercy! mercy!—I'm the dead man's prey.

PANTHUS (*peeping out*). Ha!—ha!—ha!—ha!

MELAS.—What's that?—that horrid laugh?

PHORBAS. Art thou come back to us?

MELAS. Who was't that laugh'd?

PHORBAS. Art thou come back to us?

MELAS. Did you not hear a harsh, and horrid laugh?

PHORBAS. 'I heard a thousand corpses laugh outright,
         Met in a charnel-house at deep midnight:
Their lanterns were skulls,—and their candles were marrow'—
That is the opening of a morsel of my Terrible. But, for heaven's mercy! Are you indeed not dead?

MELAS. Dead? Thou fool!—Lend me thy finger once more, and I will convince thee.

PHORBAS. Oh! blessed Melas! how do I rejoice!—They told me thou wert dead; and I have written thy elegy. Art thou indeed alive?—Oh! I have a glorious thing for thee. We'll spend the night on't.

MELAS. I'll hear nought of it. What a slave art thou,
To roar out thus because thy finger's bitten!—
Why, had thy worthless body, limb by limb,
And joint by joint, been crush'd,—what's that to thee,

Had but thy soul been noble?—Thou'rt a slave!
I will not hear thy damnèd poesy.

PHORBAS. Immortal Melas! I am but a man;
And have not commun'd oft with souls like thine,
From whom to learn the majesty of Gods:—
But thy example shall inspirit me
To deeds heroic. What thou bear'st, I'll bear.
Give me *thy* finger,—and I'll set my teeth
Deep in the bone:—and then shalt thou seize mine;
And of each other thus we'll learn to bear
Unheard-of agonies.

MELAS. Curse thee!—art thou mad?

PHORBAS. I'll gnaw thy joints—thou beautiful old man!
And thou'lt gnaw mine. Oh heavens!—immortal heav'ns!
How we'll run on our race!—I'll snatch thine eyes
Out of their sockets——

MELAS. Help!—the fellow's mad!

PANTHUS. Oh! mercy on me!—Oh! good heavens!

PHORBAS. Thy limbs I'll twist,—and wrench out at the joints!
Boil thee in molten lead!—take out thy brains,
And stir them up with sulphur and fir'd pitch!—

MELAS. Oh! heavens! what a fury!—help! help! help!

PANTHUS. Have mercy on us! have mercy on us!—my turn
will come next!

PHORBAS. Oh! 'twill be glorious! Then our matchless deeds,
Poets unborn shall sing. I weep to think
How happy we shall be.—Thou lov'd old man!
Give me thy finger—I'll take off one joint,
Just to begin with.—Come—thy beauteous finger:
Come—come—come—come:—and then shalt thou take mine.

MELAS. Phorbas, I'll take thine first; for now, methinks,
Thou'rt worthy my esteem. Then, if thy soul
Be proof to this, with nobler agonies
I will assay thee: but, if vanquish'd here,
Think not so poor a soul shall league with mine
In this high warfare 'gainst ignoble clay.
Give me thy finger.—

PHORBAS. Here 'tis, illustrious demi-god. Oh! Oh!
Enough! enough! Oh heavens! enough! Oh! Oh!

MELAS. Art thou a man to vie with me? Poor slave!
Go—get thee hence! For one poor finger roar?
Look at this leg,—this mangled shatter'd limb:
(*Enter the two* SERVANTS, *in frightful disguises; with horrid Masks, thro' which the voice may sound dreadful. They have whips in their hands.* PHORBAS *beholds them, and in speechless terror stalks to the door, looking back at them—then goes out. The two* MASKS *then go, and stand behind* MELAS.)
Here—here is agony:—yet do *I* scream,
And roar like thee? Well mayst thou hold thy peace;—
Poor heartless wretch! Hadst thou a pain like this,—
A bone that is but powder;—muscles—flesh—
Beaten and crush'd to a mere marmalade;—
Swell'd to a mammoth bulk,—immovable
As huge Parnassus,—then thou might'st exclaim.—
But where art gone?
(*He looks round, and sees one* MASK *peeping over his shoulder.*)
Ha!—What art thou?

1ST MASK. I am Podagra!

2ND MASK (*at the other shoulder*). I am Lumbago!

BOTH MASKS TOGETHER. And we are come to try thee!
(MELAS *gets up, and hobbles to the door. Just as he reaches it,* 1ST MASK *turns the key, and stares him in the face. He hobbles to the other door, but* 2ND MASK *turns the key and stares at him.*)

PANTHUS (*aside, peeping out*). Oh! thou cursed old villain!
Thou'st found thy leg at last.

MELAS. What would ye have—ye dreadful beings?—Speak.

1ST MASK. We come to undeceive thee. Bare thy leg,
And I will torture thee awhile, that thou mayst know
I am Podagra—Strip thy villain leg!

2ND MASK. And bare thy caitiff back,—so, with this scourge,
I'll torture thee awhile, that thou mayst know
I am dire Lumbago.—Strip—strip thy back!

MELAS. Oh! I conjure you by yon heavens above!
Have pity on me! (*Kneeling to them.*)

1ST MASK. We are not of heaven,
And will not pity thee.

MELAS. By earth and sea!

2ND MASK. We care not for them.

MELAS. By the immortal Gods!

1ST MASK. Thou'st nought to do with them.

MELAS. By horrid Styx!

BOTH MASKS. In *that* name will we answer thee.

(*They begin to flog him soundly. He roars out, and tries to get away; but one* MASK *puts his foot on his neck, and the other* MASK *on his leg.* MELAS *roars unceasingly.*)

PANTHUS (*peeping out*). Give him enough:—let him have Styx (sticks) enough.—Lay on, Podagra!—Well done, Lumbago!—Wilt pound my joints again? Ay—roar away.—Thou know'st Podagra now—and fiery agonies.—Lay on—lay on. That's 'much-loved gout'—and that is 'fierce Lumbago.'—Lay on—lay on.—'The immortal mind is whole, and knows no pain.'—' 'Tis but the body—pay it no regard.'—

SERVANTS (*outside the door*). What is amiss? We will force open the door——

(*The two* MASKS *leap away, and go out at the other door; leaving* MELAS *lying with his face to the ground, and roaring hideously. The door is burst open, and* LAODAMUS *enters with several* SERVANTS.)

LAOD. What is amiss? Good heavens! what is amiss? Melas, my friend—what ails thee?

MELAS (*roaring out*). Oh! Oh! Podagra! Lumbago!

1ST SERV. He's in a fit! poor man! he's in a fit!

LAOD. Then lift him up, and bear him to the air. I fear his hour is come. 'Tis the last pang.

(SERVANTS *lift up* MELAS.)

Carry his couch—and bear him to the hall ;—
The air is fresh and cooling there. Good heavens!
What a sad dash upon our joys to-night! [*Exeunt Omnes.*

SCENE IV.—*The great Hall.*
(LAODAMUS *enters, with* SERVANTS *bearing in* MELAS.)
LAOD. Tread gently, my good fellows——

(*Enter* HELEN.)
HELEN. What's amiss?
LAOD. Poor Melas in a horrid fit.
HELEN. Good heavens!
Is Asius here?

1ST SERV. Madam, he is but just gone, and we have sent after him.

LAOD. Lay him upon the couch :—then stand aside,
And let the fresh air fan him.

2ND SERV. I fear he is dead, sir.

LAOD. Poor man! his pain has kill'd him. Oh! good Asius!

(*Enter* ASIUS.)

He's gone, I fear :—seiz'd with a horrid fit——

ASIUS. Ha!—Yes—he's gone!—His heart beats yet—but that shews nothing.—Now let us open him. Dismiss your servants, all but two, who shall denude the corpse; and we will examine this phenomenon.

LAOD. Somewhat too hasty, sir. Wait till to-morrow. 'Twere scarcely decent just upon his death; even while the body reeks.

ASIUS. That's an advantage, sir,—a very great one. To-morrow I shall be away ;—and the corpse will be rotten, if, indeed, it be not so already. That limb must be thoroughly mortified.

LAOD. Did you expect his end so soon?

ASIUS. It has been my marvel that he has not died much sooner. But Apollo hath listen'd to my prayers, and accepted my sacrifices. I begg'd for Melas a sudden cure, or a sudden release; and I knew not which might come.

LAOD. We know at last.—Is he,—past all hope—gone?

ASIUS. Dead as the tree that was hewn down a year ago, and burned yesterday.—His heart beats still: but I have known a heart to thump for half an hour after death. And for *his* pulse, I should not marvel if it went on beating for twenty years after his very bones are moulded away. Come, fellows. —Strip him. I have my instruments with me. It will be a most interesting dissection.

LAOD. You forget, I think, that my wife is present. Besides, in truth, I cannot permit such a hasty, if not indecent attack, upon the body of my poor friend. To the examination of the leg I consent; but, for to-day at least, nothing farther.

ASIUS. Craving first a thousand pardons of your honor'd lady, whom truly in my hurry I did not behold, I shall bow to your pleasure, my dear sir, and commence. (*He begins to remove the bandages.*) A very extraordinary bandage this! Do you note it, sir?—You, sir, may see nothing unusual in the appearance of this canvas,—or sack-cloth—or *sail*-cloth,— whichsoever it may be:—but, sir, to an experienced eye, it tells deep matters. I would venture, sir, from the mere inspection of this outward covering, to prognosticate that the whole mass of flesh and bone beneath it is sheer rottenness.

(*Enter* PANTHUS.)

PANTHUS. What is amiss?

LAOD. Our poor friend is no more.

PANTHUS (*in terror*). Great Gods!—dead?—dead?—No— no.—

ASIUS. Panthus—how do you? Yes—yes—he's dead enough, and we shall open the body to-morrow, if indeed the state of the carcase will permit dissection.—Bless me! when shall we come to the end of this canvas?—The limb is horribly putrescent. Pity that we cannot open him immediately!— Pah!—

PANTHUS. Is he really dead?

Asius. *Really* dead?—Come, and touch him :—and note his cadaverous odour. Dead indeed?—When he rises again you may put me into the coffin in his stead.

Melas (*leaping up*). Glorious Apollo !

(Asius *screams, and runs out.* Helen *sinks on her knees and cries 'Murder !'—but soon rises and goes out.* Laodamus *starts back a step, but then recovers himself, and takes* Melas *by the arm. The* Servants *fly in terror,—and throw one another down : while* Melas *continues to stalk to and fro, calling out* ' Glorious Apollo !'*)*

Laod. My dear Melas !—pray stop one moment, and reveal this mystery.

Melas (*stalking about*). [Oh! Glorious Apollo ! I am healed ! My wounds are closed up !—my bones are made sound !—Great and glorious Apollo !

Asius (*peeping in*). He certainly lives :—and yet he looks ghastly.—This is the blessëd fruit of my prayers and sacrifices. —(*Coming in*) Melas—dost live ?

Melas. Asius, behold !—My agonies are gone—my limb is sound—my flesh is whole.—Glorious Apollo ! thee I praise for this.

Panthus (*on the ground*). Oh ! Oh ! he is come from the Shades to haunt and torture me.

Asius. I knew it would be thus.

Laod. For which reason, my good sir, you were anxious to open him before the opportunity should slip by.

Asius. Why, yes.—No—no—no—certainly—that is—but to-morrow, sir, to-morrow, sir—I will give you my reason—my reasons—which I could not—could not—make clear to—to—to unscientific co—co—co—comprehensions,—without much—much — cir — circumlocution,— and the—the lapse of many hours, the which we cannot now spare.—But, grea tand favor'd man ! declare to us how this hath been.

Melas. I have seen visions—I have heard sounds—I have felt visitations.—Great and glorious Apollo !

PANTHUS. There he is again:—talking just as when he was alive. Oh! me! Oh, me!

LAOD. What hast thou seen? What hast thou heard?

ASIUS. And what hath visited thee?

MELAS. Oh! what a glory is the immortal mind!

PANTHUS. Oh! there's that cursed old immortal mind! He'll never leave me again—Oh! Oh!

MELAS. I have seen shapes wonderful and terrible! Furies with whips, whose lashes were cords of red-hot steel.—

PANTHUS. Ay! ay!—Those were my two Furies, who flogged him to death, poor fellow!—How hearty he talks after death!

MELAS. I have heard the horrid laughings of viewless demons,—while the Furies tortured me.

PANTHUS. Why, that was me! I was the horrid demon that laughed.—

MELAS. But while the Furies scourged me, and the demons laughed and applauded,—I did but smile, and bid them do their worst——

PANTHUS. Oh, Jupiter! Who would have thought that a spirit durst lie so damnably! and within ten minutes after death too! I'll look at the poor shade.—Bless me! Just in his former shape! and as fat as ever!—and he's looking at me. Oh! Oh!

MELAS. Why, Panthus!—what dost thou there?

LAOD. My dear Panthus! I did not see you.

ASIUS. Poor gentleman! Let us lift him to the couch.

PANTHUS. Are you all living men?

LAOD. Yes—yes:—all living men, and your kind friends.

PANTHUS (*pointing to* MELAS). But is *that* shape a living man?

MELAS. Ay, Panthus! Take my hand, and feel that this is warm and solid flesh.

PANTHUS. Oh! Oh! curse you! Oh! Oh! you have crushed my joints.—Oh!

MELAS. Excellent friend! think not of it. Hadst thou known *my* agonies!—I have been scourged by Furies.—I have seen Podagra, and Lumbago,—and laughed at them.

PANTHUS (*aside*). Not half so much as they have laughed at you.—Why what a fool have I been!

ASIUS. But, my good sir, tell us how all this chanced. I am sure my intercessions with Apollo have brought it about.

LAOD. Pray you, sir, deliver us the whole, just as it fell out.

MELAS. Apollo?—Ay! Great and glorious Apollo! *he* hath done it,—and I praise him. Listen, and you shall hear.—I had retired to solitary meditation on this our life,—these earthly bodies,—and these our immortal minds——

PANTHUS. Oh!

MELAS. The pain of my limb had risen to a glorious agony, —yet did I smile upon it,—when, suddenly, a blaze like sunshine filled the room, and a shape of unutterable brightness stood before me, and spake these words——

PANTHUS (*aside*). I see he must have t'other dose before the cure is completed.

MELAS. 'Melas—thou art more than man! I have seen thy agony, and admired thy fortitude. In one thing more will I prove thee. Bear that, and thy wounds and tortures shall pass away, and thy limb shall be made whole. I am Apollo!'

PANTHUS (*aside*). He'll be for pounding my joints again—I see he will.—He *must* have t'other bit.

ASIUS. Did not this shake you, sir?

MELAS. Ay!—as Caucasus is shaken by the sparrow that alights upon it.—The God ceased—disappeared—and all was Stygian darkness—horrible blackness.—

PANTHUS (*aside*). Why, what a liar it is! I will make oath there were two good candles burning all the while.

MELAS. Mark now.—Of a sudden there stood before me two monstrous Shapes,—Furies from Tartarus.—Their eyes were like moons :—their mouths seemed fiery gulfs ;—and, as they opened them to speak, I heard thunders from out their entrails.

PANTHUS (*aside*). My poor fellows! I fear they wanted their supper.—What a knave it is! We *must* try again.

MELAS. In their hands they bore whips of fire ; and with voices like volcanoes, they told me their names,—unpronounceable by human organs.—In an instant they stripped from me my robes ; and the bandages from my mangled limb ; and on my undefended body laid the dreadful weight of their red-hot scourges. Blow came on blow ;—the air hissed with the fury of their whips :—the flesh they cut,—they lashed me to the bone ;—and, all the while, horrid demons laughed, and bade them toil on.

PANTHUS (*aside*). I wish they had toiled a little longer. Oh! thou vilest of all lying old villains ! if I durst but tell the truth of thee !—

ASIUS. I never heard the like !—Go on, pray, sir.

MELAS. To them came anon two others, whose names were Podagra and Lumbago.—One of them set fire to both my feet; —and the other tore open my back :—then shut it again ;—and then again tore it open.

LAOD. (*to* ASIUS). I fear his brain is quite turned.

ASIUS. I will not avouch that, sir. 'Tis Apollo's work.

MELAS. But at all their rage and torture I calmly smiled, and spake to them of the immortal mind.

PANTHUS (*aside*). Oh, curse thee ! I can't stand it. And yet I must, or the secret will be out.

MELAS. At length the God burst forth once more in his splendour. The Furies vanished,—and the celestial voice pronounced—' Melas, arise. Thou hast fulfilled my hopes.—Thy pains shall go from thee. Thy wounds shall be healed. Thy bones shall be made sound.' He ceased,—and a hundred lightnings flashed thro' the room ; and the God ascended thro' the roof, smiling upon me.

LAOD. But, my good Melas,—how was it that you came upon the floor again, and cried out so dreadfully?

MELAS. I was but lying prostrate, confounded with the dazzle of that glory;—and I cried out in the excess of my rapture. But now, let me go forth. I long to bound away over hill and valley.

ASIUS. Is your leg quite sound, then?

MELAS. Behold! (*Cutting a caper.*) Art thou now convinced?

ASIUS. I am. Yet must I talk farther with thee. Apollo! I thank thee that thou hast listened to my prayer. I'll go with thee.

MELAS. Apollo! Apollo! Great and glorious Apollo!

[*Exeunt* MELAS *and* ASIUS.

LAOD. What thinkest thou of this, Panthus?

PANTHUS. Nay, good friend,—that passes me. But I think he jumps remarkably well, considering the weight of that bandage. I wonder if Apollo put it on for him, as well as the rest of his clothes,—because you know, sir, those same Furies had stript him in a twinkling, that they might tickle him the better. I certainly never saw a philosopher jump better. Oh! Ah!

LAOD. Poor man! I fear his intellects are quite disordered. What dost thou want, Otus?

(*Enter* OTUS.)

OTUS (*aside to* LAOD.). They are coming, sir. Young master Adrastus has given me fifty drachms: and my honor'd lady, your wife, gave me fifty more when I had told her all that I had suffered for their sakes. And, you know, my honor'd master, you promised to give me twice as much as they gave me.

LAOD. And thou shalt have it. But go away now.

OTUS. Many thanks, my kind and honor'd lord. (*Aside*) I wish I had told him they gave me a hundred drachms each:— and I will tell him so yet,—and swear hard to it. There's nothing so much encouraged nowadays as false swearing.

[*Exit.*

(*Enter* HELEN, *and* ADRASTUS, *with a* LADY, *veiled.* ADRASTUS
and the lady kneel before LAODAMUS.)

PANTHUS. Why, Adrastus,—what mummery is this?

LAOD. What means this, sir? (*To* HELEN) Pray, madam,
what means this?

HELEN. Speak for yourself, Adrastus.

ADRAS.   Pardon me,
That, 'gainst your will, I've wrought my happiness.
I loved your daughter, sir;—and sought her hand;—
But she preferr'd another;—and, this night
Stole off to marry him. I knew the plot,—
Went in his stead,—and robb'd him of his prize:—
And she is now my wife.—Forgive us, sir,
And let us have your blessing.

LAOD.   Oh! Janassa!
Is this the duty that to me you owe?
This the reward for all my love to you?
Why speak you not?—What plea can wash the filth
From this base deed?—What!—have you *no* pretext?

ADRAS. I pray you, sir, forgive her; and excuse
That she is silent. Since the fatal word
That made her mine, she hath not spoken once,
Save with loud sobs and tears, whose keen reproach
I could not bear, did not my heart——

LAOD.   Stay—stay.
You waste your breath, young man. If such your love
That you o'er-leap all rights, and honest checks
To come at your desire, she will herself
Be dower enough for you. Then, take her, sir:—
But, of my gold, be sure no doit is yours,
Or hers whom you have wed.

PANTHUS.   My good, kind friend!
Consider better ere you tie the knot
Of your resolves so tight it can't be loos'd.
Adrastus—is this well?—But, my good friend,
Think better of it. What is done—is done:—
Let us not make bad worse. Give you the dower

You had intended,—and my son's estate
Shall double that I promised.

LAOD. While I live
Neither your son, nor that veil'd cheat shall be
A child of mine. I'll seek elsewhere for children,
That know their duties better. Ask no more.

HELEN. Husband! You are a tyrant, and nought else,—
And so I'll tell you every hour i' th' day,—
And every day i' th' year,—and every year
That we shall live,—if you abandon so
Your only daughter for no fault but this,—
Which is no fault,—for you permitted him
To make love to her.

LAOD. Prithee, Helen, cease.
When with thy breath thou canst blow down a rock,
Then puff away my fix'd resolve in this.

HELEN. I'll blow a hundred rocks away, as fix'd
As your resolve.—I tell you she's my child,
And your child—and Adrastus is our son :—
And they shall share our fortunes; or this tongue
Shall lead you such a life, you'll wish for death
A hundred times a day.

LAOD. Dear Helen—chuck—
Now, prithee, hold thy peace.—But what means this?

(*Enter* ANTILOCHUS, *with a* LADY, *veiled. They kneel before*
LAODAMUS.)

Have I two daughters stolen away to-night?
Nay—up—up—up—you can't be son to me;
For there's my daughter,—and I have but one.

ADRAS. Again forgive me, sir, that I have used
This little stratagem for my good end.
This fellow 'twas that sought to steal your child,
Whom I had wooed and loved. I knew their plot,—
The priest whom they had bribed; the place, the hour ;—
And so I feigned myself Antilochus,
And, in his stead, have married your dear daughter,
Whom, I beseech you, bless.

ANTIL.   Have you done this?

ADRAS. I have,—thou cursëd interloping knave!
And, had I fail'd, thy marriage-night had been
Thy last on earth !—She's but a slave thou hast ;
Go, take her home, and teach her tag bad verses,
To help thee get thy meagre bread.

     HELEN.   Come, sir—
This was *your* choice,—*your* hopeful son-in-law ;—
This rhyming beggar was to have our child.
Ha ! ha ! But walls have ears,—and sometimes tongues ;
Fish-ponds have water ;—garden-walks have seats ;
And, now and then, a pumpkin is afloat
Amid the rushes ; and will hear, and tell,
Most deep contrivances ;—Oh ! monstrous deep !
And masks will hide ; and priests will work for hire ;
And fathers will a virtuous anger shew
On those that cheat them ;—yet, themselves, will cheat,
And hold it righteous. Come, sir—come—come—come—
You've dug a pitfall, and fallen in yourself ;
And now you chafe, because we stand above
And look down on you there.

     LAOD.   Sweet Helen, list.
I'm in a pit, no doubt ; and thou'rt above ;—
But do not pelt me thus without remorse :—
And let me rage a little to find ease.
Thy wife, Adrastus, never will I bless,
Nor own her for my child. Antilochus,
To thee I promised her who was my child,
Because I thought thee worthy to be hers,—
And worthier far than he who calls him hers :—
And now I say,—and it unmoved shall stand,—
If she, the slave whom thou hast wed, be fair,
Healthful, and chaste,—she shall my daughter be,
And have whate'er Janassa would have had ;
And thou shalt be my son.—Take off her veil.

     PANTHUS. Now, pray you, my good friend, consider this.
     HELEN. Laodamus, while I have breath to live,

And tongue to speak,—and hand to threaten you,—
I'll wear your life out.

LAOD. Valiant love! be still.
Hey!—how is this?—I have two daughters, sure!
    (ANTILOCHUS *removes the veil, and discovers* JANASSA.
    PANTHUS, HELEN, *and* ADRASTUS *start back.*)
That *this* is mine, my eyes do witness clear :—
That *that* is mine, Adrastus is full sure ;—
Also my wife,—who must her own child know,—
And is, besides, right politic and shrewd,
And plays deep games—and cannot be deceiv'd.

    HELEN (*to* JANASSA). Are you my daughter—and this beggar's wife?

JAN. I am your child, dear mother!—and *his* wife,
But yet no beggar's bride.

ADRAS. Are you Janassa?

JAN. I am, Adrastus.

ADRAS. And this idiot's wife?

JAN. This is my husband.

ANTIL. Pray you, sir, stand off;
And, if your choler must have vent, withdraw ;
And leave my slave and me to tag our rhymes.
This is our marriage-night,—but not our last,
We hope, on earth.

ADRAS. Thou damnëd hungry wretch!

ANTIL. That fault our supper, sir, shall remedy ;
To which we bid you, will you be our guest,
And cool your fiery bosom.

ADRAS. Curse your supper!
Yourself—your bed—your wife—false, hollow cheat!

PANTHUS. Adrastus, are you mad?

ANTIL. Your vilest words
Are licens'd tow'rds myself ;—but, to this lady,
Are sins that shall have punishment. Beware!

LAOD. Come, come, young bloods :—let's have no more dispute.
Adrastus, what a strange gallant art thou!
Go to thy weeping wife :—take off her veil ;—
If there be two Janassas,—why, our fortune
Shall be two portions. Pray you, shew her face.

PANTHUS. Come, come, Adrastus, what is past, is gone.
I'll have no dagger work. Clear up thy brow.
Thou'st burnt thy fingers, and, if others laugh,
Do thou laugh too. If this match please thee not,
We'll find some remedy. Take off her veil.

ADRAS. I'll not be fool'd again.

LAOD. Come then, fair bride!
I'll draw away the cloud that veils this sun,
And glad our darken'd eyes.—Oh! beautiful!

(*He removes the veil, and discovers the face of an ugly, dirty, arch-looking* LAD. *All, but* HELEN *and* ADRASTUS, *burst into laughter.*)

ADRAS. Thou cursëd lubber !—But I'll make thee rue it!

(*He strikes the* BOY, *and hauls him about. In the struggle the female garb is torn off, and discovers the* BOY's *dress beneath. Loud laughter.*)

LAOD. For shame, Adrastus! 'Tis your lovely wife :
Kiss her, and use her well. For shame! for shame!

ADRAS. The Furies fetch you all! [*Exit.*

(*Enter* PHORBAS.)

PHORBAS. I've seen them! Horrible! Oh horrible!
Their claws were longer than my arm,
Their eyes were burning coal!

(*Enter* MELAS.)

MELAS. Stay, Phorbas,—stay awhile. Whom hast thou seen?
Podagra, and dire Lumbago ?—Come, come.
I must hold talk with thee. Didst see the God?

PHORBAS. Ha! dost thou live ?—I saw their fiery tongues ;

Their horrid fangs, red hot.   Come here,—come here—
I'll tell thee dreadful things.
  MELAS.   Didst see the God?
                       [*Exeunt* MELAS *and* PHORBAS.
  PANTHUS. Oh! heavens! that horrid madman!
  LAOD.   What! my poet?
Why, he is harmless as a violet :—
And I shall plant him somewhere, safe and warm.
But now, my good old friend,—you'll stay with us?
I'll show you all my course in this affair,—
And it shall clear me tow'rds you.
  PANTHUS.   That mad boy
Vexes me much.   I'll send him hence awhile ;
To cool upon this matter; for he's hot,
And prone to vengeance.
  LAOD.   Talk of that to-morrow.
Meantime, stay with us to our wedding-feast :
It waits us now.
  PANTHUS.   Well—well—give me your hand :
But gently.—Oh! I've had more gripes, and shakes,
Ay, and cuffs too, and horrible affrights,
These two days past than all my life before.
  LAOD. But how?
  PANTHUS.   I'll tell you soon.
  LAOD.   Well, now, sweet wife,
Let us go in to supper.   After that,
We'll talk of garden-walks, with seats therein ;
Of rushy fish-ponds ;—pumpkins floating there,—
That hear, and tell, of deep contrivances :—
Of masks we'll talk,—and priests—and pitfalls too :
And then we'll say that, tho' in most things wise,
I've been a fool in this :—and, midst it all,
We'll be so wondrous gentle,—' Cool—cool—cool'—
That is the motto :—' when she'd catch the mouse,
The cat lies still.'—Oh! we've a world of talk
For after supper :—have we not, sweet wife?

JAN. My dearest father! pray you, spare her now.
(*Kneeling to her* MOTHER.)
Forgive me, my dear mother, this deceit;—
My first, and sure, I think, my last.

HELEN. Dear child!
I cannot talk on't now.

ANTIL. (*kneeling to* HELEN). Forgive me, too.

HELEN. Arise, sir,—you distress me.—Bless you both!
May you be ever happy!

LAOD. Come away.
We'll talk of this, sweet wife, another day.
Thou see'st thy fault,—and that I hope doth shew
That, for the future, thou'lt be wiser.

PANTHUS. Oh!

Curtain drops.

Second Edition, 2 *Vols., post 8vo., with an Engraving on steel, by John Martin.* LONGMANS AND CO., 1868.

THE FALL OF NINEVEH.
A POEM.

OPINIONS OF THE PRESS.

'Having now carefully collated the Second Edition with the First, we can vouch for the justice of the words on the title-page, "corrected and improved." The entire work manifests it.'—*Durham County Advertiser.*

'.... Has just been republished after a long and careful revision by the Author, which has left hardly a single page quite unaltered.—*Bath Chronicle.*

'If enthralling interest is looked for, here, in this Epic Poem of the "Fall of Nineveh," it will be found as undeniably as in any sensational novel of the day, by the most popular of romance writers.'—*The Sun.*

'The "Fall of Nineveh" is destined to take a permanent place in the first rank of literature.'—*Manchester Examiner.*

'All the alterations, and they occur on almost every page, are improvements. The late Lord Carlisle—no mean judge—declared it to be the finest Epic in the English language.'—*Bell's Weekly Messenger.*

'It is too great a work for detraction to bring it down—too classic, too truly Homeric, ever to be much of a favourite with the mob of sensation-loving readers. Its solemn and stately march, as it sweeps onwards to its conclusion—the easy, yet powerful flow of its versification—the grandeur of its imagery—the sense of vastness, of immensity, which gradually swells the mind as the plot and narrative develop themselves, make it unlike any other poem with which we are acquainted. So carefully has the work of revision been done that it would be difficult to find a line with which even a hostile critic could find fault.'—*The Leader.*

'After careful examination, we find no alteration that is not an improvement, and this without any sacrifice of strength to "polish." . . . In regard to its subject, style, and spirit, it stands alone in our language, and, probably, in every other—the Greek alone excepted.'—*The Liverpool Mercury.*

'In his war scenes Mr. Atherstone excels. His various actions are carefully discriminated; the perils incurred are sufficiently made out; his heroes extricate themselves, or fall by intelligible accidents. His battles are, in fact, vivid and distinct moving panoramas.'—*Athenæum.*

'He is copious, melodious, and emphatic; his style is gorgeous and flowing; his descriptions are magnificent—his banquets and revelries breathe the very air of splendid voluptuousness, and his scenes of battle and of council are full of solemnity and ardour.'—*Edinburgh Review.*

'The "Fall of Nineveh" is one of those compositions which acquire fame for their author gradually, rather than by acclamation; but we think we cannot err in pronouncing that, ere many years have passed, the "Fall of Nineveh" will be found in every library, side by side with the "Iliad" and the "Paradise Lost."'—*Church of England Quarterly Review.*

BY THE SAME AUTHOR.

THE LAST DAYS OF HERCULANEUM.
A POEM.

A MIDSUMMER-DAY'S DREAM.
A POEM.

THE SEA KINGS IN ENGLAND.
AN HISTORICAL ROMANCE. 3 Vols.

BY THE SAME AUTHOR.

Three Volumes.

THE HANDWRITING ON THE WALL.

'Mr. Atherstone has caught the spirit of the Scripture narrative, and expanded it with the inspiration of his own genius. . . . He vindicates the ways of God to man, and teaches a grand moral. It is almost a Sunday book. It *is* a book which all may and *should* read, for all will find in it profit as well as pleasure.'—*Critic.*

One Volume, demy 8vo.

ISRAEL IN EGYPT.

A POEM.

OPINIONS OF THE PRESS.

'The poem contains passages that would do honour to our noblest writers.'—*Bell's Messenger.*

'As decidedly characterised by a tone of sincere piety as it is remarkable for the great facility and unconstrained power of imagination and expression which have carried the author with unflagging spirit through his long and vigorous epic.'—*Morning Post.*

'Of the general execution of the work, scarce anything too flattering can be said. It is careful and scholarlike in the last degree. The language is throughout clear, chaste, impressive; drawn from the "well of English undefiled"—the English of Milton and Wordsworth; often rising with the occasion to a long-linked music of rhythm and pictorial magnificence—never descending to the level of mere measured and stilted prose.'—*Leicestershire Mercury.*

'The ten plagues are introduced with consummate skill. We cannot too much admire the highly dramatic effect of each: the march of recorded events and the interest and progress of what may be called the story are simultaneous. Even the third plague—the most loathsome and seemingly petty among them—teaches an important lesson, and becomes terrible from the manner in which it is treated. "The hail," "The darkness," and "The death of the first-born," afford full scope for our author's own peculiar grandeur of conception and of language. His vivid descriptions of those fearful visitations are in the highest degree graphic and soul-thrilling.'—*Liverpool Mercury.*

'Of course, the closing scene depicts in gorgeous language the final overthrow of Pharaoh and all his "Memphian Chivalry" in the returning waters of the Red Sea. . . . We now take our leave of this poem, as we do of the phenomena of nature, with feelings at once of surprise and placidity; surprised at the magnitude of the work, and soothed by the ease displayed in conducting it. The language is stately, the situations are gorgeous, and the theme is of the most daring that can be conceived.'—*Downshire Protestant.*

'Taking its power and beauty in the aggregate;—its vast range of character and of eloquence; its variety of awful incident and action; the greatness of the human agency, and the terribleness of the supernatural—it is, we repeat, the boldest rush towards the MILTONIC circle of enchantment that has ever been made since;—and the one probably in which boldness has been most justified by the result.'—*Durham Advertiser.*

www.ingramcontent.com/pod-product-compliance
Lightning Source LLC
Chambersburg PA
CBHW022059230426
43672CB00008B/1228